Personality Insights

for Moms!

D-I-S-Cover communication success

DECREASE CONFLICT & INCREASE HAPPINESS TODAY!

Susan Crook

WITH ROBERT A. ROHM, PH.D.

*Joelene ~
Live an
" insightful " life!
Susan Crook
(913) 390-0565*

Regency Taylor
PUBLISHING

Published by Regency Taylor Publishing
11936 W. 119th, #159
Overland Park, KS 66213

Available in special quantity discounts when purchased in bulk to be used for workshops, retreats, and educational purposes. For more information contact Order@SusanCrook.com.

Group discussion questions available for each chapter. Download at www.SusanCrook.com/discussion_questions.htm.

Library of Congress Cataloging-in-Publication Data
Crook; Susan, 2006

Personality insights for moms! d-i-s-cover how to decrease conflict and increase happiness / by Susan Crook with Robert A. Rohm.

1. Parenting

Printed in the United States of America

ISBN: 0-9778397-0-2
2006901224 - PCN

!★±? Symbols are Registered Trademarks owned by Personality Insights, Inc. Used in this publication with permission. Portions of this book are adapted from *Positive Personality Profiles* by Robert A. Rohm, Ph.D. Used with permission of author.

The BOTS™ , OneBot™, TwoBot™, ThreeBot™, and FourBot™, 1Bot™, 2Bot™, 3Bot™, and 4Bot™ are trademarks of Personality Insights, Inc. Used with permission.

Portions of this book are adapted from *Get Real, Who You Are and Why You Do Those Things* by Robert A. Rohm, Ph.D. – used with permission of author.

CONTENTS

Introduction...7

PART 1 - GETTING STARTED

1   Alarming Communication Barriers.............................13
2   Personality History 22
3   Two Pieces of the Personality Pie 31
4   Two More Pieces of the Personality Pie 38
5   Put It All Together 45
6   Cope and Adjust Without Training Camp.....................53

PART 2 - PERSONALITY STYLES 101

7   Your Personality Style..58
8   Your Child's Personality Style.....................................68

PART 3 - MOM'S PERSONALITY STYLE

9   The "D" Mom..77
10   The "I" Mom...85
11   The "S" Mom 97
12   The "C" Mom 105

PART 4 - RECOGNIZING PERSONALITIES

13   Your Child's Ambitions 117
14   How the D-I-S-C Letters Blend Together 131

PART 5 - YOUR CHILD'S PERSONALITY STYLE

15   The "D" Child 139
16   The "I" Child 150
17   The "S" Child..162
18   The "C" Child..170

PART 6 - PARENTING STYLES

19   The "D" Parenting Style....................................180
20   The "I" Parenting Style....................................193
21   The "S" Parenting Style 207
22   The "C" Parenting Style 221

PART 7 - HOW TO HANDLE CONFLICT AND D-I-S-CIPLINE

23   Conflict and D-I-S-Cipline................................235
24   With a "D" Child...244
25   With an "I" Child 251
26   With an "S" Child 257
27   With a "C" Child 262

PART 8 - MOTIVATION STRATEGIES

28   Motivation Strategies.......................................270
29   For the "D" Child 279
30   For the "I" Child 286
31   For the "S" Child...294
32   For the "C" Child...301

CONCLUSION

33   Hope for Moms!...310

ABOUT THE AUTHOR..318
RESOURCE MATERIALS.......................................319

ACKNOWLEDGEMENTS

Special thanks:

- To my ever faithful, always supportive husband, Dale (Jay) Crook – who has completely captured my heart forever and true. Words are not adequate to thank you. This book is as much your accomplishment as it is mine.

- To my three children: Stacia, Scott, and Madison – whom I gave excruciating painful, body-wrecking, sleep depriving, birth to (and are the joy of my life). I am honored to be your mom. In addition, it has given me the idiosyncratic opportunity to recognize that moms *indeed* possess inherently different personality styles than their children!

- To Dr. Robert Rohm – how grateful I am for sharing my vision for this book and for your faithful teaching and dedication to helping others understand personality styles. It's a joy to partner with you in helping moms improve relationships with their children.

- To my editor, Penny Kubitschek – for all your meticulous efforts in making this book what it needed to be. You are not only efficient and thorough, but encompass the perfect personality for this job!

- To the eight kids on cover: Andrew, Madison, Charlie, Cate, Raymond, Chaney, Abigail, and Josh – who made the personality styles come alive! I am very thankful for your dedication, perseverance, and ability to model with such "style!"

- To Michael Coyazo – your talent as a photographer to "shoot" eight fidgety kids in what seems like eight *thousand* different poses for this cover, with limitless patience and fortitude, is amazing beyond words!

- To the many special friends and family members in my life – who've encouraged, prayed, and inspired me along the journey of this book.

- To you, the reader, for loving your child enough to want the best for them!

Author's note: Most examples throughout this book are from personal experiences, but many are from experiences shared by others. To protect their privacy, some names have been changed .

INTRODUCTION

D-I-S-Cover - "To learn by study, bringing to light for the first time knowledge of something existing, but not previously known."

*A*ll moms know that life is – shall we say – a wee bit different after having taken on the new and exciting role of motherhood. Our basic "I am woman, hear me roar" style cocoons during pregnancy, and we metamorphose into some form of new creature when our little labor of love enters this world!

Everything changes; the clothes we buy, the food we eat, and our *vocabulary*! Let me give you a few vocabulary examples of how our once very proficient, highly intellectual discussions change entirely from:

- Inbox to *Sand*box
- Wall Street to *Sesame* Street
- Starbucks to Star*bursts*
- ABC News to ABC *Songs*
- Stock Market – to *Super*market
- Corporate Reports to *Grade Card* Reports
- Fitness to Fit *Throwing*
- Ballet Performances to Ballet *Lessons* and
- Business to *Busy*ness!

In fact, moms are the busiest people I know! We hardly get a break! I don't have to tell you, kids are doing something at all times, at all ages!

I once had a mom ask me if it gets better when your kids are older. She said, "At least you can get some sleep!" I responded with, "Sleep? Oh, that doesn't change! Sure, when your teenagers were babies you wished they'd sleep through the night. But then they get their driver's licenses and you wish *you* could!" Moms have been and will forever be on call!

MOMS ARE UNIQUE

You've got to admit moms are great, in fact the best! We are literally responsible for manufacturing every human being on this planet. Pretty awesome accomplishment, huh?

And we come in all shapes, shades, and sizes – each with a unique personality style and flair! Some are trendy. Some are conservative. Some moms are bosses and wouldn't walk out the door without wearing a suit, pantyhose, high heels, and carrying a briefcase.

Other moms prefer jeans most days, and wouldn't walk out the door without carrying an ample supply of toys – eager to experience fun everywhere she goes!

Some moms are into sweats and sports, and carry around athletic gear – on the lookout for physical action! Other moms may be into sweats too, but solely for the purpose of relaxing, watching TV, reading a magazine, or lounging in a hammock. Others prefer high fashion, glamour, opera, books, and perhaps classical music.

Some moms are married; some are single. Some moms are grandmoms; some are step-moms.

Each mom, nonetheless, is a very *special* mom who has a unique personality style – for a very *special* child who has a unique personality style – and for a very *special* reason. Make no mistake, your child has been given a gift – and that special gift is you!

You may, however, not feel so special. In fact, as a mom you may feel confused, worried, and frustrated, wondering, "What in the world do I do with this child that I don't understand and I can't get a ticket to escape to another planet anytime soon?!?!!"

Do you desire to understand and develop better communication with your child? Or maybe you're not communicating at all! Well, hang on and don't give up! Reading between the lines, this book shouts, "Help is on the way!"

IT'S A NEW DAY

The greatest gift a mom can give her child is unconditional love and understanding. Each morning upon opening her eyes, a mom is faced with a choice. She can passively tolerate the nuances of the day – or launch a new and exciting day of extraordinary opportunity for her child. It's quite a profound and powerful statement to say that we can affect our child with a magnitude of such enormous potential. Nonetheless, we have been granted that kind of capability!

Moms can orchestrate relationship dynamics by choosing to be *pro*active – or battle confusing dilemmas all day, sufficing to be *re*active. Each of us faces daily personality challenges and situations that make us scratch our head, pull out our hair, or worse – attack that pint of ice cream! It's our job to get in the driver's seat and start steering our children down the road to success. And with the right communication tools, we can do it! Yes, we *are* moms, hear us roar!

COMMUNICATION IS KEY

As a mom, each of us possesses the unmistakable power to have a *huge* impact in shaping our child's day – our child's life! So, how? How do we know *what* to do, *when* to do it, and *why* we do it?

In ***Personality Insights for Moms***, you're going to find out how. We may not be *perfect* moms, but we can discover how to be really *good* moms by learning communication keys and strategies in this book. The job of being a mom is not an easy job – as we quickly discovered! We make a lot of mistakes and learn many hard lessons through the painstaking epoch of trial and error.

My goal is that this book will help you be the best mom you can be, to communicate with your child in a way you never could before, and to improve your relationship. You can *learn* to communicate effectively with your child regardless of your personality similarities or differences.

Communication is essential for a successful future with your child, but it doesn't always come naturally. In fact, communication deficiency is cited as the number one source of irritation and complaint in families, leading to damage that can last a lifetime.

I have a Master's Degree in Communication and I still haven't mastered communication (and I'm sure my three kids will affirm that statement)! It's an ongoing process to understand each other, to build on each other's strengths, and communicate love and patience in our quest for a dynamic relationship.

GET PLUGGED-IN!

I am passionate for vibrant relationships in our homes. I want to shout from the rooftops, pleading for every mom to truly grasp that greatness lives within her! But first, before we go any further, I must ask you a very important question.

Does your child have a mom who's plugged-in? Take a minute with me here. Imagine a lamp sitting on your end table. That lamp may look like a lamp, hold a light bulb like a lamp, support a pretty lampshade like a lamp, but if it's not plugged-in, it's not going to be able to do the job of a lamp.

Moms have a job too, and we have to be plugged-in to do our job effectively. Get plugged-in today! Yes, being a mom can be a challenge, but embrace the challenges! Embrace them instead of resisting or resenting them.

Maybe you don't understand why your kids are the way they are yet, maybe some days you feel like you want to escape to another planet, but let's embrace the challenges together step by step in this book, and get plugged-in with your child (and yourself) in a new and exciting way!

When I learned the D-I-S-C personality information, it changed my life as a mom. It gave me "ah-has" as to why each child thinks, acts, responds, plans, and plays differently. I used to think that motherhood was so simple. I was in control, full of wisdom, and so self-assured, prepared for every single situation. *Then* I had kids! (My "plug-in" almost short-circuited!)

In this book, you will discover surprising new attributes about your child (and other members of your family) that will change your life. I want you to enjoy the very best possible relationship with your child that you can, and enjoy each crazy, unpredictable moment. Let your light *shine*!

FUEL FOR FIRE

May this book change you from the inside out, and may you readily learn and recognize the D-I-S-C personality information and quickly respond to it – developing well-formed maturity and insight.

If the relationship with your child seems *cold* to you, this book will help fuel the flames to warm up and kindle a new communication *bonfire* in your home.

We must develop communication patterns and express love in ways that are meaningful to our children – at any age – at *all* ages – to connect and generate the kind of relationships we need and desire.

My hope is that you will *D-I-S-Cover* and "obtain for the first time, knowledge of a thing existing already, but not perceived or known before." May you look back and D-I-S-Cover that reading this book helped you gain the knowledge and personality insights that changed your life.

You, as a mom, can give your child the gift of successful communication, unconditional love and understanding at a level never experienced before. Today you can have the relationship with your child that you only dreamed of yesterday. Keep reading! You are about to D-I-S-Cover how!

This book will show you how to get plugged-in and understand why you do what *you* do and why your children do what *they* do, and give you the tools needed to D-I-S-Cover communication secrets and success for a lifetime of happiness!

1

D-I-S-COVER ALARMING COMMUNICATION BARRIERS

*I*t was late and getting dark outside. All of a sudden, I could hear footsteps running after me faster and faster. Just then I heard, "Stop!" As I spun around to see what was going on, a woman yelled, "Wait! I have something to tell you!" Animated and out of breath, she continued, "A few months ago my husband and I were exasperated with our son's behavior and we felt like we had no other choice but to send him away to a military school. Then I attended your personality training class and learned about the different personality styles. I was close to giving up on ever having a good relationship with my son, but now – it is *wonderful!*"

Sharon, a teacher who attended an in-service class I taught, proceeded, "I went to your class to receive CEUs (Continuing Education Units) for my job. I learned that my husband, John, has the personality style that is reserved, quiet and task-oriented. He always expects things to be done the "correct" way. You said his personality style is cautious and calculating, and it's very important to him to complete tasks – on time! Now I know *why* that's so important to him!"

"I am also reserved, but instead of task-oriented, I'm people-oriented. My personality style is a little shy and never in a rush *normally*! You said that I need stability and security in my life, I need to feel supported in my job – and at home, and that I dislike conflict more than anything! That's me, all right!"

"Then there's our teenage son, Matt. Matt is so…oh, my goodness! His personality is so different than ours! Matt – (imagine the *Jaws* theme song here) has always seemed impossible! He is anything but reserved or quiet, and hardly ever completes *any* task – including his homework. Every time we turn around, he's in trouble for acting like the class clown! He talks all the time, is high-strung and constantly on the go with his friends. Matt just seemed so irresponsible, disorganized, and rebellious to us. We fought all the time. It was a disaster at our house, I felt like a terrible mom, and we didn't know what else to do! But it's all changed now! Learning and understanding our opposite personality styles saved our family!"

Prior to the D-I-S-C personality training, Sharon and John felt hopeless, desperate, and were "shipping Matt out" the following semester. They felt that Matt's rebelliousness, lack of responsibility, and out-of-control flamboyant lifestyle had to stop. As far as they were concerned, Matt needed to start doing things the "right" way – *their* way – or else.

What Sharon discovered in the personality training was that her son, Matt, really wasn't rebelling against them at all; he was living life according to *his* personality style, not *theirs*. When Sharon shared the personality insights with the rest of her family, the conflict subsided almost immediately. Suddenly, they all understood their personality mêlée – the dynamics and differences that had been raging under the same roof for many years. Even Matt was surprised. He never understood why he was so different, and always felt like he just didn't fit in with his parents.

Since this exciting awareness, Sharon has felt encouraged and has a renewed confidence in her role as a mom. She now realizes that she hadn't failed in the mom role, she just didn't know how to communicate or understand the personality style and behavior differences in her son before. Matt and his parents still have completely different personality styles, but they now have a whole new understanding and appreciation of each other.

Their relationship completely turned around when they D-I-S-Covered and applied the D-I-S-C personality information. (We can stop playing the *Jaws* theme now. I'd say one mom just learned how to "Swim With the Sharks" and not get eaten alive!)

BODY-WRECKING CHILDBIRTH

If we're going to enjoy life and enjoy relationships with our children, then we need to understand them and where they're coming from – which personality quadrant, that is! We need to care about *why* they act the way they do *today*, because it affects *what* they do *tomorrow*. God has entrusted moms with a wonderful gift and responsibility to love, teach, train and bring up the best child (or shark?) we can as we discover what an awesome, yet sometimes wearisome profession it is.

Moms are the largest non-licensed group of professionals that exists. I don't know about you, we may be professionals, but I missed the training to be a mom somewhere along the way in my education! I've been winging it ever since that first excruciating, body-wrecking, sleep-depriving, painful, yet joyful moment called childbirth! (By the way, be sure and save all those labor and delivery bills! You may need them someday – when one of your kids reminds you that you borrowed a twenty!) (*See* how moms need to be on their toes?)

Being a professional mom is a highly demanding, continuous hands-on type of job that comes with no salary and no time off – not even for good behavior! However, the benefits (butterfly kisses, bouquets of wilted dandelions, and homemade mud pies garnished with roly-pollies) can be endless!

SO SWEET

Whether you became a mom by sacrificing your body or not, you are an amazing woman in the way you're selflessly sacrificial with your time, sleep, expendable income, and endless love for an endless job – all to bear the title "mom." I frequently speak to moms' groups, and have the utmost admiration and respect for moms across the country.

As I engage in meeting moms of all ages, sizes, types, and styles, I see a common goal – to be the best they can be for their children. They are champions in my book, with no contenders. No mom is *perfect*, but *perfectly made* for her child and the child for her, regardless of the communication disparity, obstacles, and overwhelming personality differences!

Considering that not all of us think the same, act the same, or express things in the same way, it's necessary that we *can* learn to appreciate and understand these exasperating personality differences. Does your child act differently than you to purposely drive you crazy – or worse, drive a wedge between the two of you? No, probably not! More than likely, your child acts differently than you because you have different personality styles and communicate in entirely different ways.

You may have wondered at times why you have been blessed with these mind-boggling little creatures called children. Are we given children as an excuse to go to parks, play in sprinklers, and purchase crayons again? No, actually we are given children for one wonderful, yet simple reason – they provide the perfect excuse for baking chocolate chip cookies (among other reasons, of course)!

So, why not try to understand them and why they do what they do – especially when they produce such a *sweet* benefit?

WHAT? NOT EVERYONE IN YOUR FAMILY IS THE SAME?

Have you questioned how in the world one child in the same environment and with the same upbringing can be so different from another? Are there personality styles running around in your family doing things as differently as day and night? How do you like to do things? How does your child like to do things? Are they the same? Probably not!

We generally do things according to our dominant personality style. First, let's take a look at the way *you* tend to operate.

Do you like to do things:

D ...the *fast* way?

★ ...the *fun* way?

S ...the *traditional* way?

C ...the *correct* way?

Now think of your child and answer the same question according to *their* personality style. More than likely, not every member in your family would select the same answer. If you and your child have the same personality style, you understand each other rather well. If you have completely different personality styles, it's as though you're speaking different languages!

Trying to understand one another's personality style is a lot like trying to speak a foreign language. Have you ever traveled to another country where they speak a different language and they can't understand you and you don't understand them? Or have you developed a friendship with someone who speaks a different language than you do?

ALARMING FRIENDSHIP

Lan, a dear, sweet lady from Viet Nam, has done my nails for the past four years. When we first met, I could barely understand her and she me. Needless to say, initially we didn't communicate too well due to struggles with our language barrier. But face-to-face every two to three weeks, we developed a friendship and a desire to try to effectively communicate and understand each other.

As our visits continued and our fondness and trust developed for each other, Lan would prepare a long list of uncertain and misunderstood English words as she anticipated my next visit to the nail salon. During my appointments, we studied for her US Citizenship exam (boy, did *I* learn a lot!). Each visit at the nail salon became a teaching opportunity to help her communicate and ascertain our very diverse and confusing English language.

One day while sitting across the manicure table from Lan, she appeared utterly baffled. She carefully articulated to me that the alarm on her car hadn't been working correctly and she had taken it to a mechanic. While filling out the form, the mechanic said, "Okay, let's see. For no apparent reason the car alarm's going off throughout the day."

"Oh, no, no," Lan kindly explained, "the car alarm's going *on*."

"Like I said, the alarm's going *off*," clarified the mechanic.

The mystifying dialogue continued. Gently correcting the mechanic, Lan replied, "No, no, it goes *on*."

"I know, I know, but it's going *off*, right?" queried the now-impatient mechanic. Completely perplexed at that point, Lan *left* – feeling confused and hopeless because she couldn't effectively communicate! It was utterly frustrating trying to understand the mechanic and make sense of a language so diverse and foreign to her.

In spite of the fact that she gave me a great laugh and joy in my heart for her sweet innocence, I explained this communication fiasco as well as I could. (It didn't exactly make sense why we say the alarm is going *off* even to me!) But the point is, when we speak a foreign language, sometimes it's very difficult to communicate without feeling confused and frustrated – possibly even angry!

COMMUNICATE YOUR PERSONALITY LANGUAGE

In a similar manner, we may be feeling the same "alarming" frustration toward our children when we don't understand or communicate in the same *personality* language. We may ask, "Why does my child always have to be so full of energy and high-strung?" or the opposite, "Why is my child so shy and quiet?" Sound familiar? When we don't "speak the same personality language," we too may experience a communication fiasco.

We must learn to speak in ways that communicate clearly with people of different personality styles. Communication with your child is not merely the process of speaking words in y*our* native language. To break down communication barriers, you must learn to speak in a way your child can understand according to his or her personality style.

Much care should be taken in understanding your child, spouse, friends, family, and co-workers. Understanding the different personality styles is not to label or put you or your child in a box. It's to help you understand why you think and do what you do, and why your child does what he or she does – when it just doesn't make sense to you.

I'LL BREAK OUT OF HERE

If personality styles are obvious, then does it mean we're born with a certain personality style? And are personality styles apparent in children? Yes, and yes. For example, my son, Scott, displayed an obvious personality style within a few weeks of making his debut on this earth (actually minutes).

When he was old enough to barely lift up that angelic, puffy little face, he focused through the crib bars and proclaimed by the mere determination in his eyes, "By golly, I'll break out of here in no time. I'll be in charge of this place and take control as soon as I can crawl out of this crib!" His quest for being in charge of our home never diminished for a minute.

He was *born* with a determined personality style, has always *been* determined, and always will *be* determined. (And please, feel free to stop and *pray* for me at any time!) For moms raising children with a **Determined** personality style (D-I-S-Cover if that's you and what it means in the following chapters), there is a light at the end of the tunnel — and it's not another freight train! Remember, determined babies do eventually grow up and move out! (God is so merciful!)

NO COMMUNICATION SPEED LIMIT

If we don't understand specifically why our children act like they do and why we respond the way we do, then we're constantly speculating. It's not easy playing the guessing game, wondering why your children act, think, talk, or behave the way they do. Most moms feel inadequate at times and wish they could do a better job of communicating with their children. But why settle for inadequate or even mediocre communication when you can amass the best?

One of your highest callings and greatest honors is to be the best mom you can be. You're amazingly gifted and talented to do so. Think about it. You can birth and grow children, conduct shrewd and profitable business dealings (even on the playground), and flawlessly apply mascara at speeds greater than fifty-five miles per hour! Obviously, then, you can also apply the D-I-S-C personality information to all aspects of your life and communicate in the fast lane!

GET THE PICTURE

It doesn't take a mom with a Ph.D. to see that not all kids act the same or prefer the same environment. Just hang out at any playground, observe and listen, and you'll get the picture. You may have a child who is high-strung and constantly on the go, climbing, conquering, and on the verge of a broken bone with every monumental monkey bar - the self-prescribed commander of the playground. (How *does* this child become the unofficial boss of the playground? Find out how in following chapters!)

Or, on the other hand, your child may be sweet and compliant, laid back, asking permission to do everything, and basically very little trouble. Shocking, but it happens.

Or does your child always have to have everything in its place? (Believe it or not, those children exist too!) It might take twenty minutes to *organize* everything perfectly on the table before he or she will even take a bite. Chicken fingers have a special place here, french fries there, ketchup in just the right place, always the drink over there, and the napkin – oh, well… forget the napkin. (Regardless of their personality style, napkins don't happen.)

Are personality differences the result of your ineffectual skills as a mother? Is it the parenting class you never took that is haunting you now? Or could it be that our children are born with predetermined personalities that impact how they interact in the world they're brought into – regardless whether we're ideal moms or not?

Understanding how one communicates takes a little time and effort – as learning any new language requires. However, after you begin to understand the four personality styles, you will be able to communicate more successfully and your interactions will become "win-win" situations. You will learn to communicate with your children in *their* personality languages, and they in turn will understand you!

This can all be done well in advance, before the "we just don't understand each other" alarm goes off – or on – off – no, on? Let's move *on* to Chapter 2!

2

D-I-S-COVER

PERSONALITY HISTORY

*H*ave you ever wondered why your child doesn't act like you – or why one child is so different than the other? Were they born that way, or is there something we can do to change them? Have you thought, "I don't understand why we're so different!" or "Why can't my child act like the other kids?" Is it baffling how one child may be a leader, outgoing, and high-energy, while another child is shy, quiet, and reserved? One may be content with silence and solitude, while another may demand constant action and attention. And wasn't it *easy*, all those years prior to having children, to swear, "My child is *never* going to act that way"? I've eaten a few of those words myself – not my favorite lunch. (*Worse* than the infamous daily mac-and-cheese!)

So when does the dominant personality style reveal itself? When my oldest child, Stacia (pronounced Stay-sha), was born, she was good-natured and easygoing. She nibbled on her fists, let out a little squeak, and I would know it was time to feed her. She seldom cried and as long as I nurtured her and maintained a consistent schedule, she was compliant and content.

Two years later my son, Scott, was born and I expected the same scenario. Big mistake! Within minutes of his birth, he instantly put those tiny little lungs into full force – screaming and demanding for things to go *his* way! In fact, every time he was hungry, he wailed! (Isn't it *amazing* how much *chaos* a little eight-pound bundle of joy can generate?) This child would not let up until his demands were met!

I was astounded by how two children with the same genes and birthed in the *same womb* could be so completely *different!* From the moment you first cradle those precious little personalities in your arms, you can see a distinctive difference! In fact, personality styles have been evident since history began!

HISTORY OF PERSONALITY ASSESSMENTS

As I mentioned, I have a Master's Degree in Communication. In graduate school I studied and participated in numerous types of personality assessments. In addition, I researched personality differences and how they affect communication in relationships. In fact, I wrote the thesis for my Master's program on this very subject.

The study of behavior and personality styles is not new. Twenty-four hundred years ago, people began to notice differences in behavior and discovered these differences seemed to follow a pattern. As early as 400 B.C. (Whoa, what was it like to be a mom back *then?* Contrary to what my kids might imply, I would NOT know!), Hippocrates, a physician, knew and understood the human body as well as temperament patterns.

He derived the names of the four temperaments from four bodily fluids: choleric, sanguine, melancholy, and phlegmatic. Even though the idea that bodily fluids determine one's personality has been discarded, a fourfold classification of temperaments is still widely used.

Then Carl Jung, a Swiss psychoanalyst and student of Sigmund Freud, sought to explain why people differ from one another, by identifying four psychological functions or personality traits rooted in biology. (I'm sure – the notorious once-a-month biological functions added puzzling discrepancies at the time! And keep in mind, PMS does not stand for Personality Malfunction Syndrome – even though it does *seem* to malfunction during this time!) Moving on, based on Jung's supposition, he concluded that each individual has a predominant personality style, which is genetically determined and can even be observed at the infant stage. (Ah-ha!)

SMORGASBORD OF PERSONALITY ASSESSMENTS

After studying various types of personality assessments in graduate school, I found there is a *smorgasbord* of assessments and labels to choose from! Some measure two dichotomous functions for receiving and evaluating information in the environment. For example, some assessment results showed that you could be an E or I, or T or J. I think there were even an N and P, possibly an S – or something like that (I could never keep them straight).

A few personality assessments use the four peculiar (and difficult to pronounce) Greek terms mentioned previously: choleric, sanguine, phlegmatic, and melancholy.

And some tests concluded that personality styles were certain types of animals! I personally feel that I've never been an animal and am never *going* to be an animal. I'm a *human being*! (Most of the time, anyway.)

A myriad of other labels or assessment tools describe human behavior. I found from the result of my communication studies that the D-I-S-C Personality descriptions (Dominance, Influence, Steadiness, and Conscientiousness) proved to be the most applicable and discernable of all the personality descriptions and labels.

D-I-S-C is simplistic, self-explanatory, and the most logical assessment label system to understand – and remember! In addition, the descriptive D-I-S-C letters easily blend together to reveal a more accurate assessment of the four distinct personality styles. (After all, moms need quick, easy, and simplistic answers to allow plenty of time for our relaxing afternoons of bonbons and soaps. Oh, sure.) Ultimately, the self-explanatory D-I-S-C definitions won out over all the other types of personality identifiers and assessments available.

WHERE DID D-I-S-C COME FROM, ANYWAY?

Awareness of the four basic personality styles, regardless of how they're labeled, has been around for a long time. (Longer than that container of greenish food buried deep in the back of our refrigerators – or the lost fries under the car seat!) As I mentioned, 2,400 years ago, scientists and philosophers, most notably Hippocrates, began to recognize differences in behavior that seemed to follow a pattern. This pattern was explored by many psychologists and scientists and ultimately defined by Dr. William Moulton Marston. After earning his Doctorate from Harvard University, he wrote *The Emotions of Normal People* in 1928. From this breakthrough work, he developed the lie detector polygraph test that is still in use today. (Something all moms should probably invest in some day, by the way!)

A catalyst ahead of his time, Marston theorized that people are motivated by four intrinsic drives. These drives direct behavior into the patterns he categorized as D-I-S-C. He defined four D-I-S-C types to show a pattern in how we act. Your skills and education may affect your opportunities and abilities, but they are not measured by D-I-S-C. D-I-S-C is a valuable instrument that helps us to understand behavior patterns in ourselves and in others.

HUMAN BEHAVIOR – SCIENCE AND ART

Human behavior is both a science and an art. It is a *science* in the sense that it's observable and repeatable. It's empirical in nature. We can objectively study it and obtain specific data from it. Research has enabled us to notice that most people have predictable patterns of behavior.

It is an *art* in the sense that we can experience it, modify it and enjoy it. We can feel our behavior and adjust it according to our circumstances and environment. Remember, your personality is somewhat like your "natural state." It is the way we are when we are operating on "automatic pilot" (like we do during those first couple of sleep-deprived months with a newborn).

Four basic personality types, also known as "temperaments," blend in complex ways to make up each person's distinct personality style. These parts are interrelated in fascinating ways, combining in multiple patterns. No one's unique personality is totally defined or influenced by only one set of characteristics. In fact, it is the limitless combinations of these elements that account for the great diversity of personalities.

BIRTH ORDER

Some researchers theorize that unique personality styles are based solely on birth order. Birth order categorically has an effect on family dynamics, but far too many inconsistencies fluctuate around birth order variables.

For example, the observation and study of twins reared in the same family have disproved many hypotheses that birth order is a consistent measure of personality styles, determined when the first- and second-born children are just minutes apart in age. In addition, it has been found that some families have a firstborn child who is a leader and strong willed, some have a middle child who is a leader and strong willed, while other families have the youngest child who is a leader and strong willed. Therefore, the results have transpired inconclusive.

Birth order certainly influences behavior, but erratic results of studies tend to disprove there's a consistent and reliable personality correlation between basic personality traits we're born with and birth order.

GENDER DIFFERENCES

Some researchers theorize that gender plays the significant role in personality behaviors. I took a Gender Communication class in graduate school, concentrating on gender communication differentiation for an entire semester. You've heard the expressions, "Boys will be boys" and "Girls will be girls." There is a significant difference in the way the two genders perceive circumstances, communicate, and socialize.

Gender does indeed affect behavior and communication, but as you have probably determined already, we see highly energized boys – and highly energized girls. We see reserved boys – and reserved girls. We see female leaders, inspirers, peacemakers, and organizers, as we do with males.

Don't misunderstand me. There is a *distinct* and definite difference in how men and women, boys and girls think, communicate, interact, and play. We can again see those differences early on, regardless of how we are affected and influenced by a socialization factor. However, research shows that both genders – men and women – have nearly the same percentage of personality styles reflected in each of the four personality groups.

Nonetheless, inborn personality traits are not a choice any more than the color or our eyes, hair, or skin. Studies have confirmed that children are born with a personality makeup that will determine how they interact with others regardless of birth order, gender, or environmental factors. Since we can't change or choose our inborn personalities for ourselves, we can learn how to recognize and work with the natural personality style we've been given!

A NATURAL TALENT

Most everyone has a primary, dominant, or natural personality style. To better understand this concept, think of someone who has a natural talent. For example, some people are naturally talented to play a musical instrument. They can pick up an instrument or sit down at the piano, thumb around, take a few lessons, and pour out beautiful music in no time. This is a natural talent. Others may diligently practice and practice, and never really achieve a *joyful* noise!

Our primary personality style is like a natural talent we're born with. Some are athletic, some are musically talented, etc. It's a dominant strength that comes easily or is natural to us with very little work. As in playing a musical instrument, one may eventually be able to develop the skill to play decent music if he or she incorporates much practice, determination, and perseverance!

After much practice, determination, and perseverance, we can also learn to develop and operate in other personality styles that are not natural to us. It takes a lot more work, but it's not impossible. In fact, the necessity to utilize all personality styles is often required to conform and communicate effectively in given situations.

LIONS AND PUPPIES, OH MY!

When I refer to personality as being our natural style, I mean it is the way we operate when we're most relaxed with ourselves. It's the way we're "wired." Let's use animals, for example. You would not expect a newborn lion to act the same as a newborn puppy. They have different natures (or temperaments). If you were to approach them, you would do so differently because they *are* in fact different! You would adapt and adjust to the circumstances their natures demand.

For example, the nature of a lion is very destructive. He's called the "King of Beasts." As a way of life, he is a predator. A lion would not make a very good house pet! On the other hand, our new little Shih Tzu puppy, Rocky, certainly wouldn't be viewed as a ferocious beast, but simply as a cute little puppy to have around the house (giving me yet another opportunity to *clean up* after somebody)! We can see in the animal world that different animals have different "temperaments," "personalities," or "makeup." They are designed to be a certain way at birth. Anyone knows that you should approach certain animals differently and treat them differently, based upon what you know about them in advance. The same is true with people. In order to have the best relationship with your children, you need to treat them in certain ways, based on how they are "wired."

As humans, we have intelligent minds – and we *should* be able to think more clearly than an animal. We may feel we should be ferocious in one situation, funny in another, quiet in another, and even pensive in still another set of circumstances. We may have the temperament of a wild lion or a cute puppy, but by the acts of our minds and wills, we can adjust ourselves to our situations.

WHAT ABOUT HISTORICAL DISCOVERIES?

It is important at the very outset of this book that we remember I'm not trying to endorse a certain personality style. Rather, we are looking at differences in behavior. The point of this book is not to discover "good or bad" or "right or wrong" personality styles. We are looking at the *differences* in personality styles.

Moms and children with similar styles tend to have less conflict and get along better together. Problems often arise when one individual has a different personality style than the other's dominant style. After all, it's our dominant personality style that we tend to operate in the most. Personality styles have a significant impact on communication in relationships and how we feel about them.

One of the most important discoveries that I found in my research regarding personality styles and communication is that many scholars, in fact, regard communication as the primary process that creates and sustains intimacy and is the cornerstone of success in our families. If we understand personality styles and the way our children communicate, doesn't it make sense that we will have better relationships with them?

I could go into much greater depth regarding the history behind personality findings, assessments, results, and conclusions, but what's most relevant is to assure you that having differences in personality styles is not as important as what we choose to do with these differences.

Understanding the D-I-S-C personality styles can help motivate us to be more patient and considerate of personality similarities and differences, resulting in more intimate relationships with our children. We can become more efficient and effective moms by seeing beyond our own limited perspective and learning to see from our children's viewpoint as well.

Now let's learn about *Outgoing* and *Reserved* personality differences in Chapter 3!

3

TWO PIECES
OF THE PERSONALITY PIE

*J*ennifer planned an afternoon of pie baking with her four daughters, each one creating her own special pie for Thanksgiving dinner. Distinctive personality styles quickly became apparent in Jennifer's kitchen on this special afternoon.

After mixing the ingredients, Ashley flung her dough into the pie pan, heaved in the fruit, plopped the top crust on, and announced, "Good enough. I'm the first one done and I'm 'outta' here!"

Alexandra was so excited for this fun afternoon of baking together. She couldn't wait to blast the music, singing and dancing while measuring, and laughing hysterically while looking at the splattered flour on her face (checking the mirror quite often). Appearing so floury cute was a prize in itself! After all, fun was what this day was all about for Alexandra.

Barely glancing at the recipe, she sporadically flung all the ingredients together! At first her pie dough was rather dry – until adding more water made it rather runny. Adding more flour brought it back to dry, then runny, dry, runny.... "Oh, who cares? I'll just throw it all in the pie pan anyway! And I'll pour some of these pretty, colorful sprinkles on top!" exclaimed the cheerful, fun-loving, pie chef, (hat and all). (Do

I need to tell you what Jennifer said Alexandra's pie tasted like?)

Abby, was happy to be everyone's assistant – and eventually finished a nice simple pie. She wanted to bake pies that smelled good like those her grandmother used to make. She often offered to help Alexandra with the directions, and was disappointed when Ashley quit so soon. All Abby wanted that day was to be together and make the day special.

Allyson, on the other hand, precisely measured her ingredients and then double-checked, careful not to measure anything incorrectly. She re-read the directions – after completion! It took most of the afternoon to finish her perfect pie. The top crust was skillfully edged, and she artistically created unique leaf designs – with, of course, the leftover crust from Ashley's pie.

Jennifer said, "Despite the fact that all four of my daughters were baking pies, all four tackled pie-baking in a completely different way! Each one is so different!"

Determined Ashley was interested in completing the job in the *fastest* way possible. Her pie may not have been perfect, but, bottom line, she had other things to accomplish.

Alexandra's main goal was to inspire her sisters to bake pies the *fun* way! It wouldn't have mattered *what* they were doing that afternoon, just as long as things were wild and crazy and they were having a good time! (Having a mirror nearby was a plus!)

Sweet Abby was content to be together, and glad to help and support her sisters with their pies. It didn't matter what they were doing, just as long as they were together baking Thanksgiving pies the *traditional* way.

Cautious Allyson approached her pie extravaganza with a completely different motive. Often frustrated and impatient, she strove for perfection and took her time (a *lot* of time) seeing to it that all the baking was done the *right* way.

How can four daughters from the same parents, in the same house, and baking pies for the same Thanksgiving dinner function so differently? Let's D-I-S-Cover their four different personality styles – as different as their four pie-baking styles!

First, we'll take a graphic overview of the four personality types. Imagine four pieces of a pie, perhaps one of mom's favorites – apple pie. (If you can't cook, don't feel pressured. Think Mrs. Smith's!)

CUTTING THE PIE HORIZONTALLY

Outgoing/Reserved

To understand the concept, let's begin by cutting our pie diagram horizontally in half, representing two simple classifications of human personality: The top half represents people who are "**Outgoing**" or fast-paced, while the bottom half represents people who are more "**Reserved**" or slower-paced.

Outgoing people are more active and optimistic. Reserved people are more passive and tend to be a little more cautious (some would say *realistic*). One disposition is not *better* than the other – they are simply *different*, and both are important.

Outgoing (Fast-paced)

Outgoing, fast-paced moms are primarily characterized by the word "Go!" It is in their blood. They love to be on the move. If a friend calls and asks, ""Would you like to go to…," they have heard all they need to hear – the answer is "Yes!" It doesn't matter if the outing is all that great or not. These moms will make it great. Rather than look for excitement, they create it. They take their "party" with them wherever they go.

They are fast-paced and energetic. They like to do everything in a hurry. You'll recognize her right away if you "do lunch" with one of these moms. You will be on the salad when she will be looking at the dessert menu!

They are optimistic and positive, looking for the diamond in every lump of coal, the gold in every clump of dirt. (After all, aren't diamonds a girl's best friend?) Generally, they like to win, and oftentimes win with flair. Outward appearance is very important to them – often, more important than inward qualities.

They involve themselves in projects, church groups, all kinds of organizations, and usually hold a leadership position. They love to be on the go and make things happen. And wherever they go, they usually make great first impressions.

They like being in charge of things, not because they like to work, but because they like to tell others what to do! This doesn't mean they are lazy – far from it. They do not know when to quit. In fact, they often can over-commit themselves. Their motto might be, "If a little is good, then more must be better!" Unfortunately, that is not always true. (Like using too much salt in your pie!)

This type of mom enjoys competition and does not lack much self-confidence. Her eyes are sometimes bigger than her stomach. She sometimes bites off more than she can chew, but to her, that's okay. She will "hustle" and make up the difference. If you've seen the bumper sticker that says, "Move it or lose it, sister," you understand it was written for the outgoing, fast-paced personality type. (It was probably written by one, too!)

Reserved (Slower-paced)

We find several ways to view those whose individual personality style is a little more **Reserved**, or slower-paced. (You might say that it takes this piece of the pie a little longer to bake.) Reserved moms tend to be your "Steady Eddies."

They may be the proverbial "tortoise" left in the dust by the outgoing, fast-paced "rabbit" type, but as in the classic fable, they usually end up crossing the finish line ahead of those who started the race with greater flourish. They have lots of patience and stamina to get the job done. They prefer to slow down, not go so fast.

Reserved types are cautious and reluctant to get involved in too many activities. They would rather look into a situation for a longer period of time than immediately jump in. This mom lives by the motto, "Measure twice...and cut once!" My grandmother was certainly not this type. To this day, I've never been able to duplicate *her* delicious apple pie because when she taught me how to bake, she *never* measured the ingredients or followed a recipe. It was a pinch of this and a pinch of that! She would have driven the precise, reserved-type grandmother crazy!

Reserved, or slower-paced individuals sometimes are accused of being too critical or picky. But this quality actually helps them to see the reality of a situation very quickly. They tend to look below the surface at what is actually under the top layer. To these moms, quality is important. More than looking good, they want to know if it really *is* good. They have an excellent discerning spirit.

Reserved moms tend to be a little quieter and operate behind the scenes. They are slower to make decisions, but get the job done and make sure everything is handled correctly. They do not like surface relationships, and often find it difficult to have a lot of friends. They would rather have one or two really close friends than a crowd around them. They are "homebodies," and do not feel an urge to be "on-the-go" all the time.

Reserved moms tend to be better listeners than talkers. They prefer to not be surprised by unfamiliar situations. The Bionic Woman is not this mom's hero or role model!

WHICH TYPE IS BETTER?

Neither type is better or more important than the other; both are significant. For example, you could compare personality styles with your washing machine. Some cycles agitate at a high speed and rapid spin cycle (like the outgoing personality style) to vigorously clean the clothes.

Sometimes, though, it's necessary to use the slower, soak cycle (like the more reserved type) to gently clean the delicate clothes. Neither cycle is better than the other. Expecting to use the same cleaning methods for all your clothing could destroy some items or not get some articles clean enough! We simply need different methods for different needs, but both are necessary.

PEACE AND QUIET

Some children are outgoing, some are found to be more reserved early on. Mindy and her seven-year-old daughter, Emily, are very outgoing. However, newborn Josh seemed to be exhibiting a much more reserved behavior. As is the custom in our neighborhood playgroup when a precious new baby is born, I delivered dinner to Mindy and her family one afternoon.

Little Josh was perfectly content in his mother's arms when I arrived. His dad and sister were running errands, leaving an atmosphere of solemn peace and quiet at home. With dimmed lights, Josh was drinking his milk (precisely at his scheduled time) in a pleasant and calm atmosphere. Life was good.

That is, until I arrived. Happy to have girlfriend company, Mindy flipped on the lights, began speaking with an animated voice, and an air of excitement instantaneously filled the room! Newborn Josh immediately started twisting, frowning, fussing, fussing, and *fussing* – until I left!

A few days later, Mindy voiced her frustration over this recurring scene, saying, "Emily was never like that! She loved excitement and activity. I don't know why Josh gets so upset!"

I explained to Mindy that Josh probably has a more reserved personality style, preferring a quiet, peaceful, and low-key atmosphere. Initially, it was hard for her to relate to such a difference in personality styles between her children, but Mindy soon recognized the need and benefit of creating a different environment for her son than for her outgoing, action-packed daughter. Once adjustments were administered, success followed.

SUMMARY THOUGHT

Outgoing, fast-paced moms can balance their own personality style by learning how to be more steady and cautious. **Reserved**, slower-paced types can balance their own personality style by learning how to be more determined and inspiring. Many moms feel some confusion when I talk about being outgoing or reserved. As moms, we're always out – going *some*where! Moms get besieged with kids' activities – games, lessons, chores, and meetings. It's a never-ending fast pace daily!

However, I'm talking about how you "feel" about your pace. A fast-paced, outgoing mom thrives on activities and is re-energized by being involved and on the go. But at the end of the day, the reserved mom will be worn out from outgoing activities – emotionally and physically drained. She needs quiet time to recharge.

We've discussed outgoing personality styles in comparison to reserved personality styles and their differences. Now let's determine if you're **Task-oriented** or **People-oriented**. In Chapter 4, we'll D-I-S-C over how to cut our pie diagram in half vertically!

4

TWO MORE PIECES OF THE PERSONALITY PIE

*K*elley never begins a cooking expedition without first accumulating all the necessary ingredients and measuring devices, efficiently organizing them left to right in the order they will be used. Each ingredient is measured accurately and directions are followed precisely according to the recipe.

One morning, some of the moms from Kelley's daughter's school gathered in her kitchen to prepare food for an upcoming teacher's luncheon. It wasn't long, however, before the situation became disorderly and extremely stressful for Kelley.

One of the moms, Terri, talked endlessly and relished the opportunity to have *fun* together – while sharing the latest *gossip*, of course! You know the "I'm not supposed to tell anybody, but…" story. While chatting nonstop, Terri mistakenly measured out salt instead of sugar, pouring it in with the other ingredients! "Do-o-o over," she announced as she laughed hysterically at yet another recipe disaster!

Their sweet friend, Sandi, was happy to be together that day, and glad she could help make a special luncheon for the teachers. She thought Kelley was very nice for opening up her house, and tried not to listen to Terri talking bad about her friends who weren't there that day.

Another mom, Tanya, kept demanding that they get back to work. Bossing everyone around all morning and eventually frustrated with how little they had accomplished, Tanya barked that the next time they would order pizzas to be delivered to the teacher's luncheon – instead of trying to work together as a team.

Terri continued to talk on the phone while the others were left to clean up the mess. Sandi helped, but was physically feeling bad at this point. Her stomach actually started aching because Terri gossiped about their friends. Feeling quite angry at the disorderly kitchen and the recipe mistakes, Kelley secretly vowed to never offer her kitchen again. Avoiding one another, they never worked on the same committee again.

CUTTING THE PIE VERTICALLY

Task-Oriented – People-Oriented

Without an understanding of why we do what we do, we don't understand why "they" do what they do. We can now cut our tasty apple pie diagram in half the other way, vertically, representing two more distinct classifications of human personality. Some people are more "**task-oriented**," while others are more "**people-oriented**."

Task-oriented moms enjoy doing "things" like making plans or working on projects. People-oriented moms like to interact with other *people*. They are more concerned with the way people *feel* than simply accomplishing *tasks*.

Task (High-tech)

The task-oriented personality finds great pleasure in a job well done. We like to call them *high tech*. To these moms, nothing is better than a fine-tuned, well-oiled, peak-performing machine. They are into form and functionality. In fact, their favorite day of the month is when their bank statement arrives in the mail. They think, "Great. I will have this thing balanced in a matter of minutes." And they usually do! They love online banking, because they can access their account balance at a moment's notice.

These moms are great at working on projects. If you need someone to be in charge of organizing a program with lots of details (such as a school function), put a task-oriented mom in charge. She will make sure every detail is covered – twice! They are excellent planners who can see the *end* of a project from the beginning. Unfortunately, they can be so concerned with getting the job done that they can easily hurt someone's feelings or appear aloof. They do not mean to be this way, but because the overall task is more important to them than the feelings of any one individual, the job must get done!

They often prefer to work alone to do things the "right" way and don't want to talk about it much. Small talk in particular is not by nature a task-oriented mom's strong suit. Task-oriented moms are not always the first to offer a hug, either. They're a little protective of their personal space. Again, they do not mean to hurt anyone, but, being task-oriented, they have a difficult time having empathy for the feelings of others if it conflicts with accomplishing the task at hand.

PLANTING FLOWERS THE TASK-ORIENTED WAY

Task-oriented moms can really get into the process of seeing a job take shape, then watching it get accomplished. For example, if you watch this mom plant flowers on a spring Saturday morning, you will observe that she first comes out with all the flowers to be planted, appropriate tools, soil, fertilizer, and wood chips. She looks the beds over (like a field marshal preparing battle plans), and then takes the task in hand. She plants one bed of flowers at a time, completing the job as efficiently as possible.

Pity her poor neighbor who is out for a nice, comfortable morning stroll. When she speaks to her friend who is planting the flowers, the task-oriented mom usually replies with a quick, "Hi," never stopping for a minute. She simply keeps digging as she secretly thinks, "Oh no, I hope my neighbor doesn't stop to talk my ear off. I'm not out here to visit. I'm here to plant and get the job done!" Should the unsuspecting neighbor continue to talk, she may find herself interrupted by the one with the shovel, "Excuse me. I'll be right back."

Do you know where this task-oriented mom is going? Yes – into the garage to get another shovel for her friend! She thinks to herself, "Two can dig better than one, and if she wants to talk, I'm willing to listen as long as I can get this job (task) completed." That is just the way she's wired.

People (High-touch)

Contrast this mom with the high-touch, people-oriented mom. They are interested in relationships with other people. Their motto seems to be, "I don't care how much you know. I want to know how much you care." After studying nonverbal communication in graduate school, I learned that 90 percent of our communication is nonverbal. Therefore, it's not difficult to detect how people-oriented moms *feel* by simply observing their facial expressions and body language.

These moms are into caring and sharing. They like a dynamic group where there is a lot of feeling, empathy, openness, and sharing of one's heart. (The task-oriented individual will listen, but will concentrate more on solving their problems rather than understanding them.)

The people-oriented mom loves to tell her story, but watch out! She can easily get off track and on to another subject! I recently traveled to a women's conference with a new friend, Debbie. Debbie, people-oriented and quite talkative, announced at the onset of leaving town that her goal for the trip was for us to complete four stories by the time we reached our destination. We were embarking on a four-hour road trip! Completing sentences is difficult with our children around, but we were alone in the car! I couldn't imagine how this would be a problem. Needless to say, jumping from subject to subject, we barely completed four stories!

PLANTING FLOWERS – THE PEOPLE-ORIENTED WAY

Because people-oriented moms are more sensitive and concerned with the feelings of other people, they handle, for example, the Saturday morning work in the flower garden very *uniquely*, with an entirely *different* motivation. Rather than being driven to get the task done, people-oriented moms are more concerned with what the neighbors might think of them if the flowers aren't planted. In other words, they feel compelled to plant flowers out of a need to be liked by others. They have a strong desire to be aware of the needs and desires of other *people*.

If someone walks by and begins to talk to them while they are planting, the first thing that goes through their mind is, "Oh, good! A friend has stopped to see me!" If the neighbor stays any length of time at all, it will not be long before an invitation is extended, "Why don't we go into the house and have a cup of coffee and visit? I didn't want to plant the flowers now, anyway!" (Which is often also why their housework gets postponed.)

Life is for the main purpose of developing and enjoying friendships with many, many people. Needless to say, many little plastic containers of unplanted flowers dry up, wither away, and never make it into the ground. (Been there!)

DAY OF THE BANK STATEMENT

The people-oriented mom behaves in a different manner than the task-oriented mom when the bank statement arrives at the end of the month. This day is almost insignificant because it doesn't affect her much, since she seldom ever balances the checkbook anyway. Frustrated people-oriented Cathy said, "My husband made me take over paying the bills each month – *before* he knew my personality style. I did the best I could. Sometimes I would be very determined, write the check, but *then* – never get it in the mail! It lasted for three months. My task-oriented husband, Richard, is very precise and meticulous. He had a perfect credit record before I took over paying the bills. It didn't take long for him to determine that I was *never* touching the bills again!"

Contrary to the task-oriented mom, on the day of the month when the bank statement arrives in the mail, the people-oriented mom's response is more like, "What? How can I be overdrawn? I still have *checks* in my checkbook that I haven't even *used* yet!"

SUMMARY THOUGHT

You have probably identified more closely with one horizontal side of the pie (or circle). Regardless which side of the circle describes you best, you can see that both types are valuable. They are different, but we need both types! We need **task-oriented** moms to get our work planned and completed. They can balance their natural personality style by learning how to be more conversational and empathetic with others.

We need **people-oriented** moms to get everyone involved and to help others feel more comfortable. People-oriented moms can become aware of the need for balance in their own personality style by learning how to plan their work, and then work their plan.

As you probably already know (because moms *know* everything), it takes a variety of ingredients to make a whole apple pie. We can't have the crust without the apples – or the apples without the sugar. And yet without spices, the pie would have no pizzazz or unique flavor. It's not how we measure that matters, but how we *measure up*!

And finally, the key *ingredient* to communication in our families is to recognize and understand the personality styles and appreciate one another's differences. Some of us are **outgoing**, while some are **reserved**. Some of us are **task-oriented**, while others may be **people-oriented**. Keep reading to learn more about this great apple pie and how the various personality styles contribute to the spice of life!

Let's look at Chapter 5 to find out how to put the horizontal and vertical pieces of the pie together!

5

PUTTING THE

WHOLE PIE TOGETHER

*W*hen we combine the two "cuts" of our apple pie diagram, we can see four personality or temperament types. (I hope talking about pies and desserts hasn't been stressful or caused you to dart toward the refrigerator at the end of each chapter! It is *no* coincidence that "stressed" spelled backwards is "desserts"!)

THE WHOLE PIE

Four descriptive letters have been added to the diagram: D-I-S-C. In clockwise order, you'll notice that the "**D**" mom (or child) falls into both categories of **outgoing** *and* **task-oriented**. The "**I**" mom (or child) is both **outgoing** *and* **people-oriented**. The "**S**" mom (or child) is **reserved** *and* **people-oriented**. And the "**C**" mom (or child) is found to be both **reserved** *and* **task-oriented**.

NOTE: It's extremely important that you "see" the model at this point. Understanding it is vital, since this model will be used throughout the book to explain how the temperaments act, react to, and interact with each other.

IN REVIEW:

"D" Type:

The "**D**" personality style is in the top half of the circle (the "**outgoing**" section), and it is on the *left* side (the "**task-oriented**" section). Thus, the "**D**" type personality is outgoing and task-oriented.

"I" Type:

The "**I**" personality style is also in the top half of the circle (the "**outgoing**" section), and it is on the *right* side (the "**people-oriented**" section). Thus, the "**I**" type personality is outgoing and people-oriented.

Both "**D**s" and "**I**s" are active and outgoing (or fast-paced), but each has a different motivation. The "**D**" mom, being task-oriented, has a strong desire to get a certain job accomplished, while the "**I**" mom, being people-oriented, wants to look good in front of people and desires status and prestige.

"S" Type:

The "**S**" mom is in the bottom half of the circle (the "**reserved**" section), and it is on the *right* side (the "**people-oriented**" section). Thus, the "**S**" type personality is reserved and people-oriented.

"C" Type:

The "**C**" mom is also in the bottom half of the circle (the "**reserved**" section), and on the left side (the "**task-oriented**" section). Thus, the "**C**" type personality is reserved and task-oriented.

Both "**S**s" and "**C**s" are reserved, but each has a different motivation. The "**S**" mom, being people-oriented, has a strong desire to please people and make everyone comfortable, while the "**C**" mom, being task-oriented, wants to focus on plans and procedures for getting the job done.

Remember, one type isn't *better* than another. We are not looking for "right" or "wrong," "good" or "bad" behavior. We are considering the *differences* in personality styles so that we can better understand ourselves and others.

WHAT DOES D-I-S-C MEAN?

The descriptive letters in the four quadrants are significant because they are your keys to remembering the **D-I-S-C** Model of Human Behavior. Each of us is a unique blend of these four types.

"D" Type:

An exclamation point depicts the "**D**" (**outgoing** and **task-oriented**) type because "**D**" moms are emphatic in everything! They have a "make it happen now" attitude! You will notice that the "**D**" is in the upper left quadrant of the circle. The exclamation point is the color green because like a green light, it means GO! Six key traits, or characteristics, describe the outgoing and task-oriented "**D**" type:

- **Dominant**
- **Direct**
- **Demanding**
- **Decisive**
- **Determined**
- **Doer**

(Chapter 9 is devoted to the powerful "**D**" type.)

"I" Type:

A star depicts the "**I**" (**outgoing** and **people-oriented**) type because the "**I**" mom loves to be the star of the show! You will notice that the "**I**" is in the upper right quadrant of the circle. Red represents the color for the "**I**" type because it is fiery and exciting and shouts, "*Stop and watch me!*" Six key traits, or characteristics, describe the outgoing and people-oriented "**I**" type:

- **Inspiring**
- **Influential**
- **Impressionable**
- **Interactive**
- **Impressive**
- **Involved**

(Chapter 10 is devoted to the people loving "**I**" type.)

"S" Type:

We use a plus-or-minus sign to depict the "**S**" (**reserved** and **people-oriented**) type because the "**S**" mom is flexible and willing to respond, more or less, the way you might ask her to! You will notice that the "**S**" is in the lower right quadrant of the circle. The plus-or-minus sign is the color blue because it is a peaceful, harmonious color, just like the color of the sky. Six key traits, or characteristics, describe the reserved and people-oriented "**S**" type:

- **Supportive**
- **Stable**
- **Steady**
- **Sweet**
- **Status quo**
- **Shy**

(Chapter 11 is devoted to the predictable "**S**" type.)

"C" Type:

We use a question mark to depict the "**C**" (**reserved** and **task-oriented**) type because the "**C**" mom loves to question everything! You will notice that the "**C**" is in the lower left quadrant of the circle. The question mark is yellow because it represents caution, like the yellow traffic light.

Six key traits, or characteristics, describe the reserved and task-oriented "**C**" type:

- **Cautious**
- **Correct**
- **Calculating**
- **Competent**
- **Conscientious**
- **Curious**

(Chapter 12 is devoted to the careful "**C**" type.)

THE TOTAL PICTURE

By now you have probably thought, "I feel like I have some of all four of the **D, I, S,** and **C** traits in me." Exactly! Don't worry! It doesn't mean you have a split personality! You are a unique blend of these four traits. Each of us is "wired" differently. Some traits are more dominant in us than others. (Much more will be said about "behavior patterns" or "blends" in later chapters.)

These interchangeable terms describe the way each mom's blend of **D-I-S-C** makes up her own unique personality. You will see how each type is different and very special. As you think more about the traits of each type, you may be aware that you really identify most with one or two of these types. Research shows that in 80 percent of the general population, people have at least *two* personality styles that tend to dominate their behavior, while the other *two* styles are less dominant.

It is rare to find a person who is solely a "**D**," or an "**I**," or an "**S**," or a "**C**." Usually we are a combination of a least two of these traits. However, one of these traits may be so prevalent that it dominates a person's life. Other personality aspects will still be present, but to a much lesser degree of intensity.

You may feel that you really do not understand one particular personality type at all. This is perfectly natural, for while we all have some of all four personality types within us, we usually have only one or two dominant or primary types, and one or two less-dominant types. It is important that we are aware of and understand our less-dominant personality types, because this is the place where we can learn and grow in our own personal lives. (It is also a great way we can learn about and understand someone close to us.)

BEAUTIFUL QUILT MASTERPIECES

From the time I was a little girl, I've always admired quilts and how they reveal many beautiful patterns, colors, and styles. You can even add photos on quilts to personalize them in such a unique way now. Due to my personality style, my own quilt accomplishment will probably never occur until I'm retired or ready to settle down a little. (Which may *never* happen!)

Regardless, quilts fascinate me. For Christmas this past year, I sufficed and tackled the popular fleece blankets where you tie strips together around the edges to form a fringe, and presto – you've got a homemade blanket!

I made a blanket with a dog on it for my son and a funky blue-and-green plaid one for my older daughter. I made a bright pink blanket (but, of course) for my younger daughter and an oversized Kansas City Chiefs blanket for my oversized (six foot four) husband. Bottom-line, they were colorful, easy, personal, and most of all – *fast* for this fast-paced personality style (quick to make, but *full* of love nonetheless)!

On the other hand, Betty, my wonderful step-mom, having a more reserved and task-oriented personality style, has taken hours upon hours to piece together many beautiful, intricate quilts. Some are made of soft pastel colors, floral, and frilly. Some are striped or checkered; and have bold or vibrant colors.

She made a contemporary queen-size quilt in masculine, geometric–shaped, black, brown, and gold tones for my son, Scott. She also pieced together a precious little pastel pink quilt with dainty buttons and lace for my younger daughter, Madison's, baby doll bed – and *many* more.

All these quilts are very different, and yet all are very beautiful – each quilt is a masterpiece handcrafted specifically for each person. God also handcrafted our unique personality styles for us – just as beautifully and specifically. And all the pieces of the quilt fit together just like the pieces of our family. When we are willing to take the time to learn and understand the individuality and uniqueness of each personality style, the end result is well worth the time and effort – a beautiful masterpiece.

Knowing my personality style helps define me, not confine me – and it will help you as well. Let's find out how all the pieces fit together in the fabric of life. We'll identify your masterpiece (even if you can't sew) and unique personality style in the next chapter (and hopefully not get tied up in knots)!

6

TRAINING CAMP -
JUST COPE & ADJUST

*Y*ou may wonder if you have to go through training or become certified as a Human Behavior Consultant to understand and recognize the four different personality characteristics. Not at all! Once you finish reading this book and begin to recognize the various styles and their definitions, you can recognize personality styles almost immediately, even from a distance!

As the Assistant Director to the Kansas City Chiefs Cheerleaders, I've had opportunities to encounter some exciting experiences. In this profession you can meet and rub elbows with a lot of "well known" people. For those of you who live in cities with sports enthusiasts (that would be *all* of you), you know the magnitude of love and admiration a city can have for a sports team – to the extreme!

Encountering autograph seekers after the games has always puzzled me. Why do fans want *my* autograph? Do they know what I just experienced? I haven't been offered the multimillion-dollar contract! During countless NFL football seasons, I've survived one-hundred-degree heat and humidity, or worse – rain, mud, or snow in freezing weather. I've battled tangled line cords (often caked with muddy gunk) twisting every which way around my legs and waist.

My mission (since I decided to accept it) is to communicate and coordinate with the Director, who coordinates with the Pack Band, NFL game production plans, television commercials, and anyone else involved in the action. We communicate by headsets – clamped onto the side of my head so *tight* that I feel like the top of my head is going to explode at any moment! There is nothing glamorous about it!

During game time, news and sports media are scattered throughout the sidelines. Every time a big play occurs, I spend a great deal of time trying to duck giant four-foot-long cameras as they race and compete for the next best play position to film. At any given moment, I subject myself to the possibility of a 350-pound lineman charging toward me (with no notice to take cover), risking the horrifying prospect of being the one tackled instead of a football player. (Now *that* would make the NFL Play of the Week!)

It's a chaotic obstacle course. It's crazy, hectic, and wild, but also invigorating, fun, and well worth the hassle. The challenge is exciting and exuberating! (Learn more about why the high "**D**" personality style *loves* challenges like this in later chapters!)

TRAINING CAMP FOR MOMS

Coaching the Kansas City Chiefs Cheerleaders is a lot like the role of a mom – raising a really large family with all girls. (I'll spare you the various challenges that occur repeatedly on a – shall we say – *monthly* basis!) Each new season brings a new squad, in other words, a new assemblage of 32 different personality dynamics.

Observing the potential cheerleaders at tryouts, judges would surmise that they all had an outgoing and people-oriented personality style. They inspire, smile, yell, wave, dance, jump around, kick, and move with a zest of high energy, obviously necessary for a successful tryout performance.

However, a few weeks after tryouts – at training camp, the true personality styles are reflected in no time. For example, during one particular session at training camp, each of the four newly formed cheer groups is required to perform skits, show evidence of creative thinking, and demonstrate public speaking in front of their peers. Stage fright instantly sets in for many. What appeared to be 32 outgoing, people-oriented personalities at tryouts generally are revealed as just a *few* legitimate personality styles of this nature in reality.

During training camp, I teach a **D-I-S-C** personality session to help the girls understand their *own* personality styles and determine why the other squad members act the way *they* do. True styles become apparent immediately. The few high "**D**" cheerleaders aggressively take control of their cheer groups. When it comes time to "perform" onstage, the "**D**" cheerleaders prefer to work, not ham it up onstage. They have things to accomplish!

The "**I**" cheerleaders, on the other hand, love performing onstage, laughing, and entertaining the whole group. They make "best friends" with everyone within minutes of the training camp weekend. They know everyone and everyone knows them in no time. They are the stars of the show!

The "**S**" cheerleaders are much more reserved and absolutely hate to perform the skits onstage in front of everyone. Some are so embarrassed that their faces turn several shades of Kansas City Chiefs red! However, they are so-o-o sweet and supportive of everyone on the squad. Everyone loves and adores the "**S**s" by the end of training camp.

The "**C**" style cheerleaders expect to follow a detailed schedule precisely, with no deviation, and are critical if things aren't done in a timely manner. In fact, a returning (veteran) cheerleader loves following the same schedule of the *previous* year. After all, consistency is something for the "**C**" style to cheer about!

"**C**s" are also exceptionally organized and practiced to perfection. This personality style has the details covered more precisely than any of the other cheerleaders. (Her favorite part is checking off each session as it is completed!) Appearing onstage is a waste of time to them, though. It is more important to complete the schedule than a potential delay caused by goofing around or having fun.

You can spot each style almost immediately. True personalities come to surface in true formation. All you have to do is watch them in action at training camp!

"C AND A"

We have a saying within the Kansas City Chiefs Cheerleaders organization that we've used repeatedly over the years. "C and A." Cope and adjust. That's exactly what is necessary to have a successful and productive year, to get through all the difficult and grueling situations. Cope and adjust. That's also what we have to do as moms with our children, cope and adjust. It's certainly not easy being a mom, while some things seem to come naturally and other things never seem to come at all! (If only we could have gone to a training camp before we became moms!)

So, what do we do? We adjust our perception and adjust our thinking, exactly like we have to do to understand our child's personality. We may be a little different than our child, or we may be very, very different. But one thing is for certain, we were all made uniquely and perfectly designed just the way we are - outgoing or reserved, task-oriented or people-oriented, **D**, **I**, **S** or **C**.

It means we alter our style temporarily to "perform" and do whatever is necessary to cope and adjust – to succeed. Even when our child is completely different and it drives us crazy, we can know that they, too, were uniquely and perfectly designed just the way *they* are. We need to remember that they weren't designed differently to irritate us, but to complement us, and to fill our family with joy by having appreciation of the similarities and differences.

MOM'S NEW SEASON

Equip yourself as a mom. Think of this book as your *training* camp for a new season. As you know, sometimes we, as moms, feel that we don't even know who we are anymore. We often lose our own identities. How many times have you heard yourself introduced as (your child's name)'s mom?" Others may not even remember *your* name! You may begin to wonder, "Who am I?"

So, who are you? Do you know? You need to know *you*. You need to know your child. After all, God, our greatest example as a parent, knows each one of His children so well – in fact, every hair on each of our heads. Why wouldn't we want to emulate His parenting?

As a mom, you can know yourself and your child. Learn the four different personality styles and see how it can change your life! (Change a diaper; change a life – all in a day's work for a mom!) D-I-S-Cover that your child doesn't act the way he or she does to do something to you, but they act a certain way *for* themselves.

Let's read on and find out how we can "C and A" (cope and adjust) to our personality differences without going to training camp! (Although almost *any* reprieve could be a welcome relief for a mom!)

7

D-Ĩ-S-COVER YOUR
PERSONALITY STYLE

*I*f you're looking for a great opportunity to identify the personality style of other moms, try playing Bunco with them. Bunco is fun and mindless – and a quick personality revelation! Let me tell you, pretenses disappear as quickly as the cheese dips and desserts, and the four personality styles become apparent almost immediately on the first roll of the dice.

"**D**" moms are identifiable (no, I didn't say certifiable) right away. They're the moms who are there to win – at all costs. "**I**" moms drive "**D**" moms bonkers at Bunco. "**Is**" are there to have fun, talk, be together, talk, show off their new outfits, talk, and talk some more. "**D**" moms sometimes have to use every ounce of control they can muster to keep from telling "**I**" moms to hush up, pay attention, and play!

"**I**" moms usually arrive late and leave last. (They don't want to miss out on any "after party" juicy gossip that might have developed at another table.) Three or four players sit at each of four different tables. If the "**I**" mom had her way, all 16 players would sit at one table so she could be involved in *all* the conversations. Sitting with only four players at a time is so conversationally restrictive and restraining!

Our "**S**" moms are so sweet, not really wanting to win at all. They just love being together. That's all that matters. In fact, they might even feel bad if they win. I've noticed that as soon as an "**I**" mom starts talking, the "**S**" mom will just stop playing altogether. "**S**s" are such great listeners. She will listen so attentively to the "**I**" mom – or anybody needing someone to listen – and forget about playing Bunco. If the "**S**" mom's partner at the time is a "**D**," the "**S**" mom is probably getting stern stares and glares to hurry up and play.

The "**C**" mom can be a little difficult to play with at times, too. The "**C**s" are the moms you refer to when you need the rules clarified. Trust me, they will make sure the rules are followed precisely. A conscientious game is a correct game to a "**C**" mom. However, there's not a whole lot to be conscientious about in Bunco. This game may be too trivial for a "**C**" mom and not "calculating" enough – a waste of her time. All in all, the food's so wonderful when you get together for Bunco, it's time well spent for any personality style, and a quick personality awareness lesson for all who observe!

HERE'S LOOKING AT YOU!

If you don't have an opportunity to get together with other moms in a Bunco game any time soon, then feel free to answer some of the assessment questions below for a better understanding of personality styles! Let's take a look at yourself first – identifying your own strengths and weaknesses, and then in Chapter 8 we'll take a look at your child's personality.

According to Chapter 3, I would say that I am mostly

☐ OUTGOING   ☐ RESERVED

According to Chapter 4, I would say that I am mostly

☐ TASK-ORIENTED   ☐ PEOPLE-ORIENTED

MINI-ASSESSMENT FOR MOMS

You will see four questions derived from the "Adult Profile Assessment" booklet. This mini-assessment is not intended to completely assess your personality style, but will serve the purpose of providing a quick personality snapshot. (For availability of the complete test, please see back of book.)

In each group of four lines of words, select one line of words that **most** describes you and place an "X" in the box next to it. There are no "right" or "wrong" answers. This is how you see yourself. It is not what you hope to become one day in the future. Neither is it about how you think others might see you. Although it could be a challenge deciding between two choices that you feel represent you well, your *first* inclination is probably your best response.

Next, select one line of words that **least** describes you in that same group of four lines of words and place an "X" in that box. Repeat this process for the remaining three groups of selections, choosing only **one** MOST and only **one** LEAST in each group. Again, you will have a total of only **two** "X" selections in each group – one MOST and one LEAST choice.

Sample:

GROUP 1 (Susan's Selections)

MOST	LEAST	GROUP 1
×	×	Fun to be with, sociable
?	?	Precise, factual, accurate
! **X**	!	Direct, speaks frankly
±	± **X**	Quiet, soft-spoken, reserved

I placed an "X" in the MOST column that represents Direct and speaks frankly," and characterized by the "!" symbol, because I feel that's the definition or line of words that defines me the *most* in that group.

I then placed an "X" in the LEAST column that represents "Quiet, soft-spoken, reserved" (I'm sure that isn't a surprise!) and characterized by the "+" symbol. That's the line of words that I feel defines me the *least*.

Now it's your turn!

GROUP 1

MOST	LEAST	GROUP 1
×	×	Fun to be with, sociable
?	?	Precise, factual, accurate
!	!	Direct, speaks frankly
+	+	Quiet, soft-spoken, reserved

GROUP 2

MOST	LEAST	GROUP 2
!	!	Restless, fidgety, easily bored
+	+	Peaceable, helps others, friendly
×	×	Well-liked, impulsive, charming
?	?	Systematic, tidy, attentive to details

GROUP 3

MOST	LEAST	GROUP 3
?	?	Conscientious, calculating
×	×	Excitable, fun-seeking
!	!	Aggressive, driven, wants to win
±	±	Accommodating, considers others, caring

GROUP 4

MOST	LEAST	GROUP 4
±	±	Moderate, easily swayed
!	!	Self-confident, makes decisions quickly and easily
?	?	Follows routine, decides carefully
×	×	Expressive, likes to talk

SCORE YOUR RESULTS

1. In the MOST columns, count the total number of "!" selections. Record this total in the box below the "!" symbol in the table called MOST CHOICES.

2. Using the same method, add up the other selections (×, ±, and ?) in the MOST column.

3. Using the same method again, in the LEAST column, count the total for each symbol (!,×, ±, and ?) and record those totals in the table called LEAST CHOICES.

MOST CHOICES:

D	★	$	C

LEAST CHOICES:

D	★	$	C

WHAT THE CHOICES MEAN

Obviously, this is not an official assessment and gives you only a glimpse into your personality style. A more accurate and extensive assessment can be obtained by taking the full assessment found in the "Adult Profile Assessment" booklet, which has an average of 90 percent face validity from its statistical validation. It is believed to be the most accurate Style Analysis available today. (See back of book for availability.)

Through choices like the ones you just made, two boxes show a potential summation of your MOST dominant D-I-S-C personality style and your LEAST dominant style. The Style Analysis describes the behavior pattern that you feel is most appropriate for you in your current environment.

Take a few minutes to consider the traits mentioned next. They should generally reflect your behavior, as a description of your personality style. The LEAST choices reveal the personality style that is not the natural or comfortable style for you to function in.

D-I-S-C TRAIT CONTINUUMS

"D" Mom

"D" MOMS LIKE:

Activities	Doing things
Bigness	Hard work
Challenge	Major productions
Competition	To be in charge
Debate	To fight

"D" MOMS ARE:

Goal-oriented	Performance conscious
Hard to please	Self-confident
Industrious	Firm

"Ds" PREFERRED ENVIRONMENT:

Upbeat, fast, powerful

"D" MOMS DON'T LIKE:

Indecision	Slow activities
Talkers who don't produce	Lazy people
Activities without a goal	Taking orders

D-I-S-C TRAIT CONTINUUMS

I" Mom

"I" MOMS LIKE:

Exposure to people
Lots of activity
Making people happy
Making people laugh

Short-term projects
To be on the go
Prestige
Selling...while they
play (golf, tennis, etc.)

"I" MOMS ARE:

Fun to watch
Great starters
Poor finishers

Likeable
Prone to exaggerate
Easily excitable

"Is" PREFERRED ENVIRONMENT:

Fun, friendly, exciting

"I" MOMS DON'T LIKE:

Being ignored
Being ridiculed

Being isolated
Doing repetitive tasks

D-I-S-C TRAIT CONTINUUMS

"S" Mom

"S" MOMS LIKE:

Peace	Friendly environments
Stabilizing things	To finish the job
To wait	Teamwork

"S" MOMS ARE:

Easily manipulated	Loyal friends
Reluctant decision makers	Poor starters
Sweetest moms in the world	Great finishers

"Ss" PREFERRED ENVIRONMENT:

Predictable, stable, harmonious

"S" MOMS DON'T LIKE:

Insensitivity	To be yelled at
Misunderstandings	Sarcasm
Surprises	Being pushed

D-I-S-C TRAIT CONTINUUMS

"C" Mom

"C" MOMS LIKE:	
Consistency	Creativity
Detail	Perfection
Excellent work	Getting it right

"C" MOMS ARE:	
Impossible to satisfy	Self-sacrificing
Meticulous	Logical
Dedicated to the task	Sensitive to details

"Cs" PREFERRED ENVIRONMENT:
Structure with procedures, accuracy, quality

"C" MOMS DON'T LIKE:	
Being criticized	Mistakes
Unnecessary interruptions	Mediocrity
Ambition without a plan	Sudden changes

Now let's take a look at Chapter 8 to D-I-S-Cover your child's personality style!

8

D-I-S-COVER YOUR CHILD'S PERSONALITY STYLE

*S*o how much personality training is required to recognize and discern the four different D-I-S-C personality styles in children? I'm here to tell you, personality styles are so distinguishable that even a preschooler can master recognizing personality styles.

My four-year-old daughter, Madison, said to her preschool teachers one morning, "Wel-l-l-l-l-l, Katelyn is an 'I' because she talks all the time, laughs a lot, gets out of her seat too much, and likes to get attention. See Trent (shaking her head); he's a 'D,' he always has to beat everybody and is kind of bossy and pushy. 'Eli-ba-beth' is an 'S' because she is really nice and really shy. Ryan is kind of shy, too, but he's always working on puzzles and making things. That's because he's a 'C.' He's quiet and really smart."

The morning after leading a D-I-S-C personality training program at Madison's preschool, her teachers were evaluating the personality styles of their fifteen students. They said, "We were *astounded* when Madison promptly spoke up and assessed the personality styles of every student in class that day – hitting each one right on the mark!"

Recognizing personality styles is fairly simple, once you understand the basic styles and distinguish specific behaviors. Obviously, if a preschooler can identify the key characteristics, we all can!

TEACHING MADE EASIER

Mrs. Young recently asked her rather shy first grade student, Audrey, to answer a spelling question in class. Mrs. Young recalls, "I was stunned! I knew she knew the answer, but Audrey quickly let out a gasp, buried her face in her hands, and started crying!"

Obviously, it can be *overwhelming* for an "**S**" child to be asked to speak up in class! On the other hand, if you are – or have ever been – a teacher, you've probably experienced the "**I**" child in class doing quite the opposite – stretching halfway out of the seat while frantically *waving* to be called on to answer the question. If called upon, an "**I**" student may have no *idea* what the answer is! The reason the "**I**" child is raising his or her hand in class is only for the attention!

The "**D**" student, on the other hand, would prefer (or demand) to be the one teaching, in fact, he or she will run the class soon if the teacher's not in control. "**D**" students *want* control and will *get* control somehow, some way. (Create ways to help them do this constructively.)

PART-TIME TEACHERS

My husband and I assisted in our daughter's preschool class at church once in a while as backups. We didn't know the kids very well, but it was easy to detect the "**D**" child right away – Kent. Kent was the one plowing down the other students to snatch the coveted favorite toys. He bossed the other kids (and teachers) around. Kent was determined to run our class, and determined to get extra snack breaks.

The "**S**s" hung on our legs, not willing to leave our sides the whole hour regardless of how hard we tried to *shake them off!* They were very sweet and helpful, but painfully introverted.

The "**C**" child, Brian, was the rule-enforcer for us, since we weren't entirely familiar with the routine. Brian made sure we knew the minute-by-minute schedule (thank goodness he wasn't wearing a *real* watch) – reporting every time Kent would leap through the air as a legendary action hero, or knock an innocent bystander down in his haste to get somewhere first. We could count on Brian to help organize the class and implement the rules. He was like a little Moses marching around, administering the laws of the preschool class!

If you don't have an opportunity to observe children in a classroom setting any time soon, but want to learn more about how your child would respond, then feel free to utilize the following three BOTS assessments to give you a glimpse into your child's personality style.

As your child makes a choice, you will often find him or her making a choice that you expect. Sometimes, however, you will be surprised by a choice. It is *this* choice that is your best opportunity to learn about your child.

HERE'S LOOKING AT YOUR CHILD!

According to Chapter 3, I would say that my child is mostly

☐ OUTGOING   ☐ RESERVED

According to Chapter 4, I would say that my child is mostly

☐ TASK-ORIENTED   ☐ PEOPLE-ORIENTED

MINI BOTS ASSESSMENT FOR YOUR CHILD

You will see four BOTS stories derived from the *All About BOTS! All About You*! profile assessment booklet designed for use with children from kindergarten age through elementary school.

(For availability of the complete child's assessment booklet, please see back of book.)

Read the three BOTS stories, have your child select only one BOT of the four BOTS in each picture that **most** describes him or her, and place a circle around that BOT.

Remember, there are no "right" or "wrong" answers in these stories, only individual preferences. This is how your child sees himself or herself. If you ask your child why he or she made a selection that you didn't expect, your child's answer will reveal how he or she thinks or feels about a situation.

Since you want to discover what your child thinks and feels, be careful to approach this in a relaxed, yet interested manner. Your child's self-awareness is growing as he or she grows. You want to encourage that growth, while allowing for their age and maturity level.

After your child has made the selections, select one BOT that your child feels **least** describes him or her in that same picture, and place an "X" on that BOT.

Repeat this process for the remaining two pictures, choosing only **one** MOST and only **one** LEAST in each picture.

Remember, this is not a test. You cannot fail! It is more like a game where you have fun learning about yourself!

BOTS Story 1 - *Thinking About a Valentine's Day Party*

The BOTS are in school and it's almost time for the Valentine's Day Party. Each one is thinking:

- **1BOT** is bored and begins to tap a pencil on the desk. 1BOT hurries through the homework and does not like to wait around for the party to start.
- **2BOT** really likes parties and wants to talk about all the fun they are going to have! 2BOT tells the other BOTS all about a new game they can play at the party.
- **3BOT** thinks people are so important and likes to give special cards to friends! 3BOT has made a special card. 3BOT is trying to think of something nice to write on each card.
- **4BOT** is finishing the homework assignment, so it will not get in the way of the party! 4BOT is being quiet, and 4BOT wishes that the other BOTS would be quiet too. 4BOT does not want anyone to get into trouble.

Draw a circle around the **BOT** you **FEEL MOST LIKE**. Then, draw an X on the **BOT** you **FEEL LEAST LIKE**.

BOTS Story 2 - *Making a Movie*

The BOTS are going to make a movie. Each one has a different job they like to do:

- **1BOT** wants to be the star of the show and knows how to make people laugh and clap! 1BOT is not shy and likes to try new things.
- **2BOT** is going to plan everything out first, so it all comes out right in the end! It is fun to come up with ideas, and then see if the ideas work.
- **3BOT** knows how the play should work and is going to be in charge of the whole thing! 3BOT tells everyone where to stand and what to say.
- **4BOT** will make sure everyone has what they need, so they can all work together! 4BOT has fun moving the lights around and helping everyone else.

Draw a circle around the **BOT** you **FEEL MOST LIKE**.
Then, draw an X on the **BOT** you **FEEL LEAST LIKE**.

BOTS Story 3 - *Finding the North Pole*

The BOTS are on a trip to the North Pole. Each one wonders if they are lost:

- **1BOT** says, "Follow me! I can find the way to get us out of here!" 1BOT likes challenges and is ready to get started.
- **2BOT** says, "I'll be happy to go along if someone wants to lead the way." 2BOT is not worried about being lost, because they will all stay together anyway.
- **3BOT** says, "We shouldn't go anywhere yet, until we can check it out first on the map!" 3BOT does not want to go in the wrong direction and get even more lost!
- **4BOT** says, "It will all be okay, so while you figure it out, I'll have some fun!" 4BOT would rather think about making a snowman while the other BOTS figure out how they will get back home.

Draw a circle around the **BOT** you **FEEL MOST LIKE**. Then, draw an X on the **BOT** you **FEEL LEAST LIKE**.

Results of the BOTS Assessment Tests are as follows:

BOTS Story 1: Thinking About a Valentine's Day Party

1 BOT -	**"D"**
2 BOT -	**"I"**
3 BOT –	**"S"**
4 BOT –	**"C"**

BOTS Story 2: Making a Movie

1 BOT -	**"I"**
2 BOT -	**"C"**
3 BOT –	**"D"**
4 BOT –	**"S"**

BOTS Story 3: Finding the North Pole

1 BOT -	**"D"**
2 BOT -	**"S"**
3 BOT –	**"C"**
4 BOT –	**"I"**

I hope that you have enjoyed the BOTS stories and have a better understanding, by communicating with your child in the stories, of how they think and feel. This mini-assessment gives you a general indication of the D-I-S-C types in your child's personality style, and can be used as a tool to generate noteworthy discussions and conversation.

(The official BOTS assessment gives a more comprehensive insight regarding your child's personality style, as well as equating your perception of his or her personality style.)

Just like you, I want your child to grow and become all that he or she is meant to be. Talking about the assessment examples in this book and respecting the choices your child makes can help you to build a relationship that is open and honest.

Let's gain an even more exciting understanding about the D-I-S-C personality styles and how we can apply the information to our lives, in Chapter 9!

9

D-I-S-COVER THE "D" MOM

he "D" mom is both *outgoing* and *task-oriented*. "D" moms eat, drink, sleep, and constantly think about power and control. Whoever said, "When the going gets tough, the tough get going!" was particularly describing a **Dominant**, high "D" mom. A "D" mom is driven to accomplish things and loves to compete.

A high "D" mom will start the ball rolling and exert control to get things done. This outgoing and task-oriented type is highly competitive. Life is a game with a series of challenges, and the "D" mom plans to achieve success. "Ds" love to play any game they can win. After all, to them, winning is the reason they play!

"Ds" are **Drivers** and **Doers**. They make the world go around. They are movers and shakers. They have things to do, places to go, people to see. With them, you had better "fish or cut bait!" Do not look for much sympathy from "Ds." They don't express a lot of warmth or empathy. They'll be quick to tell you, "Quit moving so slowly and get going!"

STAY-AT-HOME MOM

It can be difficult for a high "D" stay-at-home mom to feel content unless she establishes an outlet where she can take charge of stimulating challenges in her day. (This does not include the challenges our children can give us, such as not cooperating, especially in front of friends; throwing up in the middle of the night, after you *went* to bed dead-dog tired; or a misplaced shoe when you're already five minutes late!)

"D" moms need exciting and rewarding challenges, a channel to use their personality strengths, such as running for PTO president, managing a part-time business, or even leading a neighborhood playgroup. Basically, they need to be able to lead somebody to do something!

A high "D" mom who works *outside* the home has struggles as well. Since this mom is very driven, she has a tendency to work long hours, get overly caught up in work accomplishments, and succeed at all costs. This could lead to her neglecting the family at home if her **Driven** personality has spiraled out of control. A "D" mom sets high goals for herself and her family, and expects nothing short of accomplishing those goals.

GOALS-R-US

"D" moms can make quick decisions and do not mind taking risks on the way to accomplishing their goals. They not only set goals, they achieve them! If reaching the goal seems to be taking others too long, "Ds" can become very impatient.

"D" moms do things very deliberately and must have a purpose for doing them. High "D" moms are energetic goal seekers who choose to work with people who will help them advance. A "D" mom needs to remember, though, that others may not share her drive. If she becomes pushy, she will create resistance from the very same people who could help her achieve her desired results.

"D's" natural self-composure makes them confident and sure of themselves, so they can be very convincing when they want you to do something for them. Accomplishments and success knock at their doors.   However, if they become successful too easily or quickly, "Ds" could become conceited and give the impression that they have all the answers.   Other personality styles may quietly walk away from the "D" personality style because they feel the high "D" mom doesn't need them — or cares only for her own plans.

A "D" mom must learn that while she can do great things, she can do so much more when other people help her.

A "D" MOM EXPECTS THE BEST

"D" moms are **Dynamic** leaders at work and at home. They seek activities where they can be in charge.   Directing the efforts of everyone involved is their talent.   They never say die.   If at first you don't succeed, try and try again.

As a mom, Beth shows the same drive at home as she once did running her marketing company.   She is very efficient, determined, successful, and expects her children to operate in the same manner in their lives.   Beth sets guidelines and parameters for their behavior, with little room for deviation.   Her discipline rules are strict and above all, she doesn't want to explain something *twice* to her children.   Beth says, "I might be a tough mom, but I think kids get by with too much today.   I care about my children and will always expect their best so they can succeed in life, too."

"Ds" achieve the seemingly impossible.   Kids can count on their "D" moms for strong leadership and direction.   You can recognize a "D" mom at a meeting or church during greeting time – she's a handshaker, not a hugger.   "Ds" come across as "business-like" rather than "friend-like."

The "D" mom, exhibiting supreme self-confidence, doesn't fear hurting others' feelings.   They are firm, **Decisive**, and **Demanding** (think - Judge Judy)!   They seldom take "no" for an answer.   A "no" really means, "Ask again later!"   If you stick to your "no," they will be thinking of a way to go around you.   They are not being rebellious – they just have so much **Drive** and **Determination** that they want to keep going.   A tough assignment, stiff competition, or pressure situations actually *recharge* the high "D" personality style!

WHY AM I SO DIFFERENT?

As a little girl, I always wondered why I was so independent and driven. I grew up in a small town, graduating with some of the same friends whom I started with in kindergarten. While these relationships were very important to me, I couldn't wait to move on to accomplish and conquer all that life had waiting for me. I made quick decisions, snap judgments, and remained driven my whole life – all along wondering why I was so different than most of my friends. If there was controversy or a challenge – let me at it. The tougher, the better. Just give me the word and I would fire ahead!

I loved the competition and welcomed the challenges. They invigorated me. Having a "ready, fire, aim" personality also meant I made a lot of mistakes, though. As long as I was "firing," I was happy. My aim, however, often lacked good judgment. If I wanted it, I went after it. I made plans and expected God to endorse or bless what I thought was best! I finally figured out that it doesn't work that way. It wasn't until God got His prevailing grip on me that I aimed better, making His plan my plan. (It's amazing how *long* it took me to *figure that out!*)

MOUNTAINS TO CLIMB

"D" types have a lot of nervous energy. Their minds are always going a hundred miles a minute. They thrive on movement and involvement. They must have a mountain to climb, a project to work on, or a challenge to motivate them. Bear Bryant once said, "I would hate to give up coaching. I would be dead in six months." After retiring, he was dead in six months.

Ten irons in the fire at once are not uncommon for "D" moms. This high-energy, task-oriented personality is the kind of person who would make an excellent **Dictator**. "Ds" feel that they must be in charge. They have a natural tendency to be a "take charge" kind of person, but that does not mean that they must *run over* everyone.

LEADERS SERVE

There is a real opposition between being a leader and being a servant. A leader must be able to take control of a situation and make quick, accurate decisions. A leader must lead! However, a leader must also be a servant. Moms, in fact, spend the majority of their days as servants, regardless of their personality styles. It comes more naturally for some personality styles, though.

Think of all of our elected officials, our medical personnel, teachers, and clergy. They are all in the *serving* professions to help people. In reality, everyone is in a serving role to one degree or another. But those in serving roles with "D" type personalities will have a tendency to let their leadership ability *overpower* their serving ability. At any rate, both qualities are important, but must be kept under control. A "D" mom who understands herself will be able to lead or serve, depending upon the circumstance and situation.

CONSTANT CHANGE

"D" moms are **Dogmatic**. They take a position quickly and stick to it – unless they see a better idea or plan – then they quickly change to the new method of operation! Those who work with them, especially directly under their authority, sometimes have a difficult time knowing what is going on in their minds.

"Ds" interject change as a constant mode of operation. Because they are so "bottom line" oriented, it is easy for them to change virtually any situation in midstream. To a "D's" way of thinking, everyone should be like them and be flexible enough to adapt to any situation. "D" moms are often wrong, but never in doubt!

Ask a "D" mom a question, and she may answer you before you finish the question. Under control, she is quick to respond, directly and to the point. Out of control, the "D" mom may come across as rude because she pushes past the small talk and confronts the real issues directly.

WANNA' RACE?

A "D" mom expects to win in all things and is **Determined** to do so. A quick way to recognize a "D" mom is to observe her driving style. Driving down the highway side-by-side with another car is an immediate call for a challenge to *race*, to the "D" mom.

Recently my daughter and I were on our way to enjoy a summer movie at the mall, when a car pulled up just to the left of us on the highway. I immediately found myself, without realizing my competitive nature had kicked in, edging forward more and more, as if a race had just been proclaimed. I didn't see just another car; I saw a car about to beat me. Something had to be done!

I could not fathom that this car might win – even though I was in no hurry to get to the mall. I just needed to be the first one there – wherever "there" was! Who knows where this car was headed, but inch by inch, neck and neck, we accelerated those gas pedals.

I was just about to pass the car when I noticed that I was also about to exceed the speed limit, so reluctantly, I backed off. I didn't want to "win" a speeding ticket if a police officer should happen to be nearby. It was when I slowed down and let him "win" (urgh!) and pass me that I noticed there was a police officer nearby, all right. I had been "racing" against an unmarked police car! The driver I had wanted so desperately to beat could have given me a costly speeding ticket had I kept my "D" personality drive and determination up! "Ds" are "driven" to win and can get out of control *fast*!

WHERE ARE WE?

If you're fortunate enough (um-hum) to travel with a "D," you know she would prefer to lo-o-o-p the earth rather than stop or change direction. "Ds" have so much drive and determination that they want to keep going and will stop for nothing! Not much will change their direction if they feel they're in charge.

Jennifer and her friend Bonnie recently returned from a trip with girlfriends. They planned to leave Kansas City, drive all night, and arrive at their destination of Denver, Colorado. Now, for those of you who are familiar with this route, you know they would travel on I-70 straight west across the top portion of Kansas.

By morning, some of the passengers woke up, yawned, curiously looked around and asked, "Where are we?" (At least adults don't ask the notorious, "Are we there yet?") Just then, Jennifer caught a glimpse of a sign ahead that read "Oklahoma City 32 miles." Jennifer, being the calculating and conscientious mom that she is (knowing that Oklahoma would be, of course, the *opposite* direction), thought for moment, *gasped*, then *shrieked* in hysteria! "Bonnie, what are you *doing*? We're in *Oklahoma*!"

Come to find out, high "D" Bonnie wasn't exactly sure where they were, but she was driving and she wasn't stopping. As long as she was moving, she was fine – regardless of the direction. (A minor detail that "Ds" don't like messing with.) Needless to say, Jennifer decided to stay awake for the duration of the trip!

The "D" mom can also appear to be **Defiant**. They project the attitude, "It's my way or the highway." They do not like taking orders or being told what to do (even via highway signs). In fact, they can become *energized* by conflict. After all, a good argument gives them an opportunity to win!

Fortunately, this fervent characteristic – aimed in a right direction – sustains the "D" personality style to stand alone.

"D" types are not followers or led astray by the "wrong crowd." They might be the *gang* leader in one of these "crowds," but not a follower! (Defiance *can* be a great asset.)

PERCENTAGE OF POPULATION

Research indicates that *only* about **10 percent** of the general population has a "D" personality style. (Should we stop right now to say a special prayer of *thanks* to God for being so *merciful* to us?)

THE "D" TYPE IN REVIEW

As we have defined and described the high "D" mom type, you may have found many descriptions that fit you. If so, we would say that you have a high "D" personality style. On the other hand, you may feel that this chapter describes someone very different from you. In that case, we would say that you have a low "D" personality style. For a complete, individual assessment of your personality style, the "Adult Profile Assessment" enables you to explore how the "D" type is part of your personality style. (See back of book for availability.)

We are attracted to the "D" type because they are dynamic leaders who love to be in charge. Powerful and ambitious, they drive toward their goals (as long as they drive in the right direction). They are undaunted by difficulty or opposition, and thrive on challenges. If they find themselves in a static environment, watch out! They will pick up the pace, stir up the mix, and get things moving!

They seek an environment that includes new challenges and freedom from supervision, because they live to make choices that will solve problems. Their underlying priority in any decision is power, which they exercise in making decisions in order to solve problems and achieve their goals.

The high "D" mom, when under control, is powerful and forceful, able to bring to reality what others may feel is an impossible dream. They are never satisfied with the status quo, but are constantly looking for better ideas and bigger ways of doing things.

A "D" mom's motto is, "Ready...Fire...*Aim*!"

Now let's look at the next chapter to learn about the "I" personality style!

10

D-I-S-COVER THE "I" MOM

The "I" mom is both *outgoing* and *people-oriented*. The **Inspiring** high "I" mom loves being with people – showing up at every party! Look for the loudest mom and biggest smile in every group and you'll find her. Whether with one person or a large crowd, this type thrives on contact with others – and the more the better!

"Is" are **Inspirational**. They have bubbly personalities, great senses of humor, and the inherent ability to tell good stories! When you are with them, you feel great. They love surprises, and to them life is a good time. "I" moms help you have a "mountaintop" experience every time you are together. After all, the mountaintop is where they love to live! These moms get bored with mediocre – especially mundane details and tasks – because they would rather spend time with other people.

High "I" moms are **Influential**. They can sell snowballs to snowwomen. They make everything sound great, influencing you with their "charming" ways. Because they are good talkers, they can make you believe almost anything.

They are so enthusiastic and expressive that they may

"accidentally" make things sound better than they actually are. If they are honest, they can become great leaders and producers. If not, they make great con artists.

SUCCESS IN SALES

As a Certified Human Behavior Consultant, I have the wonderful opportunity to witness many "revivals" in families once they understand and apply the D-I-S-C personality information. It was no exception for Dawn, her husband, and their two children.

The day after learning the personality information, Dawn said, "What an eye-opener as to why my family functions so differently – and at various speeds!" Enthusiastic, she proceeded to say, "I was up half the night thinking about the personality styles and how everything began to make sense for me at home, work, church, with friends, etc. I feel like I have a new beginning! There's just one thing – I don't think that I'm really a high 'I,' even though that's what the assessment tests results revealed. I think I'm really more of a high 'D,' like my husband."

She persisted in her reasoning, "I was so successful in my career before I had kids. I won the sales awards almost every week. I enjoyed winning, like a 'D' does. I couldn't wait until every Friday morning when they posted our names on the board announcing the top sales people. That's what I loved *most*! That's what kept me going each week! I didn't like beating the others, but it was so exciting to see my name up there with a star...by...it.... Oh-h-h, yeah. That's it. I get it; I loved the *star*, the *recognition and attention!* Oh my goodness, I *am* an 'I'!"

Dawn, as any high "I" can, thrived on being the "star" salesperson for all to see!

GIRLFRIEND GETAWAY

The high "I" mom wants to be included in everything and doesn't want to miss anything. Periodically, my two closest girlfriends and I escape for a girls' extended weekend away (from all the little personalities running around in our houses, in the neighborhood, at work, etc.). Dianne, Amy and I, friends for about twenty years now, all live in different parts of the country, and fly to a central location for our annual event. We talk, eat, shop, talk, eat, shop and talk some more, covering a lot of life's eminent topics every step of the way.

Each year we reveal and establish personal goals we want to meet by the next year, review last year's goals, and discuss current issues at hand. The three of us end the weekend by sitting in a circle, holding hands, and praying for one another's families, issues, and goals – feeling rejuvenated and refreshed – before heading back to reality! (It's as good a boost as chocolate! As a precaution, however, we always equip ourselves with plenty of chocolate.)

On one particular get-away, high "I" Dianne was pregnant – need I say a whole lot more? We spent the majority of our weekend accommodating her quest for spicy food and bathroom breaks. (I know you all can relate so *well*!) Late one night, we were updating each other with all the major juicy issues going on in our lives. Dianne, as pregnant women often do, was having trouble staying awake (literally *hanging* on the edge of the sofa to keep from tumbling to the floor – while *hanging* on to every word we spoke)!

Dianne refused to go to bed. We kept insisting, but no, she just wouldn't hear of it! Dianne finally confessed (as girlfriends eventually do at slumber parties) that she didn't want to go to bed because she was afraid she might *miss* something! "Is" don't want to miss a thing – especially juicy details about someone else's life! Ultimately, to get Dianne to go to bed, Amy and I *promised* that we would save all the "good stuff" until morning. Dianne was asleep in about 30 seconds – once she knew she wouldn't miss anything.

MAKE IT HAPPEN

"Is" are **Inducing**; that is, cause agents - they make things happen. They do not feel good unless something is happening. The high "I" mom seeks a variety of activities and entertainment to do with other moms and their children. They are stimulating, stirring things up to get the party going. They are naturally magnetic, attracting a group of people to themselves. The high "I" mom is the life of the party. Her lighthearted and friendly demeanor *draws* people to her.

"Is" are also the last to *leave* the party, the last to go to bed at night, and the last to get up in the morning. They like to sleep late because they figure there is not *that* much going on early in the morning for them to miss anyway!

HELLO? LET'S TALK!

High "Is" make good speakers, actors, sales associates, comedians, etc. because they love to talk! For years I tried to convince my high "I" mom to purchase a telephone answering machine. For years she refused. That baffled me. With an answering machine, I could dial the number, leave a quick message, and be done. Mission accomplished. Instead, I had to keep calling back until I could *finally* talk to her directly.

Then one day I figured it out – that was precisely the point. She didn't *want* to listen to a machine (not that high "Is" listen much anyway). She wanted everyone to call back, and then she could *talk,* not *listen* to somebody else talk!

"Is" love to talk more than anything else! I couldn't help but overhear a conversation awhile back at a restaurant. A rather loud woman (in a rather loud outfit) said, "I don't know *why,* but I seem to talk all the time! I can't seem to quit. I just love to talk! Everybody teases me about talking too much, but I can't seem to help it. Talking is what I love to do. I could talk all day nonstop!" And that's exactly what she did for the duration of her meal. (This *can* be a test of true friendship, by the way!)

The high "I" mom can easily start a conversation or explain her point of view. Because she likes to talk and share what she knows and whom she knows, she can be gossipy, sharing private information without meaning to hurt. If you share a secret with a high "I" mom, be aware that it won't stay a secret for long! Now, if you *want* to get the word out, tell a high "I" mom and everyone will know in no time! As the saying goes, "Telegraph, telephone, tele-high 'I'!"

WATCH ME WATCH TV

The entire world is a stage to an "I" – and they are the main attraction. According to Caroline, her friend, Peggy, a high "I" mom from a small town, would never close the living room blinds or draperies on her large picture window at night. And her home was positioned on one of the busiest corners on the main street. Caroline, living down the street from Peggy, said, "I always wondered why Peggy wouldn't shut her blinds. Didn't she know that people could *see* her?"

Exactly! That's what Peggy wanted! If she left her draperies open, then it was if she were onstage for the whole town to see if they journeyed by her house. "Is" love for people to *see* them. A house on the corner in the middle of all the action was a perfect location for this high "I" mom.

TEACHER OF THE YEAR

A high "I" teacher usually wins the "Teacher of the Year" award because they are so much fun, make learning enjoyable, and therefore meet with more receptive learners. "Is" can inspire students, causing them to want to better develop themselves, their futures and careers. The high "I" students enjoy being around them and hearing their stories.

"Is" won't admit it, but they never have lesson plans. They "shoot from the hip"! In retrospect, students may look back and see that they actually did not learn much information from that teacher, but had a lot of fun!

NO STRANGER HERE

High "Is" are **Interesting**. They know so many people. Usually they know a lot of important people. People are their life, the more the merrier. They do not have to worry about going to a party – they take their own party with them wherever they go! They love to tell their stories, imitate other people, laugh, and make you laugh. When they leave a room, you can suddenly feel the temperature drop. It begins to get colder because the "on fire" high "I" stepped out.

In a matter of minutes, a high "I" mom can meet a total stranger and make them feel right at home. They are friendly and carefree, and their generous nature allows them to focus all their attention on this newfound friend. There are no strangers to the high "I" mom. They are simply friends that this interactive person has not yet met!

They usually enjoy a wide range of social relationships from many different backgrounds. Their optimistic attitude makes them fun to be with, and their happy, inspiring disposition helps them get along with almost everyone.

LEAD THE WAY

High "Is" are **Impressionable**. That is, they are easily influenced. Although they are outgoing in so many respects, they are also followers. They see what the latest fads and trends are, and then go after them regardless of how much the price tag is or how much debt they carry. (They're allergic to budgets.)

They have such a strong desire for people to like them that they will do just about anything to please other people. Many times, they will be trendsetters themselves. They dress, behave, and function basically to get attention in one way or another. Remember, show them how much you like them, laugh at their jokes, and you've got a friend!

I WISH UPON A RED STAR

High "Is" like to be **Important**. They hate little jobs or small tasks. They like to start at the top. They care more about a title and status than they do about power. If a mom tells a high "I" child to be good and she will get a *red star* next to her name, the child is really pleased and thinks, "Oh boy!"

(Tell high "Ds" the same thing and they think, "Keep your silly star and let me be in charge!")

"Is" are dreamers and schemers. They always are thinking about, wishing for, or letting their minds wander off to exciting adventures. They just know the "big event" of their life is around the next corner. If they harnessed all their thoughts, organized them, and put them into practical steps of action, there would be no stopping them.

Unfortunately, most high "Is" are severely out of touch with their own feelings and with reality. They must remember – "all that glitters is not gold!" Because they are so impulsive, they are prone to jump into the pool of life when it sounds like fun, or when they are in the mood.

Calmness is not a part of their makeup. "I" moms can be higher than a kite or lower than a skunk. Fortunately, they do not stay down very long before they find something else fun to do!

SHINING ATHLETES

High "I" athletes are captivated by the hoopla and applause they receive in the athletic arena. In football, high "Is" particularly like playing the position of wide receiver. All eyes are focused on the wide receiver as he runs down the field and catches the ball for a touchdown!

"Is" look sharp before, during, and after the game. You can easily detect a high "I" Kansas City Chiefs player. When they arrive at the stadium, they are dressed as fashionably as they come, dressed to the max. On really cold game days, many high "I" players parade down the hallway to the locker room in strikingly gorgeous fur coats, greeting everyone! (Those are really *l-a-r-g-e* fur coats, by the way!) Outgoing high "I" players linger after the games, friendly to all their fans. Security will sometimes wait for hours before the last one finishes signing autographs.

"Is" need to *shine* (not from sweat, of course)! They are good competitors, but for reasons different than the other personality styles. Coaches who understand high "I" athletes know they can get twice as much from them with *praise*. They do not like to be "put down." If you "fuss" at them, they will usually quit trying. They feel, "You don't like me, so why should I try?" When you encourage them, they think you believe in them and their abilities. That is when they will wear themselves out for you in order to show you just how right you were about them!

DID I TELL YOU ABOUT...

"Is," however, are **Interchangeable**. They are like chameleons – they can change "colors" very quickly to take on characteristics of their environment. They can be one way on Sunday (in church) and another way on Monday (at work). Many times, a high "I" will try to "one-up" you! In other words, no matter what you do, they can top it. Their weaknesses include inconsistency and stretching the truth.

When in kindergarten, my daughter Madison had a high "I" friend over one afternoon after school. Charming and gregarious Katie danced like a butterfly, and twirled and whirled. She theatrically shared how, the week before, she-e-e-e had ridden in a friend's car and she-e-e-e had gotten to watch a movie on their DVD player! Madison, unimpressed and focusing intently on building her doll castle, responded in a monotone voice, "Oh, we have a DVD player in our car, too."

Katie, determined to keep going until she got the attention that she so desired for her story, continued – this time adding a little more flair, "Oh-h-h, ah-h-h well, but they have a big screen TV in their car! It is so-o-o big!"

Madison, still concentrating on her building project, responded with, "Hum-m-m."

Disappointed by her inability to share an impressive story, high "I" Katie added, "Oh, yeah. We have one in our car, too. That's right. We have a ah-h-h, DVD and big screen, too. Yeah, we do, yeah." Still no accolades.

A few minutes later, Katie broke down in tears for no reason at all – except that she was so frustrated – almost devastated – needing *desperately* to impress her friend with her story. After observing the play date interaction, I realized how much Katie was earnestly seeking that "red star" for her entertaining story, and how discouraging it can be to a high "I" child when he or she doesn't get any kind of recognition or attention.

Exaggeration or inconsistency while sharing stories is not a big issue for some "Is." They figure everyone is **Inconsistent**, so they just don't worry about it very much. If they fail to understand the implications of their personality traits, their lives will be one long roller coaster ride of highs and lows (and getting out of hot water)!

ZAP THE FLAPS?

Tiffany, fun and delightful to be around, has the gift of hospitality (like many high "I" moms), but she *can't cook*! In fact, several years ago when she invited us over for dinner for the first time, she served – frozen pizza cooked in the microwave – and with a relatively proud expression of accomplishment. Expecting accolades to accompany this presentation, it was as though she had announced, "Well, what do you think? Do I get a red star?" Zapping frozen pizza was quite a feat for her. (Her idea of *intense* cooking involved puncturing plastic to let steam out!)

Today, however, Tiffany actually attempts to cook rather than zap. She's come a long way. One Saturday morning she invited my family and me over for breakfast (high "Is" love to entertain). Tiffany was preparing to serve us sausage and "flapjacks" (that would be pancakes in Kansas). Every *single time* she plopped new pancakes on the griddle, she would tell another story – and *fry* those pancakes to a crisp! (Did I mention that the sausage was *blackened?*)

Tiffany would get so caught up in the moment – and the story – that nothing else mattered! If we ate a well-prepared meal, fine; if not, fine! After all, the meal was just an *excuse* to be together! Being together with friends, talking, and having fun was all that mattered! (Eventually, the high "D" in me *did* have to take control, grab the spatula, and supervise the pancake duty. Pancakes are just *too* precious of a commodity to waste!)

EXERCISE AND LOOKIN' GOOD

Impressive high "I" moms project a polished image, being keenly aware of their appearance. They can overwhelm you. As soon as they walk into a room, the entire atmosphere changes. Suddenly everything begins to "lighten up" (one of their favorite expressions).

They enjoy where they are at the time. They believe life is too short to be miserable. They figure (as the old saying goes), "If you can't be with the one you love, love the one you're with!"

High "Is" are **Interested** in people. That is what makes them tick! They are particularly concerned about what everyone thinks of them. They evaluate all projects by the level of interest shown by other people. They like to travel or go places in groups. Some people are happy just to have one close friend, but not high "Is." They love people and activity. They are interested in what everyone is doing.

Julie, a high "I" friend, and I used to exercise together at a rather elite fitness center. (She would *never* work out by herself.) She amazed me with her new beautiful, colorful workout attires (credit card still *smoking* from the shopping trip to the mall to purchase her hot, new little outfit). She always managed to look dazzling!

My goal, on the other hand, was to actually *exercise* – physically accomplish an extensive workout! (With thighs like mine, it's not a choice.) In fact, I finished my workout with quite a *glow* (since girls don't actually *sweat*!). Julie, on the other hand, left with hair and makeup unscathed. She went to the gym for a different reason – to talk to everyone!

Julie had no intention of exercising; it was all about whom she was going to *see*, and more important – who was going to see *her!* (And somehow, Julie *still* managed to stay slim and trim. (It must have been from all the extra energy she burned up chasing down friends to get the latest scoop!) She had an amazing ability to get to know practically every person in the gym. (And look good while doing so!)

OUT OF THE MOUTHS OF BABES

A lot of "going and doing" can be great if coupled with maturity and self-discipline. My neighbor, Donna, is action packed, fun, and constantly on the go. There is no doubt that when she walks into a room, the room lights up!

Her five-year-old son, Andrew, is just like her – high energy, to say the least! (In fact, he's pictured as the "D" boy on the front cover of this book. Need I say more?) Ashton, her more reserved, seven-year-old son, really struggled with constantly being on the go, though. He cringed whenever his mom announced their next destination.

Finally, one day Ashton said, "Mom, look at me in the eyes," (sound vaguely familiar?) and pleaded with her, "I'm *tired* of going places all the time. Can't we just stay home? I need to do *quiet* things today."

Donna felt confused and frustrated, until I explained their personality differences. Then she understood. Sometimes we all need to be more outgoing and have fun – but sometimes we *do* need to stay home and do "quiet" things. (Out of the mouths of babes.) Understanding their personality differences helped high "I" Donna to start scheduling "downtime" for Ashton's sake, while it actually benefited everyone else in the family and helped her find time to get things done at home.

High "Is" are not primarily interested in getting a job done. Their primary interest is in how everyone gets along with each other during the job. Relationships are crucial to a high "I" mom. A stay-at-home high "I" mom may feel isolated if not able to have much involvement with others. If you're a high "I" mom in this situation (particularly cooped up with younger children), find opportunities to get involved with others in a way that is good for you and your child. Balanced according to personality styles in the family, the high "I's" enthusiasm for involvement could benefit everyone!

PERCENTAGE OF POPULATION

Research indicates that about **25-30 percent** of the general population has the high "I" personality style as their primary driving force. That is a large percentage of the population. It is certainly in harmony with the number of comedians, actors, public speakers, and entertainers in our world!

THE INSPIRING "I" TYPE IN REVIEW

As we have defined and described the high "I" type, you may have found many descriptions that fit you. If so, we would say that you have a high "I" personality style. On the other hand, you may feel that this chapter describes someone very different from you. In that case, we would say that you have a low "I" personality style. For an individual assessment of your personality style, the "Adult Profile Assessment" booklet enables you to explore how the **Inspiring** type is part of your personality style. (See back of book for availability.)

We are attracted to the **Inspiring** type because they are magnetic leaders who make life grand. No other personality type is able to set the tone or direction for activities as much as the high "I." They want to make everything friendly and fun. They love to persuade others to their way of thinking because they want to be popular with everyone. We can admire their ability to brighten almost any situation, and this ability often earns them our recognition and approval of their dreams. We all need people with **Inspiring** styles in our lives!

The "I" mom's motto is, "Ready...Aim...Let's *talk*!"

Now let's take a look at Chapter 11 to learn about the "S" mom's personality style!

11

D-Ĭ-S-COVER THE "S" MOM

The **Supportive** high "S" mom is both *reserved* and *people-oriented*. She prefers a calm, easygoing environment and enjoys making others comfortable. "S" moms run on less energy than the "on-the-go" mom of a different personality style. If an "S" mom has a child who is of the opposite, *high-energy* style, she may feel worn out by this child's drive and outgoing behavior.

"S" moms prefer one or two close relationships, and are content to stay at home rather than run around. Other fast-paced personality styles, however, may leave the slower-paced "S" mom behind, due to her lack of drive or determination to get out and do things.

Steady and **Stable,** she likes doing one thing at a time. Routine may be boring to some moms, but not to the "S" mom. It gives her a great deal of security to know things are constant and in order. If this mom feels she is being pressured to move too quickly, she may become indecisive and stubborn, holding on to what is familiar to her.

A SERVANT'S HEART
You must admire the desire of a high "S" mom to please. They are willing to go the extra mile, even the tenth mile.

Perhaps the best "S" words that describe this personality style are **Supportive** and **Servant**. "Ss" are great helpers, assiduously avoiding the spotlight in whatever they do.

"S" types make up a great percentage of our serving professions. They are "yes" people. The hardest word for an "S" type is say is the word "no." They look for ways to cooperate and help, always with good intentions. It generally takes a while for moms with this personality style to even make a decision, because they don't want to offend anyone. This mom strives for everyone to be happy.

"S" moms have an extraordinary ability to nurture and care for others. Amy, one of my closest friends (whom I mentioned in an earlier chapter) and a high "S" mom, is thoughtful and kind with a real servant's heart. Everybody appreciates a good listener, and she will listen for hours on end to my stories and situations I've impetuously managed to get my high "D" style into, with compassion and empathy.

The former homecoming queen, cheerleader, honor student, Miss "You-Name-It," now exemplifies the most devoted "S" mom I've ever known. Daily, Amy cares for her two beautiful boys, Hunter and Bryan, in a capacity that most of us don't experience.

Her older son, Hunter, currently fourteen years of age, was born with Williams Syndrome (a rare genetic condition which causes medical and developmental problems). Her second son, Bryan, now eight years old, has a severe form of Cerebral Palsy. Amy's days are filled with physical therapy sessions, two-hour feedings, bathing and dressing growing boys (who are growing bigger and heavier every day), finagling a highly technical wheelchair, researching and evaluating the latest expertise to improve or enhance their very complex lives, and in her spare time she washes clothes, cooks, and cleans house.

I could not do what Amy does and have the patience and stamina to get through each day. She is truly extraordinary. God has gifted and equipped her with the ideal "S" personality style to support, nurture, and care for her family in a remarkable capacity that the other personality styles would, without a doubt, have greater struggles living such a servant lifestyle. With a servant's heart, she single-mindedly focuses on completing her daily challenges and supporting her family by serving her husband and beautiful sons. She is an amazing "S" mom, true to her "S" personality style.

"S" moms yearn to please, are compliant, and have a gift of contentment. Adaptable, they try to do what you need them to do because they want you to feel loved and supported.

"S" MOMS CAN SPOIL

"Ss" take orders very well, perhaps too well, and can commonly be perceived as too **Submissive**. They are quick to take a back seat and give others the opportunity to be first in line. While there is just something about human nature that makes us all dislike a "know-it-all" bossy person, the "S" type comes across as just the opposite – very easy to like.

When Dianne (the other part of the threesome) and I first met twenty-some years ago, we spent a great deal of time together. I was thrilled to have such a wonderful, fun, and outgoing new Christian friend. We were "joined-at-the-hip" girlfriends.

However, there was one minor problem – Dianne expected me to wait on her hand and foot! She's anything but *lazy* (prissy maybe, but never lazy), so I could *not* figure out why in the world she expected me to do everything for her. (And at that time, my out-of-control high "D" personality style didn't function very well in a "servant" role.)

After learning about the D-I-S-C personality styles, I figured it out – Dianne was raised by an "S" mom! Having had a sweet, supportive, tenderhearted, *serving* "S" mom, Dianne had become accustomed to having *every little need* met. She had no idea she *expected* everyone *else* to wait on her as well!

After I explained the personality information to Dianne, she recognized she had been this way in every relationship, and in retrospect she realizes her expectations actually caused a few relationship problems. Dianne's mom is one of the dearest, sweetest, kindest, most giving and supportive moms I know.

She didn't mean to, but as an "S" mom she *spoiled* Dianne! (But with good intentions and a great recovery!) Even with good intentions, "S" moms have to be careful not to spoil or overindulge.

PIG OUT IN COMFORT

"S" types are **Sweet**. I have never met an "S" mom I didn't like. They are just so wonderful and endearing. What is there *not* to like about such a supportive personality style? They are not pushy or bossy, and are rarely offensive. You just like being around them – they make you feel right at home. You feel comfortable in their presence.

"Ss" take great care to please and serve. These moms find security in – and enjoy the benefits others receive from – their special efforts. The funny thing is that "Ss" don't do anything deliberately in order to make you like them. That's just the way they are. They would be that way even if no one else were around.

We spent the weekend with my friend, Elise, and her family and they took us to *over*eat at Lambert's Café. This restaurant holds the title of "Home of the #1 Restaurant in America to Pig Out" (and we managed to live up to their famous title). I absolutely love homemade dinner rolls, and the servers *throw* them across the room throughout the entire meal. (It's *great!*) I stretched my arm out like Gumby to catch rolls all evening. (That isn't *all* that got stretched out!)

As our two families loaded up in their van, High "S" Elise came running out with blankets and pillows for everybody. It was only a thirty-minute drive to this restaurant, but thoughtful Elise made sure everybody was completely comfortable for the road trip. (Another wake-up call for me!) "S" moms are intuitively sweet, thoughtful people.

SHE'LL ALWAYS BE THERE

"S" moms both communicate and desire a great deal of **Security**. They *communicate* it in the sense that they want to know you will always be there for them, because they will always be there for you. You can depend on an "S" mom in a time of need. She is loyal and thoughtful.

Regardless of our personality style, we can develop the habit of looking for the best ways to support others. It is easier for high "S" or high "I" types because they are people-oriented, but anyone can cultivate this mind-set if they will work at it. (Unfortunately, I will be working at it for the rest of my life!)

NO ATTENTION, PLEASE

Another characteristic of the "S" type is **Shyness**. "Ss" are passive and desire to go unnoticed. They prefer sitting in the back of a room so no one will notice them. They hardly speak up in a group or raise their hands to be called on. It is not that they don't like people – far from it. They love people. They just don't want to be pushy or to get a lot of attention in a group.

High "Ss" don't get easily excited, even in the midst of a crisis. They're a calming influence to others. They love to have fun and enjoy excitement – just as long as it doesn't center on them. They will sometimes avoid attending functions or get-togethers in order to escape excess attention.

SAME TODAY

"S" moms like **Status quo** or **Sameness** because they enjoy situations in which they find stability. One "S" word they don't like is "surprise"! They are more comfortable with the known and expected than with the unknown and surprising. If things stay the same, day in and day out, they feel comfortable because they know what to expect.

"Ss" drive to work the same way, eat in the same restaurants, order the same food, go to the movie they have already seen twice, and visit the same vacation spots every year. This would be boring to some, but to "S" types, it brings less stress (another "S" word they don't like!). This repetition of choices also eliminates the challenge of making new decisions.

"S" moms are also very **Sentimental**. They have favorite movies, memories, and moods. They treasure and revisit the past often. It bothers them when places from their childhood change. They like things to remain the same. "Ss" save all their old yearbooks, love notes, and other memorabilia.

ANYTHING TO AVOID CONFLICT

"S" moms can be taken advantage of if they are not strong or assertive. Linda, an "S" mom with three kids, seldom enforces rules, chores, or requires her kids to do anything "they don't like." She sidesteps conflict. Linda stays up until two or three o'clock in the morning cleaning, washing clothes, packing lunches, and taking care of everyone's needs. She is back up at six in the morning to help everyone get ready for school. She chooses exhaustion – to keep the peace.

Linda explained, "I'll do anything to avoid conflict. The kids don't like having to do the work and they complain every time." By her acquiescence, Linda's kids, unintentionally but ultimately, run over her day after day. She's worn out and stressed out most of the time. "S" moms can turn into doormats if they're not careful.

"S" MOM TO THE RESCUE

"Ss" can be "enablers." Enablers rescue and bail others out of trouble rather than let them suffer the natural and logical consequences of their actions. An enabler mom "covers" for her alcoholic friend or child, rather than raising her naturally low "**D**" personality style and saying, "Look, you need help – not more alcohol. I'm taking you to either Alcoholics Anonymous or the hospital!" That is almost impossible for an "S" mom to do. She can love and support others, yes, but enable, no.

The "S" mom can easily be satisfied just to be with you. If you need her help, she will happily help you. Sometimes she offers help when she really should not, though, particularly if the other person is taking advantage of her or doesn't really appreciate what she is doing for them.

THINKING WITH HER HEART

Finally, "S" moms can unfortunately come across as real **Suckers** and easily be manipulated to serve the selfish intentions of others. This is certainly not because they are unintelligent. It has nothing to do with their *heads*, but it has everything to do with their *hearts*. They tend to think with their hearts.

They often get talked into doing things they don't want to do – into buying things they don't need – and into going places they don't want to go. They do all these things to please other people. They easily feel sorry for someone and feel that they have to help.

PERCENTAGE OF POPULATION

Research indicates that about **30-35 percent** of the general population has this type profile. This is the largest percentage of the D-I-S-C personality styles. The supportive "S" personality type represents the most needed segment of our society. Obviously, you would expect any culture that basically runs as a service industry to have many people who have developed these skills.

Again, it is not that one personality type is qualified to serve and another isn't. It is just easier for certain types to follow certain patterns. Regardless of our profile pattern, we should be willing to submit ourselves to the needs of others in order that we may help them.

THE SUPPORTIVE MOM TYPE IN REVIEW

As we have defined and described the high "S" mom type, you may have found many descriptions that fit you. If so, we would say that you have a high "S" personality style.

On the other hand, you may feel that this chapter describes someone very different from you. In that case, we would say that you have a low "S" personality style. For an individual assessment of your personality style, the *Adult Profile Assessment* enables you to explore how the Supportive type is part of your personality style. (See back of book for availability.)

We are attracted to the supportive type because they are servant leaders who walk with us. Patient and persistent, they gently advise and guide, while they do what they can to make life run more smoothly for all of us. They are faithful to serve, and they help others to be more tolerant of one another through their steady and loyal style.

"Ss" are often the calm in the midst of a storm, offering a peaceful and rational response in a crisis. They prefer an environment that is comfortable, harmonious, predictable and stable. However, "Ss" would do well to become more goal-oriented and self-motivated.

Although the "S" type may never tell you directly, they need your appreciation for their help and affirmation of their special place in your heart. Their basic priority is predictability. They keep a steady pace and seek to provide security for their family first. The high "S," when under control, is a caregiver and teacher who stands with us through difficulty, helping us learn and grow to be all we can be.

The high "S" mom's target motto is, "Ready...Ready... Ready..."

Now let's look at the next chapter to find out about the "C" mom's personality style!

12

D-I-S-COVER THE "C" MOM

The "C" mom is both *reserved* and *task-oriented*. "C" types are **competent** individuals. They *know* that they *know* what they *know*! They have done their homework. They research the facts and track them carefully. They develop a plan of action and follow it. The "C" mom's axiom could be, "Plan your work, work your plan."

Other personality types may talk things out, but not the high "C" mom, **contemplating** and thinking things through before she takes any action. She does not offer her opinion about any subject until her viewpoint is well developed.

Their cognitive skills allow them to see a better idea, and they go to any length to achieve excellence. If, however, high standards aren't met, they can be hard to please. "C" moms question and validate information, giving full attention to details. Expect the "C" mom to be accurate and exacting, seeking precise details and expecting quality answers. Estimating, rounding up numbers, and going with your gut feeling or instinct, are all examples of shoddy work in their opinion!

MICROMANAGER MOM

The high "C" mom micromanages every part of her home and her child's life (which can be awesome and nerve-wracking at the same time)! She will give a good, objective analysis of a situation. However, because "Cs" are not people-oriented, that analysis usually will not make allowances for the feelings of the people involved in that situation.

"Cs" think that people should act on facts, not on their own irrational feelings. They are both blessed and cursed with being perfectionistic in their expectations. They simply expect that doing your best is assumed, and your best should be as perfect as you can make it – and then a little better.

PLAY BY THE RULES

"Cs" are **careful**. They proofread Xerox copies! They play by the rules, and they expect everyone else to play by the rules as well. Their rules include leaving and arriving on time.

If you don't own a watch, don't worry about it. You can determine the time by observing a "C" mom. You can set your watch by her. If you're getting together with another "C" mom, don't be late or unpredictable; she could become impatient or moody as a result.

THE ATTACK OF THE FIFTY-FOOT CORD

"Cs" are **cautious**. They look before they leap, because they don't like making mistakes. Regardless of our personality style, we can never be too careful or cautious when working behind the scenes of a chaotic, frenzied Kansas City Chiefs game. One of the "C" staff members for the Kansas City Chiefs Cheerleaders tells the nightmare story of a particular football game she was working.

To give you a little inside information, I'll explain what goes on during a typical home game. Four staff members stand in the four corners of the field, wearing headsets to maintain communication and coordination with the Director, who coordinates with the announcer, television commercials, etc. NFL game production is actually a really *big* deal. It involves intensely high pressure, national television exposure, and *astronomical* financial risks. Approximately 79,000 people deluge Arrowhead Stadium for each home game – almost guaranteeing total chaos at times – and a good chance that something could go wrong at any given moment.

During the game, one-fourth of the cheerleaders are also in each of the four corners with the staff member, rotating from corner to corner at various times. When the director gives the cue to rotate or hit the field to perform, the cheerleaders and the staff members *have* to be alert and ready to move lightning fast!

Staff members communicate by wearing headphones attached to a fifty-foot cord that extends to an electrical box on the lower side of the grandstand wall. They have to be very careful to not let their headphone cords get tangled with the other cords from the jumbo screen and television cameras.

At one particular game, we desperately needed extra help for a big performance. Soliciting high "C" Nannette, always cautious and careful and who normally *avoids* the crowds, she complied – reluctantly – for "just this one time."

The cheerleaders were anxiously anticipating the performance of their dance routine at the two-minute warning before halftime. Suddenly, the Director's voice roared into the headphones, "It's time! Tell the cheerleaders to *fly* toward the end zone! Now, now, *now-w-w-w,*" and the girls darted down the sidelines!

However, on the way to the end zone, Nanette noticed that one of the cheerleaders had dropped her pom-pom! This was *incorrect*! It could blow the routine! So, Nannette dashed down the sideline to retrieve it, and then flew around the corner of the end zone to deliver it!

Sprinting in the midst of all the other NFL chaos and *not* being oh, so careful and cautious, high "C" Nannette abruptly found herself *catapulting* into the air (it gets worse!) with her mouth *hooked* like a fish from the headset microphone! She was then *slammed* to the ground – laid-out, feet first – hoping beyond hope, by chance, that *none* of the "sold out" (79,000) fans in the stadium had noticed.

Face plastered to the ground, spewing out dirt, Nannette slowly peeked up through her tangled hair. One by one, she saw the Chiefs fans – not only *looking* at her (and high "Cs *hate* to be looked at), but also applauding and cheering *wildly*! First the bottom tier, then the second tier, and all the way up to the third tier!

Horrified and *totally* humiliated, Nannette declared, "I will never, *ever, ever* work on the field again!" And needless to say, to this date, she never has again. It was a nightmare experience never to forget!

On the other hand, if you sat high "C" Nannette down to a sewing machine to "correct" any problems with one of those itsy, bitsy, red-sequined uniforms, she would quietly, in her reserved sort of way, carefully, tediously, and flawlessly tackle (in a nonphysical fashion, of course) and repair the uniform to complete perfection.

High "Cs" will avoid, and do not want to be in front of, a crowd under any circumstances (with or without their mouths hooked by headsets!).

FIFTY-FOOT CORD STRIKES AGAIN

Dayna, a high "I" staff member, had a similar experience at a Chiefs game. But Dayna, on the other hand, *loves* to tell her adventuresome story! She said (in her dramatic, storytelling fashion), "I was on the field with the girls and it was almost time to perform! I looked like a mother duck with all my little (red-sequined) ducklings proudly marching behind me, going wherever I would go, following my every move toward the end zone!"

Dayna loved the attention of the crowd and the stunning, sparkly girls following behind her. They would have followed her into the tunnel if that were where she led them. She was the woman in *charge*, the woman of *all knowing* (thanks to the headphones), and a *leader* of all those beautiful Chiefs Cheerleaders. Wherever she would goest, they would follow! Dayna was queen!

Her head was high, her chin was lifted, her posture was perfect, her face was – her face was – *suddenly* – her face was – *in the dirt*?! Yes, she too was attacked by the headphone cord and tripped!

There's a big difference, though, in how the different personality styles reacted! High "I" Dayna promptly bounced up, *threw* her arms in the air, took a *bow*, and soaked up all the applause and cheers from her fans (er-r, ah-h, I mean the *Chiefs'* fans). She loved the attention! Good or bad, attention can be so much fun to a high "I." And frequently, relating the story for additional attention can be just as much fun!

"C" types do not need or desire to be the group leader or receive attention. It is okay with them to simply follow along and have a good time – as long as they are having a *good* time, and not a dangerous or *embarrassing* time! They enjoy being around others who are outgoing. They like the way "Ds" and "Is" make fools of themselves – just don't ask *them* to do it!

"Cs" don't like being the one in charge. It's okay if they don't get all the credit for a good job they've done. They're content with *knowing* the job was done correctly. But if you give a "C" the blame for things going wrong – watch out! She may deliberately *fold* on you!

IF ALL ELSE FAILS...

"C" moms are extremely **conscientious**. The old saying, "a place for everything, and everything in its place" was probably first spoken by a "C" type personality. High "Cs" can stay on track with a project long after others have given up. They enjoy putting together jigsaw or crossword puzzles. They see things fall into place step by step. They have little time for "horsing around." Most of life is serious to them.

"C" moms demand **compliance**. They follow instructions and can't understand why others don't do the same – do what they're *supposed* to do! A High "C' originated the phrase, "If all else fails, follow the directions!"

This mom wants order and neatness. And as all moms with small children know, order and neatness is difficult to achieve. With teenagers – it's difficult. In fact, with a family – order and neatness is difficult to achieve! This can be taxing for a high "C" mom.

CHECK IT OUT

"C" moms are **calculating**. They are task-oriented and will be the first to explain basic economics to you: "If your outgo exceeds your income, your upkeep will be your downfall." They can analyze a situation perhaps better than any of the other types. "C" moms are known for their ability to use critical thinking, as long as it doesn't become anal-retentive!

"Cs" have an uncanny ability to "see behind the scenes" and understand what is really going on. Their tactful and reserved nature sometimes keeps them from sharing their true feelings, though. They tend to focus, instead, on facts. "Cs" are the type to carefully observe an x-ray and say, "Hm-m-m. This tiny little spot doesn't look right. I need to evaluate it further." Whereas, a high "I" might see the same film, but respond with, "Hm-m-m. I don't know what that spot is. Oh well...you wanna' go to lunch?"

YOU WANT TO DO WHAT?

At a recent Kansas City Chiefs Cheerleader tryout session, I conducted one-on-one interviews with each potential cheerleader. In an interview with one particular contestant, I asked, after reading her resume, what career she planned to pursue when she completed her college education. To my surprise, she replied, "I want to be a mammogram technician."

I have to confess, I sat there dumbfounded. "I didn't realize anybody ever sought after that profession," I told her. In fact, I had no idea that someone actually *strived* to be the one who slapped a victim's breast on that freezing cold stainless steel plate, smashed it to smithereens as if being able to turn it into a pancake, and get a paycheck for it! I was amazed that this was her choice of profession on *purpose*, her plan, her goal, her destiny (besides cheering for the Chiefs, of course)!

Now, don't get me wrong, I didn't think she was a masochist. In fact, her intentions were quite honorable. She explained, "It means everything to me to be the one to carefully examine, evaluate, and possibly detect anything suspicious. There could be a time when I will identify and uncover an 'incorrect' evaluation or opinion. I want to do a precise and accurate job each time."

She may save many lives because of her competent, calculating, careful, and cautious personality style. I am so thankful for "Cs" who are wired this way to help make our lives better! They make an enormously valuable contribution to the critical medical profession.

JUST COFFEE, PLEASE!

High "C" moms love detail. High "S" moms love detail as it relates to people, but no one enjoys knowing every little intimate detail about everything as much as a high "C." I recently experienced a high "C" mom during a family Spring Break getaway to St. Louis. While waiting to board the tram to observe St. Louis from the top of the Arch, I toured the gift shop (essential to maintaining your sanity during a one-hour wait with a small child).

As I waited in line at the cash register, I noticed a rather small, unusual-looking burlap sack being purchased by the lady next to me. Curiously, I asked, "So, what's in that sack?" A single one- or two-word answer explaining the basic contents is usually a sufficient answer for a high "D" (even when shopping on vacation).

The aroma coming from the sack smelled like coffee – and it looked potentially like coffee. Bottom-line – she could have simply revealed that it was indeed – "coffee." *"Coffee!"*

That's all she had to say, but *no*! She proceeded to explain in detail (as "Cs" love to do), "These are coffee beans that were roasted in a Roure Roaster that was built in Spain. The beans come to them when they're still green. They can only roast ten pounds at a time and they don't use any steam or water like the larger companies, because it dilutes the coffee. They use a system of holes to pull the cool air through the beans to cool them down instead. It's really supposed to be good coffee. I read the details (I *bet* she did) in the paper this morning and decided to come here and pick some up."

I stood there smiling and nodding. All I wanted to know was what was in the unusual burlap sack – and got the entire *history* of that coffee! (Sorry I asked! Next time, *pretend I'm not here!)*

PERFECT STREET SWEEPER

"C" moms put a lot of emotional energy into doing things the **correct** way– not because they think they are better than other people; they just enjoy being right. To a "C" mom, "any job worth doing at all is worth doing well."

As any neighborhood full of kids, our streets become covered with little dirt piles, creative chalk drawings, and a sucker wrapper or two here and there. Fortunately, the city sends a scheduled street sweeper to take care of most of the debris. But sometimes, that's just not sufficient for our high "C" neighbor, Joan. Periodically, Joan comes out with her broom and meticulously sweeps the cul-de-sac street.

As with her immaculate yard, Joan is very conscientious about the street. Joan safeguards all the children, keeping the street very clean and orderly. She helps them to stay out of harm's way while playing ball, riding roller skates, scooters, or bikes in the cul-de-sac.

"Cs" feel that what they do makes a statement about themselves; therefore, it should be correct.

THANK YOU VERY MUCH

You can also count on the "C" type doing right and being right about almost any topic most of the time. There's a correct procedure for handling situations, and the high "C" mom will see that we follow it.

Rhonda gave a surprise party at a local restaurant for Kathy's 40th birthday. We all chipped in and gave her a group gift. A couple of weeks later, high "C" Lucy asked, "Did you get a thank you note from Kathy?"

I actually had to think for a minute to remember whether I had. "No, no, I don't think so."

"Well, me neither. I'm just so surprised she didn't send one."

I assured Lucy that Kathy loved the gift, and told her to not worry about not getting an official note of thanks. ("Ds" have a tendency to overlook details.) Yes, a thank you note is technically the appropriate and polite thing to do, but Kathy had appeared to *love* the gift. And I knew her life was extremely busy. (Kathy was accomplishing things, and *that* was good enough for me!)

However, a few days later, another high "C" friend who happened to be at the party asked the *same* question – with great concern for Kathy having done the "correct" thing. To a "C" mom, it is *very* important to do the right or correct thing. Tasks may appear to be more important to a "C" than concern for the actual relationship. Bottom-line, if you have a "C" friend, be *sure* to do it right – send a thank you note!

CALENDARS AND SCHEDULES

"C" types tend to be **conformists**, especially when it comes to getting along with the tried-and-proven. If a "C" mom thinks she can better a situation, she will make every effort to do so. "Build a better mousetrap and the world will beat a path to your door." "Cs" look for ways to take information we already possess and improve on it.

A "C" mom has a detailed, organized calendar with schedules and plans. Next year's medical checkup and dental appointments are promptly scheduled. ("Ds" go to the dentist when there's an unavoidable – usually painful – problem! "Is" go to make sure their teeth *look* good!)

That favorite yearly "mom checkup" is never delayed (guilty here!) for a "C" mom, and her kids' hair appointments are scheduled *before* the kids start looking like they could play the role of the "Shaggy Dog"! This keeps a "C" mom's life very orderly and efficient. "C" moms love calendars and checklists, and particularly enjoy checking off each item when it's completed!

"C" moms are **convinced**. They love to be accurate. They know what it means to "do your homework." If they are sure they are right, there is no changing their minds. You may think you can persuade them differently, but that is simply not the case.

MONDAY IS WASH DAY

"C" moms are **consistent**. You can usually go to the bank on what they tell you. They are hardly ever incorrect in the details of a story. Like the "S" mom, they love doing things the same way. If it worked once, why change it?

My friend Marti does her laundry every Monday with no exceptions. She likes her wash done on Monday, has always done her wash on Monday, and probably always will do her wash on Monday! I know that if I go by Marti's house on a Monday, I'm more than likely going to see stacks of sheets, towels, and clothes all over her living room. After each load is correctly washed and dried, the clothes are immediately hung on their color-coded hangers and delivered to their organized closets in perfect order again until, of course, next Monday's repeat of the ritual. It works for this high "C" mom.

High "I" Jeanie, on the other hand, washes the clothes in crisis mode (*Mom-m-m,* where's my *uniform*?!?!?!). Jeanie is thrilled when the clothes come out the same color as when they went in, and is content to pile them in a basket because at least they're clean! From there, it's anyone's pick, as long as they're willing to search and seek the iron! This cycle continues crisis to crisis!

"C" and "S" moms feel better about repetition than the "D" mom or the "I" mom, who interjects change often. "Variety is the spice of life" to the "Ds" and "Is." To a "C," variety can be dangerous – better to stick with what you know, be safe, be consistent. "Cs" usually make good moms because they are so consistent with their children. The children may not always agree with her rules, but they always know where their mom stands!

PERCENTAGE OF POPULATION

Research indicates that about **20-25 percent** of the general population has a high "C" profile. This fits accurately with regard to the number of physicians, lawyers, professors, and inventors we have in our society.

"C" types are very smart. They can do just about anything they put their minds to. They are not the majority of the population, but they are strong enough in number to let us know they exist and are ready to improve things. "C" types calculate how to have a steady, consistent, and lucrative income, too.

THE CAUTIOUS "C" MOM IN REVIEW

As we have defined and described the high "C" mom type, you may have found many descriptions that fit you. If so, we would say that you have a high "C" personality style. On the other hand, you may feel that this chapter describes someone very different from you. In that case, we would say that you have a low "C" personality style.

For an individual assessment of our personality style, the *Adult Profile Assessment* enables you to explore how the cautious type is part of your personality style. (See back of book for availability.)

We are attracted to the cautious type because they are conscientious leaders who lead from fundamental principles and they expect the best from each individual. Careful and contemplative, they see pitfalls that other styles may miss, and seek an environment with structure to maintain the highest standards and productivity. Their intense desire for perfection lights the way to the quality answers, value and excellence they need. The high "C" mom must, however, learn the difference between seeking excellence and expecting perfection, both within themselves and with others.

They shine brightest in a profession or specialty that takes advantage of their accuracy and thorough competency. Their underlying need or priority is correct procedure, working within a framework that will establish new levels of excellence. "Cs" need sensitivity to their space (and silence).

High "C" moms, when in control, are theoretical and exacting. They are able to carve out the bedrock of philosophy and facts, and they will build on this foundation to teach new heights of creative excellence.

The "C's" motto is, "Ready…Aim…Aim…*Aim*…!

We all need people with cautious styles in our lives to keep things correct! Now let's find out how this applies to your child, in the next chapter!

13

D-I-S-COVER YOUR CHILD'S AMBITIONS

Although our children may have completely different mannerisms and behaviors than we do, that doesn't make them wrong – or us right! We're all designed with different dreams, hopes, and goals. Thank goodness! What if we all wanted to be leaders? If we were all leaders, whom would we lead? Who would follow and support the "Ds'" goals and ambitions? Whom would the "Is" inspire, or the "Ss" support? And who would make sure things were correct and details complete, as our "Cs" do so well?

Now that we've identified unique personality strengths and weaknesses, we have a better understanding of why we get along with one child better than another. Different as we may be, we need to encourage our children, with their aspirant dreams and goals, according to their individual personality styles, not our own. God didn't design each child uniquely and perfectly without a distinct purpose.

GRAB THE ROAD MAP

As moms, it's our job to guide and direct our children down that road to success. Sure, we've messed up a time or two – or if you're like me, a *lot!* But with the right attitude and the right tools, it's never too late to revise and revamp!

Maybe we can't change everything, but we can change a few things, such as our attitudes, perceptions, and basic responses! Let's count our blessings and improve our lives! I want to inspire you as a mom to climb to greater heights, seek out adventure, discover new horizons, and face daunting challenges with confidence. (But don't worry, I do have my limits. Rest assured that I would never, *ever* challenge you to wear a thong bikini!)

It's so important to guide our children to find their purposes and talents, and discover how they can use their unique personality styles. We have been given a huge responsibility and *opportunity* to help our children use their personality styles to accomplish the extraordinary!

WHAT'S IT ALL MEAN?

How does your child interact? Do you have a child who is a natural born leader? Or perhaps you have a child who is delighted to sing and dance for all to watch, performing impromptu at a moment's notice? Maybe your child is more quiet, and enjoys nurturing, hugging, and assiduously caring for those baby dolls – quick to mend or nurse every scrape and boo-boo.

Or do you have a child who curiously and patiently disassembles, piece by piece, every component of a gadget (and hopefully puts it back together again)? Does he or she construct building block fortresses for hours on end?

WORLDS OF FUN

It's actually fairly easy to identify personality characteristics in children. For example, several families in our neighborhood annually visited a local amusement park together, "Worlds of Fun," in Kansas City. Personality styles erupted almost immediately at the entrance! Instantaneously, the kids broadcasted what rides they were going to attempt – or *not*!

As some of the more daring "Ds" and "Is" confronted the "scariest roller coasters ever," high "C" Megan very matter-of-factly stated that she would rather just *watch* those scary rides. After all, she-e-e-e thought it was much more fun to read the "Worlds of Fun" map instead. ("Cs" love to read maps.)

One of the best opportunities to identify personality styles soon presented itself at the bumper cars! One by one, the little "Ds" became fast and furious (more like *vicious*) ladybug racecar drivers, never hesitating to run over the oncoming drivers (or *bump* them into oblivion)! In fact, they were *driven* to bump and control during the whole session!

Our sweet eight-year-old "S" friend, Taylor, putted around like a little old lady, circling the perimeter, never allowing even an inch of her bumper to hit an approaching car. The "Is," having so much fun, eagerly waved at every adoring parent who would wave back – laughing hysterically when they were bumped. After all, it meant they got *attention*!

Next I recognized a "C" child, driving very cautiously, carefully avoiding making a "wrong turn," I'm sure. Suddenly Taylor, our softhearted "S," accidentally and with no ill intent of living up to the "bumper" car namesake, actually – yes, you guessed it – lightly *bumped* the "C" child's car. It was a gentle bump, but a bump nonetheless.

Everyone gasped. There was a piercing silence. It was as though the earth stood still for a moment. The "C" child stared. He glared. He observed any potential damage, glared back at Taylor again, evaluated that things were okay this time, and cautiously proceeded with his plan – hands at ten and two, of course. Whew! The crowd sighed, took a deep breath, and then all at once, in unison, turned their heads toward an animated voice, "Hey, look at me!" Half out of her seat, waving wildly, our attention-seeking high "I" broke the tension, and the bumper car suspense saga had a party atmosphere once again.

Ah-h-h, but there's more! Later that day, all the families rode the "Monsoon" ride together. As the name implies, you can only imagine how soaked we all got – all of us but one, our sweet little "S," Millie. After we exited the ride and recovered from the sheer *shock* of the drenching we had just encountered, every personality style was a buzz! Laughter, stories, and exhilaration were abound for all – all but Millie. Somehow she had miraculously avoided the torrential downfall.

To give you an idea of how important it is for "Ss" to feel included and that they belong, Millie pleaded to go on the ride again. She desperately wanted to get soaked (*saturated*) – to be like everyone else in the group. Even though she was the only *fortunate* one who was dry and comfortable, it was *more* important to this "S" not to be left out. Recognizing personalities in children at play can indeed be "Worlds of Fun"!

DREAMS AND ASPIRATIONS

Did you know that it's possible to catch a glimpse of your child's dreams and desires unfolding – even when he or she is a small child? Children often express or act out their future career goals and aspirations when they role-play. Stand back and observe their creative play time when they don't know you're watching.

See how your children express their dreams. Help them move toward those dreams to achieve all they can aspire to be! Take a look at the following charts to view a few prospective career options you might recognize!

"Ds" Make Good...

Administrators	Gangsters
Army Rangers	Law Enforcement Officers
Athletes	Lawyers
Boxers	Marines
Builders	Military Officers
Business Owners	Motivators
Coaches	Navy Seals
Cowboys	News Anchors
Developers	Private Investigators
Directors	Producers
Drill Instructors	Race Car Drivers
Entrepreneurs	Real Estate Developers
Executives	Sales Managers
FBI/CIA/DEA Agents	Supervisors
Fighter Pilots	Truck Drivers
Foremen	Moms!

"Ds" ARE MADE TO WIN

"Ds" live to compete, that's why they make great athletes. With a killer instinct, they will hang in there until the bitter end, doing whatever it takes to win. Regardless of the odds against them, "Ds" don't want to give up, don't want to give in, and they don't!

Professional athletic teams, who have gone through the undertaking of specifically hiring "D" personality styles, have found enormous success by the end of the year. (Enormous battles, as well.) Team dynamics may not include team cohesiveness, but if coaches can tolerate the "D" players and persuade them to participate and recognize the value of working together as a team, without stifling the "D" determination, the team will undoubtedly experience a championship season.

SAME CAREER, DIFFERENT DRIVING FORCE!

Having a particular personality style does not limit you or exempt you from being able to obtain certain career aspirations. It simply helps you understand why one type of career may be appealing to some – and painful simply *thinking* about it to others!

Kendrea, a Kansas City Chiefs Cheerleader, and Lorin, who attended the Young Married Sunday School class my husband and I taught, were each in law school. Both had the same desire to become a lawyer, but for completely *different* reasons – resulting from completely different personality styles.

Kendrea (high "D") wanted to be an attorney because she loved the challenge of debate. She said, "I don't want any job that would involve pleasing someone else."

Lorin (high "I"), on the other hand, aspired to become an attorney after watching the Ally McBeal television show. "It was not until high school and the creation of the Ally McBeal television show, as well as other popular TV shows featuring interesting and dynamic female lawyers, that I became interested in becoming a lawyer," shared Lorin. Television lawyers represented fun and excitement to her – complete with people, glamour and glitz!

Obviously, both had the same *dream* of becoming lawyers, but with polarized goals and aspirations – for the same profession. That's where the distinction comes in – where we understand the motive and reason behind the dream.

"Is" Make Good...

Actors	Politicians
Airline Attendants	Preachers
Auctioneers	Public Relations Directors
Broadcasters	Public Speakers
Car Salesmen	Radio Personalities
Circus Clowns	Reporters
Coaches	Salespeople
Comedians	Speakers
Con Artists	Storytellers
Entertainers	Teachers
Evangelists	Telemarketers
Masters of Ceremonies	Telephone Operators
Meeting Planners	Travel Agents
Peace Corps Volunteers	Wedding Consultants
Performers	Moms!

"Is" WANT TO BE SEEN

Julia's six-year-old daughter, Mattie, had a standard answer every time she was asked what she wanted to be when she grew up. "That's easy," she would dramatize, "When *I* grow up, I-want-to-be-e-e-e – *popular!*" In addition, she would prance around the house, singing to her little sister in her theatrical fashion, "I'm going to be *popular* when I grow up!"

Julia, her high "C" mom, reserved and uninterested in popularity, shook her head every time. "It was baffling to me as to why popularity was so important to Mattie," shared this reserved-type mom. Working in a conventional-type job gave Julia ample opportunity for her conscientious personality style to be meticulous and calculating. She saw no benefit in her daughter's desire to be "popular." In fact, Julia considered spending so much time with friends a waste of time.

However, it was Mattie's dream! Julia did not understand her daughter's dream, and they had many battles in their home over their differences. It was a constant source of conflict.

But when Julia understood their personality differences – and that it was *okay* to be so different – she understood the value of helping Mattie grow. She began to share in her daughter's enthusiasm. Julia realized that learning to accept Mattie for her personality style was essential to helping Mattie feel secure and loved, regardless of their differences.

MOTIVATION BEHIND THE DREAMS

We need to be careful to discern where our children's inspiration originates and what their motivational factors are derived from. For example, high "I" Elaine wanted to be a nurse when she grew up. (Notice this profession is not listed on the "I" career list.) She said, "I lived in the moment and don't remember wanting to be anyone other than a nurse."

She continued, "My desire to be a nurse originated from reading an intriguing book series about an exciting nurse who always had romantic and mystery-oriented experiences in the hospital. It sounded so exciting – sort of like Nancy Drew!"

Elaine soon discovered, "I took a nursing class, and decided very quickly that nursing wasn't for me after all. I found, though, that I was comfortable with and enjoyed speaking and acting in front of others."

This discovery proved to be a "shot in the arm" toward a fulfilling career encompassing Elaine's outgoing personality style. Elaine became the Director of the Kansas City Chiefs Cheerleaders. She frequently speaks to groups and is seen by or "in front of" thousands of people at every Kansas City Chiefs home game. A perfect personality career fit after all!

"Ss" Make Good...

Artists	Painters
Chefs	Pharmacists
Child Care Workers	Pastors
Counselors	Planners
Customer Service Reps	Real Estate Agents
Department Heads	Researchers
Diplomats	School Teachers
Elementary School Teachers	Secretaries
Flight Attendants	Social Workers
Funeral Directors	Supervisors
Homemakers	Teachers
Human Resource Directors	Technicians
Librarians	Veterinarians
Managers	Waiters/Waitresses
Nurses	Moms!

FULFILL YOUR DREAMS

Janet is living her childhood career dream. She explains, "I always wanted to be a mom – just like my mom, who stayed at home and made cookies with her kids. In high school, I took the 'Careers' class and was told that a full-time stay-at-home mom was, 'Not a job option, please choose something else.' A test indicated I had an interest in helping others, so I was directed to nursing and/or teaching. My degree is in education, but I have never desired a job outside of what I am doing now."

Today, Janet is perfectly content (and probably always will be) in her career as a stay-at-home mom. What a blessing she is to her family and friends! She sought after – and is fulfilling – her admirable dream.

A PERFECT CAREER MATCH

High "S" mom Sharon, on the other hand, also aspired to be a nurse. She says, "I never thought about being anything but a nurse, my whole life. I remember as a small child, maybe four or five years old, my mother made me a nurse's uniform, and I had my medical bag. As I grew up, I selected the classes I needed in high school to get into nursing. I graduated a semester early from high school in order to pursue my dream as soon as possible."

Sharon's childhood dream came true – and continued throughout her entire adult life. She explains, "I worked as a nurse all of my professional life and always loved nursing. I retired after thirty-one years as a school nurse to become a Director of Nursing at two different psychiatric facilities. My entire career was spent working as a nurse."

When the personality style corresponds with the career, dreams are conceived and achieved!

"Cs" Make Good...

Accountants	Mechanics
Architects	Military Intelligence
Artists	Musicians
Authors	Philosophers
Bankers	Photographers
Bookkeepers	Physicians
Camera Repairmen	Pilots
Composers	Professors
Computer Programmers	Scholars
Consultants	Scientists
Dentists	Statisticians
Engineers	Surgeons
Finishing Carpenters	Teachers
Hospital Administrators	Theologians
Inventors	Theoreticians
Lawyers	Tool & Die Experts
Librarians	Watch Repairmen
Machinists	Moms!

BUDDING CAREER

Madison, my eight-year-old "C" child, aspires to become a teacher some day. She loves to role-play, placing her studious stuffed animals in their assigned seats – promptly on time. She then lectures them on the many ways to follow the rules and how they should correctly play with the other toys. Every time I suggest the *possibility* of any other type of career, she insists, "No, mom, when I grow up I'm going to be a teacher."

So, we designed personal business cards with cute little animal graphics and an admirable title of "Madison Crook, Stuffed Animal Teacher." Her budding career is well on its way. (The pay's not very good, but the benefits these obedient, miniature students receive are endless!)

GIRL SCOUT CAMP LEADERS ROCK!

Another great opportunity to distinguish personality styles is by volunteering at a Girl Scout camp. You get to experience a variety of personality styles in not only the girls, but also in the other moms! While spending the day with Madison's first grade troop (the "Trouts"), "D" personality styles became apparent right away. They had missions to accomplish, such as hiking trails to scale, fires to build, and zip cords to zip on.

"D" moms would do things the *fastest* way, taking control and running the show in no time. And the precocious little "D" Girl Scout camper was right there with her. Logan, a high "D" first grader, tried her best to boss around the other girls – and didn't hesitate to tell all the "non-D" leaders what they should be doing next. With her hands on her hips, she proceeded to direct the day's activities by barking out orders and snapping at everyone to get busy – doing things *her* way! Needless to say, she made a few enemies (as high "Ds" can do) by the time the flag was lowered on the first day.

The high "I" campers, on the other hand, loved doing things the *fun* way – even if it meant wandering off the trail a time or two and getting lost. The "I" moms exchanged more "Swaps" (decorative hat ornaments) than some of the *girls!* It gave them an opportunity to make many new friends! They led animated camp songs with clever and creative stanzas, always happy-go-lucky, and would do just about anything to earn those beads at the end of an event – relishing every form of recognition and applause. Sometimes, though, it was like having an extra first grader around when trying to get something accomplished!

The little high "I" campers loved marching past other troops, singing and dancing for all to see and enjoy. That is – until they marched by an older Girl Scout troop. This group abruptly informed the high "I" first grade showgirls, "You aren't really the 'Trouts.' You're really the '*Fish*!!!!'"

Standing in dismay, Cina bellowed, "Ah-h-h-h! She doesn't *like* me! She called us fish!" She buried her face in her hands and sobbed. Cina's show was over, her fun diminished. In fact, life was awful. Camp was awful. Being a fish stunk, and so did Girl Scout camp. Tears could have filled the nearby mossy pond.

Fortunately (and thank goodness), our sweet little "S," Olivia, came to the rescue to console Cina. The attention was *good*, life was *good*, and camp was *good* once again. Cina was happy, laughing, and playing. And "S" Olivia was happy to make a new special friend and introduced Cina to "Blueberry," her other friend at camp. Blueberry was, however, a caterpillar. The two girls and Blueberry became fast friends or "family" (as they explained), spending a great deal of time together chatting, discussing "s'mores," and the latrine situation.

Next we heard, "Line up! It's time to go on our next scheduled adventure!" from our high "C" leader, as she motioned with her efficient, organized, laminated schedule and map – ingeniously attached to her belt holding a compass and small flashlight. The "C" Girl Scouts were eager to follow the rules and promptly lined up as told.

We were about ready to hike to the next event when I noticed that "C" camper Grace was crying. When I inquired of her mom whether Grace was okay, Jennie told me, "Grace always wants things perfect. She was upset because she spilled a little juice on her sit-upon. Grace thinks her sit-upon isn't 'right' anymore, but don't worry. She does this a lot, since she believes *everything* has to be perfect."

Just then, as we lined up, I heard a commotion around the picnic table where Blueberry resided. Curiously, I approached our "Trout" troop and found two of the "S" girls crying! (Early mornings and long, hot days make for a long, hot and *crying* week!) Typical of their tender hearts, the girls were feeling sorry for Blueberry and didn't want to leave "him."

They tenderly shared through little tear-stained cheeks, "We feel so bad that he can't go to rope-making with us," clearly wanting to stay and support him and protect him from the adversity of –*loneliness.* ("Oh my," *this* 'D' mom thought, "the good Lord knew my limit was one day, not the whole adventurous week!") Praises and blessings go to all Girl Scout leaders. They are beautiful angels (disguised in knee socks and vests)!

20/20 HINDSIGHT

Many years later, we can look back at the interests and desires of young children and find that they're involved in careers very similar to their playtime interactions, activities, and dreams.

Please keep in mind, seldom is anyone ever just one personality style. Each of us is a blend of all four styles. So, let's look at Chapter 14 to find out how the **D-I-S-C** letters can blend together!

14

HOW THE D-I-S-C LETTERS BLEND TOGETHER

*Y*ou may have recognized by now that you have some behavior characteristics from all four D-I-S-C types. For example, you may feel that you are Direct and Influencing, yet sometimes Steady and Conscientious. Your unique Style Blend represents the dominant personality styles or types consistent with the degrees of their intensity.

About 80 percent of the population has more than one high, or dominant, type in their personality styles. This means that they have more than one D-I-S-C style which they can identify. But only one type is dominant. One or two other styles may be strong types as well, but not quite as strong as their dominant styles.

For example, my most predominant trait is the "D" style. My secondary high type, the "I" style, is also above the midline on my Adult Profile Assessment graph (for availability, please see back of book). This is an important distinction that helps me better understand which personality style I will revert to and what I will do under stress.

The secondary high type in your personality style helps your primary type by using those behavior traits together to serve and accomplish your passion. For example, because I am a high "D" type, I will naturally try to drive very hard and decisively in order to reach my goals as quickly as possible. Since my secondary type is "I," written as "D/I," I will also try to influence other people in a very persuasive manner in order to reach my objectives.

I am painfully aware that my "C" trait is the lowest. Therefore, to be able to succeed in my "C" quadrant, I must establish an atmosphere that will be conducive to productivity when it comes to, say, writing books. I often go to different restaurants (after the busy lunch hour) and sit for the afternoon, working on a "C-type" activity (writing). This is necessary in order to accomplish my "D" goals. If I satisfy my secondary "I" personality style by working around people and being served iced tea in beautiful environments (especially outdoor patios in the warmer months), my "C" work can appear tolerable, or even enjoyable.

Otherwise, it's a struggle for my "D/I" personality style to remain secluded in my office, sitting in front of a computer in an office chair all day. But my passion is inspiring and helping people through my writing and speaking. Therefore, I must find alternative opportunities to set myself up for success, and accomplish these goals by forcing myself to do the ABCs (Applying Buns to Chair)!

UNDERSTANDING STYLE BLENDS

We can observe two different kinds of Style Blends: Complementary and Contrasting. Looking again at our D-I-S-C circle, we learn that the most common Style Blends are with D-I-S-C types that are adjacent to or bordering on the model. These are called **Complementary Style Blends**.

D/C or D/I   I/D or I/S

C/D or C/S   S/I or S/C

Complementary Style Blends:

- **D/C** or **D/I**
- **I/D** or **I/S**
- **S/I** or **S/C**
- **C/D** or **C/S**

These Style Blends are complementary because the behavior traits in these types seem to complement each other. They have one part of the D-I-S-C circle orientation in common. They are both Outgoing or Reserved, or they are both Task-oriented or People-oriented.

"D/I" Personality Style

The "D/I" – **Dominant** and **Inspirational** – combination is outgoing, and is both task- and people-oriented. This combination results in a highly optimistic and outgoing mom who is energized by people, driven by dominating and influencing. Skilled in their vocabularies, these moms can confront and entertain at the same time, persuading you toward their points of view. This is also true for "D/I" children. They are charismatic and talkative in all that they do, sometimes convincing others to do it *for* them!

"D/Is" are quick and decisive and rarely challenged when giving orders. They have a sharp sense of knowing others' needs and desires.

This personality style is driven, and loves to talk to people. As a "D/I," life is at its best for me on the days that I have a speech presentation. I am driven to help others live life to its fullest and be the best they can be, and I'm determined to help them get there. It just gets even better if I can accomplish this goal while *talking!*

" D/C" Personality Style

The "D/C" – **Dominant** and **Cautious** – combination is task-oriented, and these moms work well on *planning* committees. Task skills come naturally to them. This combination can achieve great things, doing things fast and correct, and can be instrumental in bringing about change. They have an ability to see the big picture as well as the details of the picture, and critically develop systems to make things better. When you meet these people, they may seem cold, distant and aloof, when actually they are preoccupied with their tasks. They must focus on developing people skills; otherwise, they may go through the day ignoring everyone and becoming very bossy or critical because others can't keep up.

"D/Cs" influence others by setting the pace for new ideas and goals. My husband, (Dale) Jay, has the "D/C" type personality. He and I both are driven, but he almost exclusively prefers accomplishing and completing tasks. Our primary personality styles are the same ("D"), but our secondary personality styles are opposites ("I" and "C"). (It's not unusual to marry our opposites, by the way!)

Every New Year's Day, we eat a late lunch at a local restaurant away from the demands and responsibilities at home (I know you *know* what I mean) and establish, project, and write down in detail our yearly goals. (This takes approximately three to four hours). As "Ds," we both love goal-setting, exciting new challenges, and accomplishing things. By doing this, we can identify, pray for, and assist with one another's goals throughout the entire year.

As high "Ds," we're much alike in that respect, but completely different in our secondary personality styles. In reference to our "goals list," most of Jay's "D/C" goals are centered entirely on tasks. Some of my "D/I" goals are centered on tasks, and some of my goals involve people.

Consequently, I'm often dragging him out into the cul-de-sac to visit neighbors, visit friends, visit anybody! Jay, on the other hand, methodically and consistently pays the bills and keeps orderliness in our household by completing those necessary tasks that I have a tendency to – ah-h-h – overlook. It makes for a great team. As "Ds," we can accomplish a lot – as long as we remember to place relationships as a priority, too! (That doesn't always come naturally for us.)

- **"I/S" Personality Style**

The "I/S" – **Inspirational** and **Supportive** – combines easily and is very relationship oriented. Making friends effortlessly, these moms work well on *welcoming* committees! Primarily interested in people, they are approachable and understanding. The "I" moms are generally fun with great senses of humor, while the "S" moms are very easygoing. These "I/S" moms have the ability to see the good in others rather than focus on their weaknesses.

While the "D/C" lacks people skills, the "I/S" needs to become more task-oriented. "D/C" types and "I/S" types often clash when they begin working together. They are attracted to each other because of their differences, but those differences can soon become like oil and water.

While the "D/C" moms focus on getting the job done with "do it now" determination, we can see that the "I/S" moms concentrate on building up people and developing better relationships. It is more difficult to see a need if you don't *want* to see it, or if you have not been trained to *recognize* it. However, we need each others' personality styles for balance.

- **"I/D" Personality Style**

The "I/D" type – **Inspirational** and **Dominant** – is generally open and friendly with others, and more driven then the "I/S" type. This is an exciting personality blend. Their fast-paced challenges are stimulated by sheer fun! They are the moms who love parties, speak to anybody on the elevator, and know people everywhere they go!

- **"S/I" Personality Style**

The "S/I" – **Supportive** and **Inspirational** – moms are highly people-oriented. This style has very similar traits as that of the "I/S" type, but not as outgoing. They prefer a small group or one-on-one relationship, rather than the party atmosphere the "I/S" loves. The "S/I" type tends to follow rather than lead, and warmly extends a helping hand to others.

- **"S/C" Personality Style**

The "S/C" – **Supportive** and **Cautious** – type is reserved, but also both task- and people-oriented and easily attracted to a "D/I" type. The "S/C" types are faithful and loyal team players, good at finishing what they start (once they start).

They maintain traditions and have a complete commitment to quality and orderliness. They are conscientious about living in a stable environment and needing time to adjust to change. Avoid surprises for this more serious type. Instead, help them feel supported and have freedom to express their feelings when they're ready to speak – after thinking about it.

- **"C/S" Personality Style**

The "C/S" – **Cautious** and **Supportive** – personality type is more reserved, less excitable, and becomes drained by highly energized people activities. There can be a noticeable difference in personality styles between a "C/S" blend and a "C/D," **Cautious** and **Dominant**, blend. Both styles expect correctness and are conscientious and calculating, but the "C/S" is more supportive in helping accomplish this.

- **"C/D" Personality Style**

The "C/D" – **Cautious** and **Dominant** – personality type is more assertive and outgoing than a "C/S" type. "C/Ds" are determined to see that things are done and done right. They will approach a project with a step-by-step commitment to accomplish the feat. Focusing on such a commitment to excellence can manufacture negativity, however, by innocent people-oriented bystanders.

Contrasting Style Blends:

- **"D/S" and "S/D"**
- **"I/C" and "C/I"**

Less common Style Blends are types that are across from each other on the model. These are Contrasting Style Blends because the behavior traits in these types often seem opposite and contradicting. The two types in these Style Blends are opposite for Outgoing or Reserved, and they are also opposite for Task-oriented or People-oriented. This personality Style Blend is a walking contradiction and unusual, but not impossible.

This combination does not occur often, but such blends can be somewhat confusing internally, until they gain an understanding of their personality style. People with contrasting Style Blends may feel that people misunderstand them, for they can behave in seemingly conflicting ways. These people may also feel more conflicted in decision-making, for they have two contrasting perspectives to balance within their own personality style.

- **"D/S" and "S/D" Personality Styles**

An "S/D" – **Supportive** and **Dominant** – combination is unique and unusual (and not very common) in that it is both reserved and people-oriented at times, while outgoing and task-oriented at other times. These people are both tough and gentle. Think of a nurse's vocation, requiring toughness and gentleness.

A "D/S" mom wants to be in charge (**Dominant**), but also really enjoys helping (**Supportive**). When in charge, she is frustrated when no one else helps. When helping, she is frustrated when no one is in charge.

- **"I/C" and "C/I" Personality Styles**

An "I/C" combination is unique in that it is both outgoing and people-oriented at times, while reserved and task-oriented at other times. The "I/C" type really loves people (**Inspirational**), but knows how important it is to research the facts and do a job correctly (**Cautious**). When they are having fun, they feel guilty for not working. When they are working, they feel guilty for wishing they could be with people having fun.

These types can be the life of the party and also the hardest worker of the group when completing a project. Think of a really good salesperson, warm and friendly, able to make you feel good while also handling details in completing the sale.

Technically, these moms don't have "split personalities." These are simply moms who have a blend that is more difficult for them to understand. Interpreting their temperament's conflicting signals causes them (and their loved ones) a little more frustration at times. Knowing how to use and control the power of your personality Style Blends is the secret.

To reiterate, the "D/S" and "I/C" combinations are uncommon, but they do exist. Typically, a mom who is primarily a "D" is secondarily an "I" or a "C." And a mom who is primarily an "I" may secondarily be an "S" or a "D."

Likewise, one who is primarily an "S" might secondarily be a "C" or an "I." And a mom who is primarily a "C" typically is secondarily an "S" or a "D." Refer to the Model of Human Behavior graphic again for a visual reference, and you can see how this flows.

Understanding our personality blends helps us understand our strengths and weaknesses. When we recognize our strengths and grow in our weaknesses, we can progress and profit immensely. Now let's look at Chapter 15 to learn more about the Determined "D" child!

15

D-I-S-COVER THE D CHILD

*W*HY IS MY CHILD SO DEMANDING?

The BOTS are going to make a movie. Each one has a different job they like to do:

- The "D" child **(3BOT)** knows how the play should work and is going to be in charge of the whole thing! The "D" child tells everyone where to stand and what to say.

THE "D" TYPE CHILD SAYS:

"Mom, as a high 'D' child, I often make plans because I like to make things happen. I want to show you that I can do things myself. I love to take charge of myself and others. When I work, I work hard; when I play, I play hard. I will try almost anything if I think it will work. I like to make decisions and I don't like doing the same old things all the time, so I question the way things are done.

"I can be demanding when I think that I have a better way, or if I feel that your decision may not be in my best interest. I tell you what I think and I get straight to the point. I don't understand that I may make you feel challenged, mom; I just want to know who's in control. I need to learn that in order to be in authority, I must learn to be under authority. As you know, I am full of energy and want to do great things with my life!"

YOUR "D" CHILD'S STRENGTHS AND WEAKNESSES

The "D" type represents 10 percent of the population. "D" children (the ones who make you feel like *they're* letting *you* live at home) are very determined, purposeful, and look for the opportunity to conquer any challenge. As with all personalities, however, their strengths can become their weaknesses if out of control.

With a strong desire and preoccupation to win, a "D" child will race to be first at anything, regardless of how trivial. Even in something as simple as getting to the water fountain first, this child may become impatient, if not belligerent, if someone is in front of him or her.

THE "D" CHILD

STRENGTHS:	WEAKNESSES:
BABY:	**BABY:**
• High energy	• Impatient
• Bright	• Demanding
• Born leader	• Precocious
• Determined	• Stubborn
CHILD:	**CHILD:**
• Adventuresome	• Hard to please
• Take charge	• Angry
• Busy and productive	• Cruel
• Strong-willed	• Sarcastic
• Assertive	• Rude
• Optimistic	• Pushy
• Persistent	
TEEN:	**TEEN:**
• Decisive	• Crafty
• Competitive	• Arrogant
• Confident	• Inconsiderate
• Leader	• Self-sufficient
• Responsible	• Domineering
• Independent	• Prideful
• Productive	• Insensitive
• Goal-oriented	• Unemotional

The "D" baby can be very demanding when it comes time to eat, drink, or sleep. The powerhouse "D" child is very active and often in charge of the home already! No debate class in college ever prepared any mom for a standoff with a six-year-old "D" child! The "D" teen can make quick decisions and after a while, outsmart the parents!

"Ds" have never met a group they couldn't lead. They naturally gravitate to leadership positions in school, work, etc.

"Ds" usually prefer to fly solo. People with this personality style would benefit from consciously training themselves to bring others into their decision-making processes. To succeed in leadership, they must become aware of the needs and drives of others.

EASTER EGG HUNT

The assertive high "D" naturally takes charge in a situation, but this can be perceived as aggressiveness in "D" children. They take quick action when they recognize an opportunity. For example, have you ever watched children on an Easter egg hunt? Because of their different personality styles, each child approaches the pastel little treasures hidden in the grass with a different motivation.

The "C" child follows the rules, stays within the designated boundaries, and counts out the exact number of Easter eggs each child is allowed to keep. To take an "S" child on an Easter egg hunt is an experience full of love, graciousness, and reaffirming kindness. "Ss" don't hesitate to share any excess eggs they've gathered with the other children; they're so sweet. (It's actually more fun to hug the bunny anyway.)

The "I" children miss a lot of the eggs because they're so excited about skipping and waving to all their friends. They have such a good time – especially if they can talk to all their friends while they're hunting for the eggs! In fact, hunting for *friends* can be more fun than hunting for *eggs*!

Taking a "D" child on an Easter egg hunt is a whole different story. My high "D" son, Scott, embellished me with some of the most embarrassing Easter egg hunting moments of my life. He was out for the kill! He would *elbow* his way to snatch every egg in sight, and then hurl them into his Easter basket as if shooting hoops! Being forced to put some of the eggs back was one of the most difficult "acts of kindness" this "D" child ever experienced. When other moms repeated the promising Easter message, "He's Alive! He's Alive," they weren't referring to Jesus at the time! They were warning their kids about Scott!

"Ds" need to win, and win they do. That's where we, as moms, have to encourage our high "D" child to act like a caring, sharing child – and not *hog* all the eggs! (By the way, this event required action that involved more than the "Mom look"! I had to assist with a little *elbowing* of my own! Hm-m-m...and we wonder where they learn these things!)

WILD, WILD (JAY) WEST

"D" children are busy and productive from the time they get up in the morning until they fall fast asleep that night. They love to conquer problems, with a strong drive to get a lot done! They set their mind on something and courageously charge after it with everything they have, enjoying freedom from controls or supervision. Such was the case when my husband, Jay, was eight years old.

Jay spent day after day re-enacting scenes from his favorite television show, the "Wild, Wild West." (Why *wouldn't* that be a "D" child's favorite show?) Jay, impersonating Jim West, the main character on the show, went about humming the theme song and replicating the latest stunt or rescue.

One Thanksgiving Day, Jay's family gathered at his grandparents' home. Outside, all by himself (which is fine for a high "D" child because they can find challenging things to do on their own), Jay (aka the notorious Jim West) tells the story, "I concocted an exciting episode of my own: I would hoist myself up into a big tree in my grandparents' front yard and hang upside down by my feet with a rope. My strategy was to stash my pocketknife in my boot and *just* as I needed to escape, I would *drop* the knife down from my boot...*catch* it... *cut* the rope...and *escape!*" (His voice even became quite animated as he recounted his exhilarating plan. Guy thing.)

Continuing, "As I reached to grab my knife, it dropped to the ground! There I was, hanging upside down – with no knife and no backup plan for "Wild, Wild 'Jay' West" to escape!

Dangling by my feet, I tried to break loose by swinging back and forth, back and forth – to no avail! I tried to climb up the rope, twist around, anything, but I was determined *not* to give up and call for help. Eventually worn out and out of options, I just hung there – spinning in slow circles around... and...around."

Just then, as Jay spun around facing the house (did I mention that this tree was also in front of the living room picture window?), he saw the draperies slowly opening. As he twirled around for the final time, Jay confesses, uh-h-h – I mean – *continues*, "I slowly looked up from the brim of my cowboy hat and saw my entire family holding their stomachs, bending over, and laughing hysterically! I was defeated – and my Wild, Wild West days were history."

Keep in mind, my husband has very *little* "I" in his personality, so all this attention and performing the "Wild, Wild West" show for others was *not* part of his "D" action plan. At last, his grandfather came out, retrieved the knife, and rescued the little "D" hero from the tree, but *not* from the humiliation. (Thank goodness he wasn't mimicking *Superman*! Who *knows* what he would have tried!) A "D" child is an adventure waiting to happen!

ENTREPRENEURS AT HEART

Persistent and busy, "Ds" are born entrepreneurs. Their independent nature enjoys responsibility and challenges. An unproductive, sedentary lifestyle would be boring to this personality type. Even young "Ds" seek the bigger picture, a broader horizon, and opportunities to be industrious.

For several summers, I planted two or three tomato plants in our backyard. My "D" son, Scott, saw a potential opportunity in this, so one spring when he was about eight years old, he solicited (begged) to plant a *few* more. "Ds" know how to get what they want. This driven child *somehow* ended up with 16 plants! Now if you've ever planted tomatoes, you know you can get quite a few tomatoes off of just *one* plant, let alone *sixteen* plants! Surprisingly enough, though, throughout the summer Scott continued to water and weed. (Keep in mind, this child didn't even *like* tomatoes!)

One morning in the grocery store, I overheard him ask the store clerk for a handful of small brown paper sacks. Later that afternoon, he took off down the street with his entire wagon loaded with sacks of tomatoes (priced sky high) – and came back with a sack of *cash*! That was his first step down the road as a successful entrepreneur.

And it didn't stop there. At age ten, high "D" Scott came running into the house one afternoon yelling, "Mom, mom! The neighbor said he would pay me to mow his lawn!" At first I was hesitant (fearing mowed toes), but decided to give him a chance. "You can't use the weed eater, though." (Afraid he would mistakenly weed-eat the newly formed fuzzy hair on his ankles instead!) Determined to complete the job and trim the yard with *something*, he resourcefully supplemented (as "Ds" do so well) the weed eater with my *antique* scissors instead! "Ds" find ways to accomplish their goals.

This taste of success and money subsequently launched Scott's lawn mowing business, "I'd Like to Get to *Mow* You." He started his first business that summer, mowing approximately fifteen lawns per week thereafter. High "Ds" have an entrepreneurial spirit and drive to make money, that's almost unstoppable.

"D" TEEN UNDER AUTHORITY

"D" teenagers seek leadership and solving problems, but can get into trouble if they overstep the line. The fast-action "D" personality style at any age likes to make quick decisions, but can fail to weigh all the alternatives or consequences adequately.

Geared up for a challenge, "Ds" walk around with their "dukes up," ready to take on any potential opponent. My "D" son, Scott, as a teenager, could see a conflict, or "smell trouble," and take it on as a challenge even though it had nothing to do with him. He would not hesitate to charge full speed ahead into the middle of the situation to conquer it. I constantly had to remind him, "Sta-a-a-a-ay out of it before you end up being the one in trouble!"

It's good to act fast and step out in faith, but with sensitivity and good judgment. (Remember, the "D's" motto is, "*Ready, Fire, Aim!*") "Ds" will not dodge pressure or confrontation. In fact, they will deliberately put pressure on themselves. Other personality styles can be very uncomfortable with pressure or altercations, and purposely avoid "D's" combative, aggressive attitude.

CONTRACT FOR CONTROL

Because "Ds" don't like being told what to do, it is important to let them feel they have choices. Again, my high "D" son, Scott (believe me, he's given me a *lot* of material), was very aware that he had choices. Obviously, he could choose to do the "right thing" – or choose to do the "wrong thing" – with an established consequence. To help him feel he had some power in his choices and consequences, I let him help me construct a contract. This allowed him to have ownership and control of the consequences if he chose not to act responsibly. Amazingly, sometimes he established tougher consequences than I would have! (Again, his goals were high!)

Get "D" children to agree beforehand on the discipline they will receive if they violate the rules. For example, with their strong desire for control, you can tell your "D" child they have a choice in what they do first, brush their teeth or put their pajamas on, but bedtime is 9:00. Ask, "What do you choose? It's your choice."

Learn to ask questions rather than make dogmatic statements. "How much time do you think you need to spend on your homework?" is much better than, "You must spend at least one hour on your homework." Let them be a part of the decision-making process, negotiating weekday and weekend curfews, chores, activities, etc.

WHO'S THE BOSS?

The sometimes bossy, strong "D" personality can be perceived as a rebellious spirit. "Ds" think that if they don't tell everyone what to do, it will never get done! Stephanie said to me after a personality workshop, "I don't know what to do about our situation at home. My son, Jason, is controlling our family!"

To learn more about her situation, I quizzed her about the circumstances to determine the consequences. "Let's see," I asked, "Can you take away the car keys; increase his curfew? How about a phone restriction? How long before he will be moving out anyway (*anything* to give her *hope!*)?" She replied in a panic, "He's only *four!*"

"Ds" will control you if they can get by with it. They will stretch the limit; you must let them know what the limitations are. They need parameters for their behaviors and actions. By establishing this ahead of time, you can be *pro*active rather than *re*active to situations. The "D" child will try to wear you down, out argue you, and outlast you. But remember, you're the boss! Outlast them, and they'll learn it's pointless to manipulate.

"Ds" don't like being submissive, but freedom comes through submission to authority rather than fighting against it. They must learn to respect authority figures in their lives, such as moms, teachers, and police – even when these people seem to make life difficult for them. If you keep them busy and productive with constructive interests, they'll stay out of trouble. If you let them get bored, they'll create trouble!

LITTLE REAL ESTATE TYCOONS

"D" children are confident, driven, and determined to reach greatness. As a child, that confidence can be considered precocious. As an adult, a "D" can be overwhelming with their goals and ambitions. *In* control, they win – and help others win. *Out* of control, they step on toes and smash hearts while achieving their dreams.

"Ds'" dreams are full of confidence and certainty that they can accomplish them. Late one night when Scott was about ten years old, I walked down the hall near his bedroom about an hour after the bedtime ritual. "Mom," he whispered. "Ca' mere. I can't sleep because I've been thinking – I know what I'm going to do when I grow up." "Oh yeah, what's that?" I inquired, waiting to hear a cute story about becoming a cowboy, astronaut, racecar driver, etc.

He said, "I'm going to the local community college for the first two years so I can live at home longer (*yikes!*) to save money. Then I'm going to buy a duplex and live on one side, and the people who live on the other side can pay the money for it. Then I'll buy some more houses and have all those people pay for those houses. Isn't that a good idea? Ga' night."

That was it. He was asleep within minutes. "Ds" don't fret about things; they know they'll find a way. Today, as I write this book, Scott is in his early twenties and co-owns twenty-one rental houses. "Ds" find ways to make their dreams come true.

FOLLOW THIS LEADER

An obstacle most "Ds" face, however, is that they are used to succeeding and expect to succeed, and demand that they continue to succeed. They haven't experienced the pain of failure. Oh, they've experienced failure all right, but it is so short lived that there isn't time for pain. It isn't long before they have another dream; they hardly notice they've failed. Not having been broken, they can be so full of themselves that they can lose effectiveness in identifying with and helping meet the needs of others.

When "Ds" are pushed too far, they can become overly aggressive and lack sensitivity in their words or behavior. "D" types think everyone should be like them. They have minds of their own and want to control everything and everyone, but they must first learn to control themselves.

At recess, the "D" child wants to play follow-the-leader as long as they're always the leader! Otherwise, they lose interest and quit playing. If taught how to handle this strong desire for leadership, these determined children can grow up to be great bosses, needing little motivation or inspiration. They have a great desire to work for themselves in pursuit of their own agenda. If they're working for others, they need to be in control of some aspect of the project.

A "D" child will keep you on your toes (and wear you *out!*). His or her drive and ambition will challenge anyone they're around, including you! "Ds" are full of high energy, and quick to make decisions. Tell them it can't be done, then stand back and watch them get it done! It takes a lot of energy to stay on top of "D" children, but channeled in the right direction, you can propel them to prosperity and success!

THE "D" CHILD'S REPORT CARD MIGHT LOOK LIKE THIS:

√ He has a lot of energy and is a good leader.
√ He is determined to get the job done and likes to take charge.
√ Your child could work on not being so competitive and bossy at times.
√ He gets angry easily and can be sarcastic or rude if things don't go his way.
√ He is very responsible and productive, often working independently.

Now let's take a look at Chapter 16 to learn about the Inspiring "I" child!

16

D-I-S-COVER THE ⭐ CHILD

*W*HY DOES MY CHILD GET SO DISTRACTED?

The BOTS are going to make a movie. Each one has a different job they like to do:

- The "I" child (**1BOT**) wants to be the star of the show, and knows how to make people laugh and clap! The "I" child is not shy and likes to try new things.

THE "I" TYPE CHILD SAYS:

"Mom, as a high 'I' child, I love surprises! Parties and having fun things to do are what make life exciting. I like to talk about what I think and feel. I love being with lots of people – and hearing them say that I am doing a good job. Quick jobs are best for me because I seem to forget details and I sometimes forget to do things.

"I like to do things when I'm in the mood, so I may not like it, mom, if you just tell me what to do. I may try to talk you into letting me do it when I'm ready, or letting someone else do it. I hate it when people fight, and I try to make sure everyone has a good time.

"To me, a stranger is just a friend I haven't met yet! Having other people like me is important, and I need to feel important to you, too. And mom, you can help me learn that it's nice to be important but it's more important to be nice."

YOUR "I" CHILD'S STRENGTHS AND WEAKNESSES

The "I" type, representing 25-30 percent of the population, has never met a stranger. This personality style seeks attention from birth, crying if left alone. As a child, he or she will follow you from room to room to be with you.

Sociable, outgoing high "I" teenagers, looking for attention and approval from everyone, might as well surgically install permanent telephones in their ears. As with all personalities, however, their strengths can become their weaknesses if out of control.

Every move an "I" child makes is one step closer to having fun! As children, they seek fun and games throughout the day until the moment they collapse in bed at night. Their happy, cheerful, and friendly personalities attract them to others, who flock to be around them. Conversations with this inspiring type are stimulating because they are so expressive and full of life.

THE "I" CHILD

STRENGTHS:	WEAKNESSES:
BABY:	**BABY:**
• Bright	• Wants to be held a lot
• Playful	• Into everything
• Precocious	• Cries for attention
• Imaginative	
CHILD:	**CHILD:**
• Happy	• Disorganized
• Enthusiastic	• Distracted easily
• Affectionate	• Emotional
• Many friends	• Doesn't follow through
• Imaginative	• Impulsive
• Good communicator	• Over-active
TEEN:	**TEEN:**
• Friendly	• Doesn't complete things
• Charming	• Gullible
• Joiner	• Talks endlessly
• Life of party	• Needs attention
• Popular	• Gossipy
• Optimistic	• Succumbs to peer pressure
• Spontaneous	

"Is" enjoy life at its best. The last movie they saw is their *favorite* movie. The last restaurant they ate at is their *favorite* restaurant. The last book they read is their *favorite* book (as long as there were plenty of pictures). The last friend they met is their *best* friend – until the next one comes along!

The "I" child is very affectionate, holding hands, *hugging* – even first acquaintances. My daughter Madison was almost knocked down recently by a big bear hug from a high "I' girl, whom she had just met for the first time. The little girl was absolutely thrilled and overjoyed – because her name was Madison, *too*! *Wham!* The affection exploded like spontaneous combustion!

My eight-year-old "C" Madison looked at me (peering through her new-found friend's little arms *squished* around her neck), rolled her eyes, smiled, and said, "Mom, she's an 'I'." Madison became the other Madison's "best friend" for the whol-l-l-le *hour*!

STAR OF THE SHOW

High "Is" love surprises more than any other type, and actively seek social recognition (to be popular). For example, you can quickly spot an "I" child onstage. "Is" are entertaining and attention grabbing at any performance. They don't hesitate to wave, giggle, or wiggle onstage. They can get by with so much more than other children (or their siblings) because they're so entertaining. They love to be the star of the show – and really want to be a star to you. Give them your undivided attention, and then watch their creative charm go to work.

"Is" want everything they do to be important to you. An "I" needs attention and will *get* attention somehow. They can make glib or witty remarks that can hurt for the sake of gaining attention. Refusing to give them your time and attention may cause them to eventually give up. They need affirmation that you love them and accept them for their delightful and amusing behavior. If you strip them of this opportunity to feel loved and accepted by you, they may engage in inappropriate relationships with others who will affirm them as they are.

Attention is healthy; however, if "I" children are successful at achieving too much attention, they may be shocked someday when they discover they're not the center of the universe after all.

ME, ME, CALL ON ME!

Madison's kindergarten soccer coach petitioned the girls to select a new team name. Sitting in a circle on the practice field, all the "C" girls carefully thought and contemplated the perfect name for the team. The "Ss" really didn't care; any name would be fine with them as long as they were together.

A high "I" teammate waved her hand fervently until she caught the coach's attention. Her response? "Uh-h-h – I don't know, *but* I'm going to a birthday party tomorrow! I can't wait! It's my friend, Halina's, birthday and…(gasping for air) I'm invited!" It didn't matter that she had absolutely *no* team name to offer, she just wanted to raise her hand, get noticed, and talk!

A "C" teammate was quietly thinking (as "Cs" love to do) about the new team name. Finally, after much "C" contemplation, she politely raised her hand and recommended, "Red Spirit." And so, with a unanimous, "Yea!" the new team name was birthed, while the "Is" performed spontaneous cartwheels across the soccer field! (All kindergarten coaches must have the patience of Job!)

Referring to the important birthday party announcement, if "Is" get left out of a birthday party, they're devastated! With popularity and social status or acceptance as an overwhelming drive, belonging to group activities and social functions is their passion – almost obsession. You can encourage your "I" child to sing, dance, speak, or play sports (although it doesn't take much persuasion).

Because of their short attention span, education may not be as high a priority as theatre, cheerleading, drill team, or anything that provides an opportunity to be "onstage." Younger high "Is" love playgroups, outings, visiting friends, children's theatre, and particularly – birthday parties!

YOU'RE WEARING THAT?

"I" children love clothes at an early age. They are obsessed with how they look. They opt for bright and colorful outfits. Again, it's attention getting. Madison's high "I" friend was at our house for a play date recently. Passionately, the six-year-old asked, "Oh, my! Have you seen the newest Gymboree line?" (My "C" daughter was clueless.) "C" and "S" moms prefer more conservative and subdued beiges, whites, or soft pastels, and don't understand the flamboyant flair of their "I" children.

Let "I" children have choices in selecting their outfits (in a style that's not *too* unflattering). Pick your battles with an autocratic sensitivity to their desire to get attention. Teach the value of flattering and appropriate fashion. Otherwise, as a teen this child could grow up dressing very sexy or inappropriately as a way of getting attention. Choose modesty and moral values as a battle to fight, not fabric or color preferences. After all, a colorful outfit might even brighten *your* day as well!

"SH-H, SH-H, SH-H!"

High "Is" have an endless supply of conversation ability and a gift for meeting people. They will go to a party and know everyone there before they leave! Talking to strangers is merely talking to new friends they simply haven't met yet! More reserved personality styles don't always understand this behavior.

High "I" Kathy said, "My mom was constantly shushing me when I was a child. I talked a lot while growing up, and what I remember hearing most from her was 'Sh-h, Sh-h, *Sh-h-h!*' I always wondered what was wrong with her, because I loved talking to people and she didn't. She wouldn't take me to a lot of busy places because I made her so nervous. My mom often said that I stressed her out a lot!

Now that I'm an adult, she tells me how much it scared her to go out in public with me. Friendly to everyone I met, she knew it would be very easy for a stranger to approach me and take me away – and I would have been happy to go!" (That's a situation where a child-harness might come in handy!) High "Is" meet and know a lot of people in their lifetimes!

A BIRTHDAY CELEBRATION

High "Is" love to be the center of attention, and assume everyone else loves for them to be the center of attention as well. They know life is full of surprises and exciting things to do. Life is constantly changing, and the high "I" adjusts easily to change.

Soon-to-be-seven, high "I" Emily mailed invitations to her outdoor birthday party over a month in advance. It was very exciting that all her friends were coming to celebrate with her. What fun the beautiful "Princess Castle Moon Jump" would be for everyone. It would be the "best birthday party ever!"

The big day came with anticipation at its highest. The princess cake and brightly colored balloons were ready, presents were wrapped, and excitement loomed. Everything was perfect – that is, until the morning forecast predicted severe *storms* that afternoon!

Having an optimistic attitude when her mom, Mindy, asked for alternative party ideas, high "I" Emily eagerly suggested (certain that everyone would be crazy about her new party plans), "I think all my friends would *love* to come over (presents in hand, of course) and watch home movies of *me* instead!"

Hum-m-m. High "I" children aspire to be the center of attention and are enthusiastic to make it happen!

FRIENDS OR FOES?

"Is" are impulsive, spilling things or falling easily because of it. We can help them to not feel that they are strange or different when this happens. "Is" also have a tendency to exaggerate or str-r-r-retch the truth just a li-i-i-i-i-ttle bit. It's not that they're choosing to be deceitful, but that they're striving to tell an *exciting* story – to be liked, accepted, and get attention.

"Is" hate silence and can monopolize all conversations. Friends are very important to an "I," but those friends don't like it when their "I" friend talks too much. You can help your child practice listening instead of talking. (After all, that's why God gave us two ears and one mouth. It's twice as important to listen!) ("Ss" understand that so well.)

Friends are also the most important determinant in measuring what they're doing. If an "I" child lacks self-confidence, she could get involved with the wrong crowd in order to feel accepted among friends. This personality style can spend too much time with friends when seeking acceptance. Stay involved and informed, give your child limits, and remember to keep it fun, adventuresome, and desirable at home, too!

MESSY/CLEAN

High "Is" procrastinate like no other type. If it's not fun, they don't want to do it. They, more than any other style, want freedom and flexibility. Striving for social recognition and being popular supersedes their desire to meet a schedule, responsibility to details, or complete their task.

Jennifer said, "My twin daughters look so much alike that sometimes I have to look twice to see the difference. However, there is a distinct difference in their personality styles. For example, one is so outgoing and the other is quite shy. You can also see an obvious but invisible line down the middle of their room. Rhonda's half is a complete mess all the time. She can never find anything! On the other side, Rachel's half is immaculate, neatly organized, and perfectly kept. Rachel likes things organized because it helps her to be on time for everything. In contrast, Rhonda is never on time for *anything*! She puts everything off until the last minute and then, because her things are so disorganized, she can't find anything when she needs it. Rhonda's procrastination puts a lot of pressure on everyone else in the family, too. We always have to search for some misplaced item of hers just so *we* can make it on time!" The high "I's" messiness can affect the entire family if left out of control.

ACTIVE OR HYPERACTIVE?

Due to their high-energy, outgoing, and rowdy behavior, sometimes "I" (and "D") children are misdiagnosed and misunderstood – particularly by those of dissimilar personality styles.

Recently I read an advertisement in the local newspaper, seeking children to participate in a clinical research study:

ADHD

The Following Symptoms May Signal Attention Deficit Hyperactivity Disorder:

√ Difficulty completing homework or other tasks

√ Not listening when spoken directly to

√ Easily distracted, restless, can't sit still

√ Fidgets, runs around, and/or talks excessively

√ Blurts out, interrupts

√ "Forgets" to do things (homework, chores, etc.)

(All doctors and medications will be provided at no charge.)

Does this behavior sound vaguely familiar? Interestingly enough, this advertisement also describes the same general characteristics of a high "I" child. We can only speculate that some children are certainly prescribed medication because their personality styles are misinterpreted. This outgoing personality style can be understandable to the "D" or "I" mom, but exhausting or overwhelming to the "S" or "C" mom!

High-energy, compulsive, and distractive tendencies can be misunderstood by parents and professionals. They may revert, instead, to depend on the medication to do the job of discipline and structure. Obviously, an ADHD misdiagnosis isn't the situation for all children, but certainly in some instances a percentage of our children are over-medicated.

RIGHT PRESCRIPTION

I spoke to a group regarding the personality styles and conveyed that I believe some of our children are misdiagnosed as having ADHD rather than identifying potentially high "I" (or "D") behaviors. A lady approached me afterwards saying, "My son's school counselor insisted that we put him on Ritalin. The counselor said that my son was immature with inappropriate outbursts in class, never wanted to sit still and listen, and often interrupted. So, at their insistence, I had him tested for ADHD. Although he didn't officially test out as having ADHD, they suggested we put him on the medication anyway."

Shaking her head, she continued, "Also at their recommendation, I held him back a year – even though he was already one of the oldest boys in his class. That didn't help either; in fact, it seemed to escalate the problem somewhat. Now I *realize* that my son has a high 'I/D' personality style. He is high energy and craves attention, and he's strong willed, determined, controlling, and demanding! Some days have been fun and productive, and some have been awful. It has been extremely confusing to me why he does what he does!

But now, knowing I'm a 'C' mom, I know I never understood his behavior or recognized his personality style before!"

Since that first encounter, this mom learned that she needed to quit fighting against the way her son is wired and start redirecting his plethora of energy toward a productive result! Now she knows there's a potential alternative to medication. She can work on helping him release (in a positive way) his intense energy, have agreed-upon control and consequences, and build his self-esteem!

EXTRA EFFORT PAYS OFF

A similar experience occurred with an observant teacher, Mrs. Oehlers. She explained, "On a particular day, if a student forgets to take his or her ADHD medication, it makes for a challenging day. The important thing is that I understand what I need to do to keep his or her attention and interest. I strategically 'prescribe' fun, leadership opportunities, and physical activity outlets throughout the day. This helps develop concentration – and control the power struggles. It's more work for me, but well worth the extra effort.

"However, when the same student comes back the next day after having remembered to take his or her medication, I am back to dealing with a student who walks around like a zombie! Granted, students are a lot less maintenance when they just pop a pill, but it seems sad and overtly wrong to me! I have actually experienced the difference in students who are supervised according to their personality styles, not just medicated to get through the day. I can see a big difference when personality styles are taken into account."

STRINGENTLY EVALUATE

Taking medication for a true diagnosis of ADHD is not a "wrong" thing to do; it's certainly necessary in specific cases. I've even heard amazingly positive stories regarding the effects of appropriate diagnosis and medication. However, it's essential and crucial to stringently evaluate the child's personality style to determine why he or she has trouble staying focused, chooses fun over work, or is high energy – before medicating them.

We just learned that the "I" child demands much attention, but they can be great helpers for you as a mom or teacher if you thank them and appreciate what they do. They can soar to new heights if you recognize their abilities and encourage them to achieve their greatest potential.

THE "I" CHILD'S REPORT CARD MIGHT LOOK LIKE THIS:

√ Your child is very outgoing and friendly with her classmates.

√ She is learning to talk at more appropriate times now.

√ Homework needs to be completed on time.

√ Please work on tardiness in the mornings.

√ She loves to have fun and is often the life of the party.

Now let's take a look at Chapter 17 to learn more about the Supportive "S" child!

17

D-I-S-COVER THE $ CHILD

*W*HY IS MY CHILD SO SHY AND LAID BACK?

The BOTS are going to make a movie. Each one has a different job they like to do:

- The "S" child **(4BOT)** will make sure everyone has what they need so they can all work together! The "S" child has fun moving the lights around and helping everyone else.

THE "S" TYPE CHILD SAYS:

"Mom, as a high 'S' child, starting new jobs is hard for me, but I do like to work on one thing at a time and finish what I start. I don't mind being told what to do. I really like for people to work together and get along. I like sticking with what works, and I don't like it when things change too quickly. I need to feel comfortable, so I like knowing what will happen next.

"I love kind words when you appreciate me, but angry words upset me terribly, so please be gentle with me. I hate arguing and confrontation, so I may do things for others that I really don't want to do in order to keep the peace. When I feel pushed, I can be very stubborn because I want to please people so much. I may need your help, Mom, to learn that I can say no to people at times and it will be okay. I just love to be with you! I am a kind, gentle, and easy child."

YOUR "S" CHILD'S STRENGTHS AND WEAKNESSES

The "S" type, representing 30-35 percent of the population, is reserved and people-oriented. This type likes to do one thing at a time. Desiring a great deal of security, the "S" style is very supportive, sweet, family-oriented, and likes where there is a predictable routine of things remaining the same.

They are the least demanding of all personality styles. Whatever you suggest is fine with this child; yes (plus sign), or no (minus sign). It's okay either way to an "S," just as long as you're together. As with all personalities, however, their strengths can become their weaknesses if out of control.

THE "S" CHILD

STRENGTHS:	*WEAKNESSES*:
BABY:	**BABY:**
• Easygoing	• Shy
• Sweet-natured	• Reserved
• Undemanding	• Timid
CHILD:	**CHILD:**
• Harmonious	• Slow
• Affectionate	• Low energy
• Lovable	• Lazy
• Easygoing	• Insecure
• Sweet	• Gullible
TEEN:	**TEEN:**
• Pleasing	• Hates conflict
• Good listener	• Sucker
• Caring	• Indecisive
• Sentimental	• Submissive
• Dependable/Loyal	• Unmotivated
• Stable/Steady	• Resists change

HAMSTER CARE

"S" children are softhearted, sensitive, and dependable. They have a built-in radar detector that focuses on the needs, feelings, and desires of others. They feel good when they can care for or nurture others. They love sameness because it makes them feel comfortable.

One morning after I spoke to a MOPS International (Mothers of Preschoolers®) group, Judy, a lady in the audience, darted to the podium, exclaiming, "I've *finally* figured it out! Now that I understand the personality styles, I've *finally* figured out my three daughters and our family hamster situation. You see, my high 'I' daughter, Ellie, begged for months to get a hamster, 'Ple-e-e-ease, mom, I *promise* I'll take care of it!'" (We've all heard *that* one before!) Judy gave in to Ellie's incessant pleas with the hope that it would help her daughter improve in responsibility and accountability.

Judy continued her saga, "It wasn't long, though, before my 'I' child quickly *bored* of having to care for Harry, the new family hamster, so Shelly, my 'C' child, volunteered to take over. Shelly is extremely organized and responsible. I thought she would be a perfect hamster caregiver. Shortly thereafter, however, my 'C' child became extremely *stressed out* taking care of this tiny little hamster. She was paranoid she would do something wrong! This was a major crisis to her! Alas, my daughter, Kelly, volunteered to rescue the hamster from her two sisters."

Judy went on to explain that Kelly (who she now realizes is an "S") has always loved to play with her dolls, cook fabulous plastic meals for them, change their diapers a dozen times (boy, will *that* change!), and nurture all her stuffed animals. Harry, the hamster, became cared for, loved, fed, and nurtured.

Judy said, "You would have thought it was Kelly's own child! She enjoyed the opportunity to help support and rescue Harry from his troubles. Because of Kelly, we had a happy hamster from that day on – and Ellie and Shelly never looked back!"

SHE'S YOUR FAVORITE

"S" children are easy to please and strive to help everyone they can. They have a strong sense to belong, be with and be like others. Remember Millie at Worlds of Fun? She was willing to get *drenched* just to be like everyone else. "Ss" simply enjoy being together. Kind words of appreciation come easily to them.

"Ss" are considered much easier to raise than the other styles. In fact, if you've raised only one child and he or she is an "S" child, it's not the real world! (Wouldn't it be *great* if we could place an order for our child's personality style?) I recently overheard a mom say, "Two of my three kids often complain, 'Mom, you like Angie more. You always favor her.' And I tell them, 'Well, maybe I do, but it's because she's always *sweeter* than you two are!'"

Can you guess what Angie's personality style might be? If a mom could have a favorite, the "S" child just might fit the bill! If the "S" child feels loved, accepted, and secure, you've got yourself a very amiable and pleasant family member.

ANCHORS AND SPONGES

"Ss" are relaxed and willing to do whatever you need. They are anchors, because they like to stay in one place and sustain you when you need them. Life may be constantly changing, but "S" children remain the same. Because they are sensitive and patient, they allow for your mistakes as a mom (and we *all* make them!) and graciously forgive your human frailties.

The "S" child's sensitivity can be pushed to an extreme, though. He or she absorbs the friction in the home like a sponge. Perhaps more than any other type, an "S" child will protect harmonious family relationships. If there's disharmony in your home, this child will try to solve the problem and carry the load – taking on far more than he or she should emotionally. This can literally affect an "S" type physically. Due to their need to feel secure, "S" children can be damaged easily, leading to withdrawal and shutting down emotionally.

WHY DOESN'T SHE KEEP UP?

"Ss" are ready for a nap shortly after they get up! They have little motivation and low energy. Resting and relaxing is their primary goal. When not in the security of the home, younger "S" children may appear clingy and need you close by their sides.

The "S" personality style does not act or react as fast as the high-energy personality styles. Life operates and equates to more of a snail's pace. "S" Polly, daughter of an "I" mom, a "D/I" dad, and an "I" brother, was continually tagging behind her family members. It used to be a source of contention and aggravation for the rest of this high-energy family, because Polly was lackadaisical, slow moving, and never in a hurry.

Her mom, Dianne, said, "When we get out of the car to go into a restaurant, we can be halfway up the sidewalk before we notice that Polly hasn't even unfastened her seatbelt! It used to be so frustrating for us. I used to get extremely irritated at her, but now, after understanding her personality style, I realize that she's not deliberately trying to manipulate us or drive us *crazy*. She's an 'S'. It makes a difference to know that she's wired that way!"

Polly, in fact, would more than likely have preferred something different – to stay home, snuggle, and watch television together. With a household of two "Is" and a "D/I," it's hard for her to not *feel* different, because she *is* different from the rest of her family members. In reality, she could feel something is *wrong* with her because she's not like the others (and will *never* be like them).

"S" children can secretly be worried or scared that their family wishes they had a different child! Avoiding conflict at all costs, "S" children won't speak up and could ultimately act out their frustrations on others in passive-aggressive behavior. In addition, if "S" personality styles feel things are indeed moving too *fast*, they may stubbornly dig in their heels to *slow* things down.

AFRAID TO ASK

If you ask "S" children to do something, show them how to do it step by step. If they don't know how, they may be too shy to ask. "Ss" don't want to impose upon or bother anyone with minor issues or questions. Five-year-old Jordan wanted to please her mom by surprising her with a bowl of cereal for breakfast one morning. "Ss" are such pleasers and are so thoughtful. They were out of milk, though, and Jordan didn't know what to do. So, rather than impose, she improvised with her own version of milk – flour and water! When asking your "S" child to do something, remember that he or she prefers that you explain exactly what to do next.

"Ss" have an innate desire to find the easy way! Solving a complex problem may be difficult and overwhelming for them. They may appear to be the strong, silent type, but the "S" child desperately needs your support with affirmation, approval, and acceptance.

SPEAK UP

Most "Ss" are very compliant and easygoing, but can be gullible or a sucker in the wrong crowd. Joan told me the story of her teenage daughter, Bethany. She said, "Bethany could always be trusted, and we had very little concern about her. That is until, as a teenager, she started arriving home after her curfew. We gave her consequences for this, but she repeatedly showed up late. Her grades dropped because she didn't have time to do her homework and she was exhausted all the time. We couldn't imagine what was happening. We became concerned she might be involved with drugs, drinking, or some other seriously wrong choices. So, we prohibited Bethany from going out with this group of friends. At first she blew up, but a few days later – after things calmed down – she confessed."

Fortunately, Bethany wasn't involved in drugs, drinking, or anything like that. Come to find out, when it was time for Bethany's curfew, she struggled with how to tell her friends that she needed to *go* when they wanted to *stay*. She avoided the conflict with her friends, but was trapped without transportation. She didn't want to bother her friends or feel like she didn't belong, so she took the rap at home (where she felt secure) instead.

Joan and I discussed other alternatives for Bethany. We determined an investment in a cell phone would give Bethany an opportunity to call when she couldn't get a ride home. We also role-played with Bethany ways she could stand up to her friends when necessary, regardless of the outcome.

JUST SAY NO

It's very important for "Ss" to feel accepted by their peers, but we, as moms, need to teach them how to take that hard step and break loose. They have to get tough before the crowd they want to belong to leads them down the wrong path (because an "S" will *follow*)!

"S" teenagers, who are typically easy, compliant kids, have unintentionally gotten themselves into trouble with drugs, immorality, or wrong decisions, simply because they have such a hard time saying "no." Is it any wonder the "Just Say *No!*" anti-drug campaign works so well for some students and does not work for others? "Ss" want to please and cooperate without causing a rift. Steer their compliant, sweet spirits down the right path by first giving them the tools and guidance they need to feel strong and safe.

THE "S" CHILD'S REPORT CARD MIGHT LOOK LIKE THIS:

√ Your "S" child is very compliant and mannerly – shy, but well liked.
√ If another child needs assistance, she's the first person I think of to help.
√ She's a little slower paced and quite sensitive.
√ She will not raise her hand to be called on in class, preferring to be a spectator.
√ She may be a slow starter, but always finishes what she starts.
√ If every child in my class were as sweet as she, my job as a teacher would be a dream!

Now get ready! Let's take a look at Chapter 18 to learn about the Conscientious "C" child!

18

D-I-S-COVER THE **C** CHILD

*W*HY DOES MY CHILD ASK SO MANY QUESTONS?

The BOTS are going to make a movie. Each one has a different job they like to do:

- The "C" child **(2BOT)** is going to plan everything out first so it all comes out right in the end!

THE "C" TYPE CHILD SAYS:

"Mom, as a high 'C' child, I like to know exactly what you want me to do. I like clear plans and directions, so I may ask a lot of questions to be sure that I understand. I hate mistakes. I really want to do everything right, and I expect myself – and others – to do a good job. Small things can be very important to me. I like to make sense of things and I like things that make sense! I like to think about things; in fact, sometimes I worry about things a lot.

"I do things that I know I am good at. Mom, you may need to encourage me to try to do something new, because I will hesitate to do something until I am certain that I can do it. I don't express my feelings in words; I prefer to show you how I feel through what I do. I actually like to be included in the family or group activities, Mom, even though I may seem aloof. I need you to help me learn to relate to those close to me and learn how to show my love!"

YOUR "C" CHILD'S STRENGTHS AND WEAKNESSES

The "C" type, representing 20-25 percent of the population, is very cautious, calculating, and relishes the opportunity to correct and arrange things in order.

The "C" baby dislikes too much stimulation, noise, or activity. The "C" child demonstrates curiosity and enjoys learning the facts.

Teenage "Cs" think things through before deciding or acting, because they like things to be precise. They may appear antisocial and uninterested in people, but they're focusing on a project. As with all personalities, their strengths can become their weaknesses if out of control.

THE "C" CHILD

STRENGTHS:	WEAKNESSES:
BABY:	**BABY:**
• Quiet	• Timid
• Curious	• Cries easily
• Prefers schedules	• Clingy
CHILD:	**CHILD:**
• Responsible	• Moody
• Perfectionistic	• Sensitive
• Intense	• Unsociable
• Gifted/Good in arts	• Moody
• Loyal	• Critical
• Content alone	• Closed
	• Rigid
TEEN:	
• Cautious	**TEEN:**
• Deep thinker	• Critical
• Conscientious	• Negative
• Orderly	• Inflexible
• On time	• Easily offended
• Idealistic	• Worrisome
• Analytical	• Doubtful

You can recognize a high "C" child at an early age. They are organizing blocks, toys, Legos®, and even their food in a systematic order. As a toddler, my high "C" Madison would sit in her high chair, organizing and separating her peas and carrots, lining them up in rows in sequential order before eating.

When taking a bath, she would line the foam alphabet letters by color sequence (she didn't yet recognize the letters) along the side of the bathtub.

She's always played with Legos®, Ellos®, or building blocks of any kind. She enjoys crafts, coloring pictures, or drawing – for hours! It's sometimes *harder* for me to sit still than it is for her! (Rainy days are not difficult with a "C" child.) High "C" children are efficient and orderly in everything they do. They're detailed and organized, and follow through to completion.

HIGH STANDARDS

"Cs" value school for the opportunity to learn. They enjoy reading (or being read to) more than any other child. "C" children set high standards and can be very hard on themselves if they don't reach their own expectations. It's exciting (if a "C" can get excited) to come up with correct answers and figure out problems. This is fun for a "C" child, frustrating to an "I" child.

"Cs" ask a lot of questions because they need a lot of answers – *quality* answers. "C" children have curious minds and *need* opportunities to learn and discover answers or solutions to problems.

As moms, we want all of our children to soar academically, to say things like, "Calculus was so much fun today! I *enjoyed* figuring out the problems and answering the questions!" (Don't hold your breath. Those words may *never* brush your child's lips unless you have a "C" child!)

CARTOON DETAILS

"Cs" enjoy solitude, details, and organization. When my high "C" daughter Stacia was a child, she would not just sit back, relax, and watch cartoons on a typical Saturday morning. Referring to her "PDT" (Personally Designed Television guide), she carefully recorded all the detailed cartoon specifics.

She also (on her own) developed an organized checklist for her school clothes and activities each week – in the second grade! (This could be quite beneficial for a high "I" mom!)

"Cs" have a propensity to keep their rooms clean and organized. I never had to tell Stacia to clean her room. Today, her apartment is perfectly organized and clean. With or without a mom's threats, "Cs" will keep things in order.

Sometimes "Cs" are considered too serious about life. An "I" mom might think that her "C" child is sad and needs to have more *fun*, to lighten up! Regardless, allow "C" children time to think and recharge – to have alone time to plan and calculate matters. Really, it's okay! Don't pressure them to talk a lot or participate in outgoing activities just because you – or their siblings with other personality styles – think differently.

TRICK OR TREAT

You can recognize different personality styles at Halloween or fall festivals fairly easily. In their wild and crazy costumes, the "Is" are shouting, "Hey, look at me! Look at me!" They're excited for the opportunity to draw attention, pretend, have fun, and party! But the more reserved "Cs" have developed a Trick-or-Treat *plan*, methodically collecting candy from house to house, following the rules and staying on the sidewalks. "S" trick-or-treaters are polite at each house, and quit when they have appropriately filled their orange plastic pumpkins.

My high "D" son, Scott, on the other hand, would use a large *pillowcase* and fill it to the top – until it was bursting at the seams! He, too, had a methodical plan, darting from house to house, then from neighborhood to neighborhood, collecting more candy than all of the other kids combined!

After my "C" daughter Stacia arrived home from Trick-or-Treating, she would organize her candy into small plastic bags according to the brand or type of candy bar, gum, suckers, etc. I would stand back and watch with amazement that she would take the *time* to do this essential task. (Just *give* me the *chocolate*!) "Cs" love to categorize and organize, insisting everything should be in its place.

HOMEWORK HURRAHS!

Capitalizing on a child's personality style will benefit both the child and the mom. I'll never forget one day when my high "C" daughter Stacia was in the second grade. She came running to the car after school with such enthusiasm and excitement. Jumping up and down, she squealed, "Mom, Mom! Guess *what?*"

Whoa! I couldn't imagine the exciting thing that might have happened that day, and couldn't wait to hear the news!

With a great big, toothless grin, she sang, "I've---g-o-t---*homework!*"

That's right! She was absolutely *thrilled* to finally have homework with assignments to complete each day. Every day afterwards, self-disciplined Stacia would plop herself down after school at the kitchen table with her snack, and promptly complete all of her required homework. It was part of her plan – on her list, I'm sure! (This may really be a shocker if you don't have a high "C" child!)

High "D" Scott, on the other hand, was a completely different story. His homework was put off until he had no choice. He was relentlessly busy building his two-story fort, creating major sand projects, or competing in sports.

For high "I" children, homework often goes unnoticed and unfinished (unless they want to *look* good in front of their peers)! We know how the high "Is" operate. When do they write their six-week term paper? That's right, the night before it's due!

OBSESSED WITH PERFECTIONISM

"Cs" are worriers and perfectionists. "C" students are generally good students – seldom making "C" grades. Tanya's sophomore son, Carter, lived with continuous headaches preparing for his college exams. Tanya said, "It was imperative to Carter that he test out at the top of his class. In fact, in Junior High he wouldn't participate in activities without an argument, because he was worried about college even *then*! As a perfectionist, he was obsessed with studying all the time and oblivious to relationships."

One day his frustrated mom, Tanya, said to him, "Carter, you *have* to release this worry and anxiety." Tanya suggested that he close his eyes and imagine that he failed the exams, was kicked out of college, or never even made it into a big school. Then she had him think of possible alternatives. This was a big step to stop the worry and headaches for conscientious Carter. Once he realized and accepted that it wouldn't be the end of the world and there *were* other things of importance in life besides college, he was able to relax and enjoy his family and friends more.

"Cs" want to *do it right*. Help them to recognize and appreciate other significant factors in their lives. They'll be thankful – *some* day!

THINKING AHEAD

"Cs" naturally love to *think* things through. They'll contemplate, strategize, theorize, and formulate plans – before they get out of bed! One morning when I woke Madison for school, she said in a quiet whisper, "Mom, I need to lie here a little longer."

I replied, "Oh, okay, but why?"

In a serious six-year-old response, "My head has been thinking about something and it still has to finish two things, then I'll get up, okay?"

"Sure," I responded – knowing how *important* it is for "Cs" to think things through to completion. (And I certainly didn't have to remind her to not be late. "Cs" hate to be late!)

PRACTICE MAKES PERFECT

"Cs" tend to avoid doing things until they are assured of competence and high-quality success. Riding a bike; playing miniature golf, soccer, or softball; and jumping rope was put on hold it until high "C" Madison *knew* she could do it and do it well (age appropriate, of course). Once "Cs" are assured they can do it correctly, they enjoy the new opportunities. They will drag their feet until they feel competent.

Madison had always refused to ride her bicycle, which was astonishing to me because I've always loved to ride bikes. To our surprise one morning, she *insisted* that her Dad take off the training wheels – she felt confident. Then, she didn't just want to ride around in the cul-de-sac – her *first* ride consisted of a ten-mile ride on the bike trails to go out for breakfast. "Cs" are very cautious until they feel confident and assured of success.

"Cs" KNOW WHAT THEY KNOW

"Cs" are convinced they are correct, and firm in their conclusions. My friend, Jenn, was elated when she announced at Bible study that she was expecting her third child. With two boys, she was hoping for a girl, but happy nonetheless when the sonogram confirmed that the baby was indeed another boy. Week after week, we prayed for her pregnancy with this precious baby boy, discussed potential names (as we moms *love* to do), and showered her with lots of blue baby gifts.

Jenn's four-year-old high "C" son, Carter, on the other hand, *insisted* they were having a girl – regardless of the proof with the sonogram picture. As high "Cs" do, Carter *knew* he was right and kept repeating, "No, I *know* it's a girl…Jesus told me." This conviction continued week after week, month after month. High "C" Carter felt he knew what he knew and wouldn't let up. Jenn and her husband, Kevin, were concerned about how to handle Carter's disappointment when his new baby brother would arrive.

Ultimately, the big day came for Jenn to deliver. In *position* to help him enter into the world (and you *know* what I'm talking about!), the doctor announced, "He-e-e-ere comes his *head!* He-e-e-ere comes his *shoulders!* He-e-ere comes… *whoa…wait a minute! He's a she!* It's a *girl!*"

Wow! What a shocker! However, when Jenn announced the astonishing news to Carter, in his very matter-of-fact "C" response, he confidently stated, "Yes, Mom. I already *knew* that."

"Cs" know what they know! (And Daddy went straight home as fast as he could to turn the blue nursery into a beautiful pink and frilly princess room – while mommy and baby princess slept. And yes, we replaced the many *blue* train and truck outfits with *pink* lacey princess and ballerina outfits right away!)

CHESS OBSESSION

"Cs" really enjoy excellence in workmanship and artistic endeavors, both as observers and as artisans themselves. They can take hours analyzing an idea, work of art, or design with a quest for excellence. After I taught a D-I-S-C Personality Insights training session, a mom came up to me with tears in her eyes and shared, "My teenage daughter and I barely speak to each other. She is utterly obsessed with the game of chess! All she thinks or talks about is calculating her next winning strategy. I *hate* chess! She's ruthless and quite honestly, before today I found her *boring!*"

This mom continued, "But now I see that I'm an "I/S" mom wanting to go places and have fun, while she's obviously a "C/D" who prefers staying at home, studying and contemplating the game of chess. Her dreams and motives are so different than mine." Notice how their personality styles are completely different.

She said, "I realize now that I haven't appreciated *her* personality style. I need to stop nagging and just let her be herself. No wonder she acts like she doesn't want me around! Granted, I may not love chess, but I do love my daughter and I want us to have a good relationship – even though we're so different. I've *got* to change my thinking about her and I'm *going* to – starting today! Thank you for showing me that our relationship *differences* are okay – before it's too late!"

As all moms know, it's *never* too late to express love, appreciation, and understanding to your child. Regardless of what happened yesterday, we can change today to affect tomorrow!

THE "C" CHILD'S REPORT CARD MIGHT LOOK LIKE THIS:

√ Your child is quiet, shy, a deep thinker, and content to play alone.

√ He is sometimes moody and unsociable.

√ He completes his work, but seems to question me or worry easily.

√ Your child is a great problem solver.

√ Unlike the other students, his desk is amazingly neat and orderly.

Next, we'll take a look at Chapter 19 and find out about the Determined "D" *parenting* style with *each* personality style!

19

D-I-S-COVER THE D

PARENTING STYLE WITH A...

 ERSONALITY CAPSULE FOCUS:

TYPE:	THOUGHT PATTERN:	BASIC NEED:	IDENTIFIER:
"D"	What?	Control	Dominance
"I"	Who?	Recognition	Interaction
"S"	How?	Appreciation	Support
"C"	Why?	Quality answers	Correctness

- **Dominant**
- **Direct**
- **Demanding**
- **Decisive**
- **Determined**
- **Doer**

Basic Need: *CONTROL!*

Why do we get along with one child better than another? Moms who don't understand their children with different personality styles will try to make all the children in the family act the same. Looking at the Personality Capsule Focus chart, it's apparent that each personality style thinks differently. A "D" type may think, "*What* can I do to take control?" An "I" type may think, "*Who* is going to be there?" An "S" type wonders, "*How* can I help?" while a "C" type asks, "*Why* are we doing it this way?"

Again, the issue is not so much the actual information or factual data as it is our perception and perspective regarding that information. We see things from our own perspective, but we also need to understand the way our children see things from *their* perspectives. Stepping into their shoes (out of high heels and into Velcro-strapped tennis shoes) helps us take a journey down their road – and understand why some kids stomp in those mud puddles and others steer clear!

"D" MOM – THINKS, "WHAT?"

A persistent "D" mom thinks, "What? What can we accomplish? What can we do about this?" She believes everyone should want to work and accomplish many things – like *she* does. The "D" mom is on a mission – a mission where she is more interested in accomplishing things than getting people to like her. Sometimes she's so goal-oriented that relationships take a back seat. Jeopardize this mom's goals, and you will reap her wrath!

Conflict is a motivating factor for a "D" mom; in fact, she is energized by it! This mom must learn that it's best to operate as a nurturing and supportive mom, toning down her determination to bolster her children to win.

"D" moms naturally take charge in relationships. They quickly respond to opportunities to try something new, and tend to direct their children to do the same. They take quick action and make quick decisions when they recognize opportunities. They make sure their children gain full advantage of their opportunities as well. For "D" moms, relationships need to become a priority, remembering children need a mom, not a drill sergeant!

Life is constantly changing, and the high "D" mom deals well with change. In fact, she often creates change to get the results she wants! She has great problem-solving abilities and draws on her strength to help her children get through any situation.

A "D" mom who works outside the home accomplishes great things at work as a leader or director. However, sometimes she accomplishes so much at work that her family gets her leftovers at the end of the day (and this time I'm not talking about food).

To a dominant-style mom or child, a good relationship is one in which he or she has freedom from controls or supervision. They want to experience many varied activities, so relationships will probably center on doing things they want to do and accomplishing goals. "D" moms are attracted to people who help them get things done. They naturally evaluate you based on the results you achieve.

"Ds" *expect* aggressiveness. What is an argument to others is usually a discussion to them! Personal friends usually provide them with fun, stability, or expertise in an area of interest. They are most interested in working with people who do the parts of a job that they don't have the time or desire to do. This mom loves a challenge; the more she can accomplish, the better.

"Ds" are high-energy people. In fact, physical activity is how they *unwind* after a hard day at work! You will feel the strength of her drive!

GOALS-R-US!

Because a "D" mom often doesn't view spending quality time together as *productive* enough, she struggles in relationships with her children. She establishes goals for her children and knows how to move them into action (by sometimes displaying anger or impatience when they don't measure up). Her high standards and expectations can be detrimental to a child whose goals are much more subdued. A child can easily feel discouraged, worthless, and like a failure because he or she can't measure up to the high "D" mom's incessant ability to perform.

Life is for accomplishments to "D" moms, but they do go on vacations. But a "D" mom's definition of a vacation consists of something to conquer, setting the pace for exciting challenges. A vacation would never consist of lying around in the sun all afternoon. That doesn't accomplish anything (except skin cancer)!

Living the "Super Mom" syndrome, a high "D" mom often lets winning get in the way of the loving, caring, "I'll always be there for you" mom that children need. The "D" mom must be brave enough to sit down with her children and ask them what they need from her. She has admirable strength others yearn for, and can accomplish more than anyone else if that strength is used with a measure of consideration and respect.

"D" MOM IN PARENTING RELATIONSHIPS

 *Mom - Parenting a* *Child*

> **"D" – TASK-ORIENTED AND OUTGOING *MOM & CHILD*!**
>
> **Strengths**: This self-motivated dynamic duo is fast-paced and likes to get things done! They accomplish many different things together and find stimulating challenges to experience!
>
> **Struggles**: Blending of the "Ds" can be volatile if their goals are different. Respect and appreciate those differences. Remember, the relationship is more important than the accomplishments!

This energetic combination likes to achieve a lot of goals,

but can butt heads if they are not eye-to-eye and on the same team. A power struggle in a house with two "Ds" is similar to two lions vying for power of the den. "Ds" like to be in control, and this mom is generally in control of everything – except her "D" child!

This powerful combination strives for success, achievement, and takes responsibility. Both mom and child are competitive and can conquer just about anything if they work together and restrain their need to win autonomously. "D" teams in the household would fair well to adopt the motto, "One team, one dream," displaying respect and admiration for each other.

Self-motivated "Ds" don't need to be pushed to keep going (pray they're headed in the right direction)! Decisive "Ds" will resist being controlled. Don't threaten them or force the issue. Use short, one-sentence commands, giving choices whenever possible.

D Mom - Parenting an ★ Child

"D" – TASK-ORIENTED AND OUTGOING *MOM*!
"I" – PEOPLE-ORIENTED AND OUTGOING *CHILD*!

Strengths: The determined "D" mom and inspiring "I" child combination is outgoing and energetic. Accomplishing goals while having fun is the key to this relationship success!

Struggles: The direct "D" mom is bottom-line oriented. Games and theatrics of the fun-loving "I" child could exasperate this impatient, goal-seeking mom. Outspoken and demanding, hurt feelings end up as the main accomplishment.

This powerful combination is confident, optimistic, and looks for action. "Is" strive to play and have fun, while "Ds" strive to accomplish. A "D" mom can learn to lighten up and take time to play with her "I" child! The key for the "D" mom is to refrain from becoming frustrated when the "I" child is unorganized, fun loving, or lacks the same drive.

If you're a "D" mom, talk and have fun while you're accomplishing your goals! Be prepared to listen enthusiastically to the "I" child's creative stories and ideas – it may take a while! Insist on the facts. Keep goals simple, easy, and fun to do. Reward your "I" child with praise and affection. Overall, your strong personality to accomplish things can be a wonderful role model for this playful type.

WHAT'S THE POINT?

"D" moms prefer one-line answers. When asking, "How was your day?" they expect short, concise answers. "I" children, however, may elaborate with long, drawn-out stories about their day – and everyone else's day! Hold back and listen, but help them learn to stick to the point. Bottom-line communication is good, but feeling loved and accepted is more important to an "I" child.

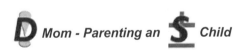

***D* Mom - Parenting an *S* Child**

"D" – TASK-ORIENTED AND OUTGOING *MOM!*
"S" – PEOPLE-ORIENTED AND RESERVED *CHILD!*

Strengths: This is a mega personality contrast! Striving for status quo, slow and easy, the "S" child can steady the fast-lane "D" mom to cruise control if she's not too impatient!

Struggles: This determined mom is driven to accomplish many things – leaving the "S" child in the dust. Her dogmatic determination could easily squelch feelings of stability and security in this reserved child, annihilating the relationship.

This combination, having little common ground, is a more difficult personal relationship because of their contrasting styles. If the "D" mom is too controlling, the "S" child could easily be intimidated and crushed by the "D" anger, curtness, or tone of voice. Sensitivity is necessary when a "D" mom speaks to this hypersensitive child.

"Ds" like to lead and "Ss" like to follow, as long as they feel stable, secure, and close to you. The "S" child can offer steadiness and warmth and is a practical help to the "D" mom. A "D" mom needs to give "S" children plenty of attention and acceptance for who they are, not who she thinks they should be. More than other personality styles, "Ss" want to please, support, and *feel* supported by their moms.

A "D" mom could crush and break an "S" child's heart. Show love and support first. A "D" may be on a mission, but the laid-back "S" just wants to be together, sharing and caring. Instead of dictating what needs to be done, help your "S" child get started, and work together. Enjoy the process – as the "S" style is prone to do.

RELAX, CONVERSE

Driven "D" moms need to remember that it's okay to relax. It's not a crime! "Ss" know how to relax and enjoy. They desire a slower pace. High "S" Melody said, "I hate going home. After school, my mom has a list a mile long of things for me to do before dinner. So I go to my friend, Lynette's, house whenever I can, especially if I'm tired. Her mom always makes me feel comfortable and relaxed. I know she cares."

We want *our* homes to be safe havens, places of peace, where our children feel loved. Find a hobby or project that you and your child can work on, but take it easy. (Make sure that project doesn't consist of changing your "S" child to become more like a "D".) Even with great ideas and leadership ability, it's not as important to make something or someone better, as it is to listen to your child. My "C" daughter Stacia has said, "Please just listen, don't instruct." (Ouch!)

ADD SOFTNESS

An "S" child may shy away from asking questions because of the "D" mom's abrasive verbal responses. Denying your child an opportunity to ask questions or request details can close the door to communication and future loving relationships. This child eventually could isolate or desert the relationship. It may be a major challenge, but the "D" mom can add softness to her natural style, to keep from being too hard on the "S" child (or any child).

D Mom - Parenting a *C* Child

"D" – TASK-ORIENTED AND OUTGOING *MOM*!
"C" – TASK-ORIENTED AND RESERVED *CHILD*!

Strengths: This is a highly task-oriented relationship. These two independent people like to get things done! This driven mom gives direction and the conscientious child follows through!

Struggles: The "C" child wants things done *right*, and the "D" mom wants things done *right away*! The more cautious "C" child wants to make sure every detail is correct before making decisions. The "D" mom's short-tempered impatience could hurt and immobilize this child.

This highly task-oriented combination is a very difficult *personal* relationship because they both focus on *tasks!* "Ds" like to take risks and make adjustments as they go, while "Cs" like to comply with rules and make a plan before they start! Since both perspectives are valuable, they can learn much from each other.

As a "D" mom, give your slower-paced child an opportunity to make plans and think through a strategy without rushing him or her. Avoid surprises, and give plenty of time to adapt to changes. It's very important to the "C" child to have the facts and make the correct decision after carefully contemplating the risks. This child will never be a risk taker, but enjoys a calculated move that he or she feels will be successful. If you push (as a "D" mom can do so well), you risk damaging his or her self-esteem.

INSTRUCTIONS NOT REQUIRED (EXCEPT FOR "Cs")

"Cs" will always take time to read instructions and consequently, put things together in about half the time as those who "wing it." If we have a new item that needs to be assembled, my eight-year-old daughter, Madison, actually *likes* reading the instructions. This makes her feel confident we're doing the job right.

As a "D" mom, on the other hand, I enjoy the challenge of figuring things out without reading those minor, little details. But let's face it, things just don't always turn out the *correct* way when I do it *my* way! (Not to mention all those leftover parts!) I've learned that reading the instructions and the *time* it takes – can actually be a good thing! (But "Cs" already *knew* that.)

SOCKS TO MATCH

"C" children want things to be perfect. When I was a child, my "D/I" personality was emphatic about particular things. I've been told that at age four, I stubbornly refused to go outside each day unless my socks matched my outfit. (Enter – the "D" stubbornness and the "I" attraction to clothes.)

My "C" daughter Madison also cares very much about her socks, but for a different reason – a "C" reason. It is important to her that her socks *fit* just right (seam perfectly straight across the top of the toe, etc.). If we have delays in the morning, it's usually because her socks don't fit perfectly! I don't know how many battles we've gone through because of this! A "C" child will pull, stretch, rearrange, roll down the tops, and then *pat* in place until the socks are correct. (Thank goodness for flip-flops in warm weather!)

"C's" clothes must fit just right, too. Tags are irritating and often removed. "Cs" require perfection – not because they want to *look* right, but because they want it to *be* right! Since school delays are at significant risk because of this, we started working on Madison's socks *first* thing after hopping out of bed each morning, so she would have ample time to adjust and readjust her socks during breakfast and "Clifford"!

FOLLOW THE RULES

"Cs" strive for correctness and perfection. They expect you (and themselves) to live by precise standards. They naturally evaluate you based on the accuracy you maintain, and are attracted to people who do almost anything with excellence.

"Cs" play by the rules – and expect everyone else to play by them as well. When Madison was younger and wanted to play outside, she'd say, "I'm going outside, okay, Mom?" A few steps closer to the door, she'd repeat, "I'm going outside now, okay?" Then, as she stepped out the door, she'd peek back in to affirm again, "I'm outside now!" (Okay! *Okay!* Just *go!* – I'd often *think*, but not *say!*) It's very important for the "C" child to do the *correct* thing.

Madison also makes sure that I'm following the rules, too, by asking, "Mom, are you wearing your seat belt?" or "Mom, are you going the speed limit?" ("Well, *ye-e-e-es!*") It's very important to a "C" that rules are followed. (It's also important that "we" answer these meticulous children with patience and understanding toward their intense dedication and obedience to rules.)

When conscientious "Cs" are overly focused on the "correct" or the "right" way or thing, they have a propensity to worry too much. A house full of conflict, matters of health concerns, or situations they don't understand can ignite a fury of worrisome thinking in a "C" child. By working within parameters of the "rules," we can boost the confidence and build the self-esteem in these little thinking machines.

STRENGTH FROM ILLNESS

Sherry struggled through the discovery and recovery of cancer. It was a frightening, yet eye-opening experience for Sherry and her family. As those of us who have fought the cancer battle can attest, it's a nasty, intrusive, and unwanted disease. Through difficult situations, however, sometimes new doors open.

The process of doctors' visits, surgery, and chemotherapy seemed endless, but as a high "D" mom, Sherry was determined to get through one day at a time, regain her strength, and come out on top. One afternoon after Sherry's final chemotherapy session, her "S" son, Brendan, sat next to her bed and tenderly revealed that he had dropped out of law school. Brendan desperately hoped to pursue an art degree instead.

Brendan explained, "Mom, I never wanted to be a lawyer and I've always wanted to be an artist. I've always loved art, but you never would have accepted it as a challenging or productive enough profession. Your having cancer has taught me to value life. It has given me the strength to do what I *want* to do, not what you *expect* me to do." Apparently, Sherry's high goals had never been Brendan's high goals.

Coincidentally, a couple of weeks later, Sherry's "C" daughter, Molly, revealed, "Mom, there's something I need to tell you. Your having cancer has made me face the truth about my own life. You need to know, I've been silently struggling with bulimia for over two years." Sherry was shocked.

Resolving to change her life, Molly said, "I'm going to learn to accept that I can't ever be perfect or achieve anything near your magnitude of accomplishments. I want my life to matter to you *and* me!"

Together, they made plans to get counseling for Molly. Eventually, Molly began working with younger girls who were struggling with eating disorders. Sherry's illness had opened the doors for her children to re-evaluate the previous choices they had made – choices based on their *mom's* high goals for them. Ultimately, their lives were changed and directed down paths more conducive to their own unique dreams and desires.

"D" moms must let their children function in their own personality quadrants at rates and styles that fit them. Otherwise, these moms are setting their children up for failure to meet expectations that are extreme – undesired, unhealthy, and unattainable.

INSIGHT FOR "D" MOMS

"D" moms carry out remarkable accomplishments, but they can be bossy, domineering, and impatient. They generally formulate successful tactics, taking it personally if their judgment is ever questioned. Missing out on a leadership position, promotion, having a serious illness, or raising a rebellious child is a negative situation for this controlling mom. She evaluates her child based on the results achieved. She wants others to cooperate with her decisions and work hard to be successful. Oppose her, and you've declared a bitter war.

"Ds" expect instant obedience to their demands, "Follow my orders immediately – it's my way or the highway." "D" moms have to be very careful to not try to win every verbal battle. ("Ds" hate to lose *any* battle!) "Win the battle, but lose the war."

A "D" mom's parenting style is, "Give me the bottom line – do what you're supposed to do and that's it – no exceptions." But she needs to let her children make mistakes. After all, how do we learn best? From our mistakes! Many "D" moms have a tough time letting go and learning to quit bossing their children around – even when they're adults (cough, cough)! I often have to remind myself that my two adult children are exactly that – adults now. It hurts to bite the lip sometimes, but important to respect and value them for who they are.

"D" moms can lead their children to aspire to new heights and accomplish things they would not have otherwise accomplished. Children of a "D" mom – in control – are often proud of all that she accomplishes when she does so with grace and control. The responsible "D" mom is a determined mom who propels her children to work toward being the best they can be!

Now let's take a look at Chapter 20 and find out more about the Inspiring "I" parenting style with each type of personality!

20

D-I-S-COVER THE ⭐
PARENTING STYLE WITH A...

$\mathscr{P}$ERSONALITY CAPSULE FOCUS:

TYPE:	THOUGHT PATTERN:	BASIC NEED:	IDENTIFIER:
"D"	What?	Control	Dominance
"I"	Who?	Recognition	Interaction
"S"	How?	Appreciation	Support
"C"	Why?	Quality answers	Correctness

- **Inspiring**
- **Influencing**
- **Impressionable**
- **Interactive**
- **Impressive**
- **Involved**

Basic Need: *RECOGNITION!*

"I" MOM – THINKS, "WHO?"

Preferring group activities to being alone, "Is" desire to be liked or popular more than anything else. They think, "Who? *Who's* going to be there? *Who* am I going to see? Better yet, who will see *me*?"

"I" moms are fun moms and love to play, entertain, tell stories, and participate in activities. Getting attention is an essential ingredient to their enjoyment in life. "I" moms make their children laugh! They want their children to enjoy them. Consequently, trying desperately to please or be *liked* by your child can be a detriment when parenting.

To remain disciplined and authoritative over her child, an "I" mom needs to understand that she must parent first, not strive to be her child's best friend (until that extraordinary day when the child becomes an adult).

The "I" mom seeks an adventurous, fun, and social lifestyle, racking up more miles in her red convertible (or family van) than the other three styles put together! The problem lies in getting there on time – including getting her children to school and appointments on time. "I" moms must work on responsibility and structure in the homes.

Chores and responsibilities at home are just *not* fun. (Don't we know!) With too many fun things to do *outside* the home, the family may find themselves void of a mom. If life becomes too serious, boring, or demanding, an "I" mom might end up MIA! (We need milk cartons for missing "I" moms!)

"Is" IN PERSONAL RELATIONSHIPS

 *Mom - Parenting a* **D** *Child*

> ### "I" PEOPLE-ORIENTED AND OUTGOING *MOM!*
> ### "D" TASK-ORIENTED AND OUTGOING *CHILD!*
>
> **Strengths**: This is an optimistic combination! The "I" mom is great at inspiring her "D" child in all his or her endeavors, and she is enthusiastic to share the spotlight in all accomplishments.
>
> **Struggles**: The "D" child's struggle for power can overwhelm this happy-go-lucky mom. Role reversal could occur if the "I" mom becomes too permissive. The "D" child could control the home shortly after birth!

This is an exciting personal relationship. The "D" child can be a great asset alongside the "I" mom to accomplish things she would not have otherwise accomplished. However, on a mission to gain power and control, a "D" child may take control of the "I" mom – particularly if she's afraid she won't be liked upon enforcing rules. "I" moms must remember who's in authority.

"D" children are clever in achieving "yes" answers (drive the car, squeeze out more money) from their "I" moms. They scheme to become "best friends" – all to take control of the house. A "D" child could quickly establish role reversal in no time! A controlling high "D" teenager with a fun-loving high "I" mom will manipulate bedtime rules, dating restrictions, allowance, curfews, church attendance, vacations, dinner plans, and more!

Allow your "D" children appropriate power and control by offering choices. Remind them that respectful requests and suggestions are welcome, but a condescending tone shows a lack of respect. "I" moms need to remain fun and fair, but firm.

DESSERT, ANYONE?

It's no secret that *all* personality styles know how to push their moms' buttons. Some kids just happen to be really successful at it. Recently I observed two ladies with a little boy who looked to be almost three years old, out to eat in a not-so-kid-friendly restaurant. The dazzlingly dressed mom seemed exhilarated to be out of the house, talking and laughing the whole time. (Within minutes she and the server were "best of friends".)

Suddenly her rebellious child announced, "I don't *like* this food and I don't want to be here anymore!" He appeared determined to gain control by screaming and jumping. The mom continued chatting, oblivious when he threw his fork, hitting a lady at the next table.

Then it happened. The desperate "I" mom caved. Frantically, she motioned for the server and pleaded, "Okay, okay! He's just not happy. He doesn't want to eat here and he's throwing a fit. Will you just bring him some dessert instead?" (It worked!)

Kids have a strong need to have order and balance, and permissiveness can promote rebellion out of frustration for a lack of security or structure in their lives. Love isn't giving in to your child and giving them everything they want. Love is disciplining them, becoming the "heavy" when necessary, and teaching them to show respect and obedience in all situations.

ACTIVE FROM THE BEGINNING

Even at birth, the "D" child is physically and mentally active. As a high "I/S" loves to do, Tammy enjoyed holding hands, hugging, and snuggling. She loved being together and having fun. Zack, on the other hand, would only sit on Tammy's lap for a few minutes before he jumped down. He was on his way to conquer the world every chance he could. You know the type, CEO of Planet Earth!

Tammy said, "I should have recognized his personality style when he was a baby, vigorously kicking his legs and waving his arms. I now know not to take it personally when he doesn't want to sit still and snuggle with me. I'm no longer afraid that it's because he doesn't like me. I know he needs his freedom to go and conquer things. And it has nothing to do with *me*!"

 Mom - Parenting an  **Child**

"I" – PEOPLE-ORIENTED & OUTGOING *MOM & CHILD!*

Strengths: This outgoing, adventurous "I" combination enjoys people! Animated and affectionate, they give and receive plenty of love, often wearing their emotions on their sleeves. "Is" are intuitive about other's feelings, generous with compliments, and most of all – enjoy making people laugh!

Struggles: "Is" can talk too much and compete to be the center of attention. Enjoying fun activities and time together can deter them from getting things done. Impulsive and disorganized, they see possibilities, but can be oblivious to possible failures.

This is an enthusiastic personal relationship. "Is" fast-paced activities are stimulated by sheer fun. They live life to the fullest with optimistic expectations and enthusiasm. With these two stars' zest for life, life is like one big surprise party. With great fun and a sense of humor, they are confident and excited about life!

"Is" find that talking is essential, and they're sure to tell every detail. This combination needs to work on taking turns talking, because they forget to listen! Two "Is" in the same household have to be careful to not compete for the limelight. Organization is not a strength for the "I" mom, but she must make an extra effort to help the "I" child value order and responsibility. Otherwise, overspending and financial issues could become a serious problem in their home.

BUT I'M SO-O-O HUNGRY, MOM

Generously giving and showing love can build self-esteem in any child. However, a high "I" mom, intensely desiring to be accepted and liked, can make poor decisions and become slack in discipline.

Being liked was very important to Jamie, a recently divorced mom. Jamie is fun and outgoing, a high "I" mom who fits every definition of this fun-seeking personality style. She was determined to help her two kids have fun and accommodate their every wish and desire after all they had gone through.

One weekend, Jamie loaded up the kids, clothes, toys, and snacks for a trip to visit her out-of-state friend, Gwen. When they arrived, the 104-degree temperature was scorching (114-degree heat index) and unbearable, with warnings to stay inside. But Jamie's children were complaining, "I'm bored," (heard that one!) and insisted, "We want to go do something." Fearful they were not having *fun* with her, Jamie agreed to take them to play miniature golf – *outside* – in the *horrific* heat! (I'm thinking the kids could have done something *inside*, but…)

Then at about eleven o'clock that night, Jamie's two children were begging for a snack. "Mom, we're so-o-o-o-o hungry." (You've heard the bedtime saga.) So, this fun and accommodating high "I" mom pulled out two Cokes® and two large Hershey® chocolate bars! (Uh, huh. You get the picture.)

An hour later, while watching the kids *leap* through the air from chair to chair (*vibrating* from all the caffeine), frustrated Jamie said to her friend Gwen, "I just don't understand why they're so wound up and won't settle down! I try to make them happy, and then they won't listen or go to bed when I tell them to!"

"I" moms need to evaluate the consequences of their "fun" decisions *first*, before suffering the consequences *later*. Oftentimes they are not firm enough with their children (even in the happiest of marriages). Permissive moms want to do things for and with their children, sometimes making the mistake of giving them too much freedom and ultimately becoming ineffective.

COMPETITION IN THE HOME

The optimistic "I" combination complement each other (and themselves) about everything. They can also compete for attention or the spotlight. If a teenage daughter brings home a new boyfriend, these two could become competitive or jealous of each other.

The familiar words Trudy generally hears from her attention-getting "I" mom are, "How do I look? Does my makeup look okay? Do you like this outfit?"

Trudy said, "I want her to notice how *I* look, for once!"

IMPULSIVE SWIMMER

"Is" are spontaneous and lively, embracing excitement at every turn. They jump in with both feet and ask questions later – literally! My daughter and I were swimming at a hotel recently when a child, about five years old, skipped toward the indoor swimming pool singing and dancing for all to hear and enjoy. The little girl's mom was down the hall, chatting away. The child leaned over with her eyes on the water (admiring her reflection, I'm sure) when my six-year-old cautious "C" daughter Madison said, "Look, mom. She shouldn't do that. She's not being careful. Watch, mom. Something's going to happen."

Just then, the "I" child kicked off her sandals and, sure enough, *jumped* into the pool – the five-feet-deep section! Her mom was oblivious, still chatting and laughing. The little girl disappeared under the water and bounced up gasping for air. "Help!" she yelled! I swam as fast as I could! (Ever have that nightmare where you're moving in sl-o-o-o-ow motion?)

She went under again while her Mom was, yes, *still* chatting. Frantically, I pulled the little girl to the side of the pool as she coughed and spit out water. Her Mom approached, looked confused, and said, "Oh, wow! I was talking and didn't even *notice!*"

The high "I" child's impulsive behavior strikes at the speed of lightening. They live from moment to moment, finding new adventures wherever they go. They choose what seems like fun at that moment. A high "I" mom has to "notice" and structure the environment to limit decisions or fun intentions that could lead to disaster from illogical thinking.

Mom - Parenting an 💲 Child

"I" – PEOPLE-ORIENTED AND OUTGOING *MOM*!
"S" – PEOPLE-ORIENTED AND RESERVED *CHILD*!

Strengths: This combination is highly people-oriented. The "I" mom likes to do fun things together, and the "S" child is happy to follow her lead – or finish what she starts!

Struggles: The "S" child would prefer a slower pace and time together without action. Tasks and organization are not a top priority for this combination and must be considered to avoid Pandemonium in the home!

An "I" mom with an "S" child is a comfortable personal relationship because of their love for people. Since both are people-oriented, this relationship can be very meaningful. "S" daughters love tea parties, cooking together, playing board games, and making crafts with each other. In addition, "S" sons will cooperate with all of the above (with the exception of the tea party).

The "I" mom's enthusiasm and outgoing nature helps the "S" child feel comfortable when trying new things. The high "I" mom prefers having many people around, which is precisely what the "S" child tries to *avoid!* An "S" child wants to be together, but not on the go. The "S" child wants stability and security, and the "I" mom thrives on spontaneity and change. If the "I" mom remembers to slow down and allow her "S" child to keep up, she fosters a feeling of support, encouragement, and value.

ALONE AND SELF-CONSCIOUS

It wasn't until Carol understood her own personality style that she recognized how she was instrumental in affecting her ten-year-old daughter, Hazel's, insecurity. Hazel often woke up to no clean clothes and her mom still fast asleep – because she stayed up late (as "Is" like to do) watching television. Hazel would often leave for school alone and self-conscious with no breakfast and no support – disheveled and sad.

After Carol attended a personality workshop, things began to make sense. She knew what she needed to do about her undisciplined lifestyle to help her daughter. Carol sacrificed late night movies and telephone conversations in exchange for an opportunity to get up earlier, help Hazel get dressed, fix her hair, and prepare a little breakfast. After making those adjustments, she sent Hazel off to school happy and secure.

As a result, Hazel felt good about herself. She no longer felt insecure because her mom hadn't helped her feel special and supported. Carol's sacrificial love for her daughter paid off. An "I" mom can balance responsibility with enthusiasm, once she understands it takes extra effort!

"I" MOMS NEED INTERACTION!

Faith wants to sit on her mom, Natasha's, lap all the time, but high "I" Natasha wants to "be free and on the go"! High "S" Faith prefers to stay home, content to color, play with her dolls, or watch television. Being a stay-at-home mom is frustrating for Natasha. Natasha recharges by talking and interacting with others. Faith recharges by sharing downtime together.

Recognizing her daughter's more reserved personality needs, Natasha knew she needed to make some adjustments. Needing interaction with other moms, Natasha worked it out so that every morning she and her friends can walk together before their husbands leave for work.

During Faith's naptime, high "I" Natasha talks on the telephone with her friends – without interruption (while she enthusiastically enlightens another mom with one of her newest *great* stories). And Natasha *really* comes alive if there's a school meeting to attend at night with other moms. Stay-at-home, high "I" mom Natasha learned to cope and adjust!

WORDS OUT OF CONTROL

The "I" mom does things on the spur of the moment – the louder and crazier, the better. But she could embarrass the "S" child when too loud or funny. The "S" child dislikes having attention drawn to them.

Benjamin thought his mom, Melana, was so much fun when he was a child. "My mom created fun games, sang and danced, played with us, and was quick-witted. She was entertaining; I never knew what was going to come out of her mouth. But that became a huge problem when I became a teenager. I never knew what was going to come out of her mouth!"

Benjamin continued, "My mom's loudness and desire for attention worried me so much that I became reluctant to invite my friends over. I had to plead with her to stay away when I did. Also, I would have liked for her to come and support me at my basketball games, but when she did she would stand up, scream at the referees, and make a spectacle of herself. She loved the attention and didn't care how she got it, even at my expense. I was always so embarrassed. Now that I'm an adult, I see that she really hasn't changed and I still avoid being with her. I care about her very much, but I don't care to be around her very much."

An outgoing, talkative, loud, or flashy dresser high "I" mom could painfully embarrass a shyer "S" child to the point of a nonexistent relationship. This doesn't mean that reserved "S" children don't love and adore their moms, but can be embarrassed by their out-of-control, outgoing behavior.

Mom - Parenting a C Child

> **"I" – PEOPLE-ORIENTED AND OUTGOING *MOM!***
> **"C" – TASK-ORIENTED AND RESERVED *CHILD!***
>
> **Strengths**: The outgoing "I" mom prefers spontaneous excitement, while the cautious "C" child wants alone time and schedules. The "I" mom can learn to implement schedules, while the "C" child can learn to have more fun!
>
> **Struggles**: The significant differences between the "I" mom and "C" child can lead to frequent misunderstandings. Unless the "I" mom takes time to slow down and listen, her child can feel rushed, uncared for, and misunderstood.

This is a very difficult personal relationship because they have contrasting styles. The bubbly "I" mom needs excitement and fun, while the no-nonsense "C" child likes to keep things consistent and structured. Since both perspectives are valuable, they can learn a lot from each other.

The "I" mom loves to talk, while her "C" child chooses to use words sparingly and precisely – until he or she knows the words are correct. An "I" mom can tone down her enthusiastic responses and lower her expectations for lively conversations. The "C" child will stick to stating the facts and details. Recognizing her child's need for correctness, this is a great opportunity for the "I" mom to listen carefully to what her child has to say, and understand his or her cautious nature while arriving at the conclusion.

"Cs" NEED A PLAN

"Cs" get physically and emotionally uncomfortable in an unorganized environment. The "I" mom can find creative ways to organize and be productive. She can develop a system (using bright-colored file folders) to make appointments, return library books, or sign school papers. "Cs" at any age want to be on time. Arriving late for school or events can be devastating for a "C" child. However, the "I" mom and "C" child have different concepts of time.

Alisha enjoyed her junior high Sunday school class. Every week, "C" Alisha was dressed (clothes laid out the night before) and ready to go by nine o'clock as planned. For her high "I" mom, Jan, leaving at nine o'clock meant leaving at "nineish."

Alisha hated to be late for her class. Jan, however, actually *liked* walking in late – in fact, *preferred* walking in late. After all, it drew attention to herself! But Alisha felt upset and embarrassed because everyone noticed her when she walked in late. Frustrated, they battled weekly Sunday morning blowups. Alisha revealed, "I felt that my mom did that on purpose to embarrass me."

The "I" mom can be oblivious to her child's feelings, thinking the child should lighten up – be just like her! We have different expectations according to our own expectations.

Jan and Alisha have come to understand this. In fact, together they created a plan to start getting ready earlier. They picked out a fun and crazy timer to count down the minutes before it's time to leave for Sunday school. Jan said, "I now understand and appreciate Alisha's organized, quiet, and 'on time' nature, and I wouldn't want my daughter any other way."

Jan added, "And there's an additional benefit. Now that I get to church earlier, I can drink coffee, eat goodies, and talk to a lot of my friends prior to going to class. I wasn't aware earlier that they did that!"

LITTLE LEAGUE STATS

"Cs" may be one of the sharpest tools in the toolbox, but they're not the friendliest or the most outgoing. Tracy's son, Raymond, quiet and reserved, loves baseball. He practices consistently, perfecting every pitch. ("Cs" like to practice. After all, practice makes – you got it.) Tracy said, "Raymond also records the Little League stats perfectly at all the games .

He carries his clipboard and pen in hand wherever he goes, to write down every detail of a game. He's very serious and doesn't talk to anybody!"

Talking to or meeting people are not priorities for a "C." Tracy found frustration at its peak, however, when she tried to introduce Raymond to new friends at the ballpark. She said, "Frozen like a statue, Raymond stared at the other person, barely responding. It was so embarrassing! I loved meeting new people and I talked to everyone. That was my favorite part about going to Raymond's games! I didn't know what was the matter with him!"

Following one of my personality conferences, Tracy said, "I used to get so frustrated by Raymond's lack of an outgoing personality, but now I realize it's very hard for him to be friendly. He doesn't project a lot of warmth and can appear rude and unfriendly – in fact, cold! But now I know why."

Raymond has a "C" personality style. He is not actually cold or rude at all. His heart is warm, but his behavior can be perceived as cold. Tracy began teaching Raymond to feel safe, show friendliness, and speak up. As moms, we can use special coaching to help our "C" children develop important and necessary people skills.

PRACTICE MAKES PERFECT

We can explain the logical reasons why more reserved "C" personality styles feel as they do – and let them know that we understand. "Cs" can come across as standoffish or rude, but basically this task-oriented personality style is simply not interested in talking to people, chatting on the telephone, or even smiling for the camera! And it's okay that they feel that way.

In the past, I have done role-playing (and reverse role-playing) with my "C" daughter Madison to help her understand how *others* feel when she doesn't respond with a friendly smile or responsive words. We've practiced what she could *force* herself to say upon being introduced to someone new, how to speak up and order her food at restaurants (Restaurant Rule #1: If she wants to eat, *she* needs to order), and appropriately answer a question when asked.

It has helped her feel more comfortable with *what* to say, to practice her response *before* the situation arises. (This can be especially helpful when your child meets your husband's boss for the first time!)

CAUTION! SLOW THINKERS!

"Is" walk into a room and it's as though someone had turned on the light switch! This personality style has the gift of persuasion and is full of ideas. They love to entertain and delightfully inspire others to join in with them. (As in Hollywood, they start the trends and others strive to be like them.)

Conscientious "Cs" are, however, slower paced and do not like to be rushed or *inspired* by their "I" moms to make a quick decision, complete a project, or inspire the world! "Cs" are deep thinkers, and will logically analyze and weigh the facts before making a move (unlike the "I" mom, who acts, *then* thinks)!

The good news is that the curious "C" child asks a lot of questions and the "I" mom likes to talk! However, this mom desperately needs to work on correct and quality answers, avoiding flippant or silly remarks, to communicate effectively in this relationship.

INSIGHTS FOR "I" MOMS

Preferring freedom from details and schedules, the "I" mom needs to put extra energy into establishing guidelines and boundaries. Make a game out of completing what is unpleasant! Learn how to stay focused and finish things you've started. The results are dazzling!

Now let's take a look at Chapter 21 and find out more about the Supportive "**S**" *Parenting* style with *each* type of personality!

21

D-Ĭ-S-COVER THE  PARENTĬNG STYLE WĬTH A...

𝒫ERSONALITY CAPSULE FOCUS:

TYPE:	THOUGHT PATTERN:	BASIC NEED:	IDENTIFIER:
"D"	What?	Control	Dominance
"I"	Who?	Recognition	Interaction
"S"	How?	Appreciation	Support
"C"	Why?	Quality answers	Correctness

- Supportive
- Stable
- Steady
- Sweet
- Status quo
- Shy

Basic Need: *APPRECIATION!*

"S" MOM – THINKS, "HOW?"

The "S" mom is supportive and nurturing, and cultivates a peaceful, stabilizing environment at home. She thinks, "How? How can I help?" This calm, easygoing mom is dedicated and strives for harmony in the home. She considers an interruption from her child as an "opportunity" to show support. It's so hard for the "S" mom to say, "No!"

This sweet mom is the one who ends up buying fifteen boxes of Girl Scout cookies every year and a dozen tins of popcorn from the neighborhood soccer team.

The "S" mom would rather follow than lead. She does not like to be the center of attention. She can be found behind the scenes. Committed to her children, the "S" mom will volunteer to bake several items for a bake sale. She's happy to *serve* at a spaghetti dinner, as long as she doesn't have to organize it! People could take advantage of the "S" mom because of her cooperative and sensitive style.

This mom is compassionate, wants everyone to feel included, and gets her feelings hurt easily. She is re-energized by relaxing, watching television, taking a bubble bath, or taking a nap. Some equate the "S" mom's quest for a slower pace as lazy. Striving to avoid conflict, she has to be careful not to be perceived as a doormat or pushover by other, more overbearing personalities in the family.

This mom could inadvertently rescue her children from trouble and bail them out, instead of allowing them to suffer the logical consequences. She does not like change and will struggle when forced to do so, even when it's the best choice.

"S" MOM IN PARENTING RELATIONSHIPS

 **Mom - Parenting a** **Child**

> ### "S" – PEOPLE-ORIENTED AND RESERVED *MOM*!
> ### "D" – TASK-ORIENTED AND OUTGOING *CHILD*!
>
> **Strengths**: This is a more difficult personal relationship because of their contrasting styles. The "S" mom offers wonderful encouragement and support to the goal-oriented "D" child.
>
> **Struggles**: The "S" mom can feel exhausted with an action-packed "D" child. Avoiding conflict at all costs, this mom can be too easygoing and lenient, allowing the power-seeking "D" child to have too much control in the home.

This combination can be upside down if the "S" mom doesn't take command of the decisions and discipline in the home. The determined "D" child is hard to discipline, and could run the household in no time if this mom doesn't establish and maintain control from the beginning. She may feel she can't keep up with this determined child! Allow your "D" child areas of insignificant control, as long as he or she is not controlling you!

This child is very independent, whereas the "S" mom likes to do things together. As a born leader and natural director, the "D" child can offer initiative and determination to the "S" mom. Preferring the back seat, the "S" mom can be supportive and helpful for the goal-oriented "D" child, but must establish rules and guidelines and stay in control.

Preventing the "D" child from bossiness and running roughshod over the "S" mom is essential to teaching him or her how to have patience and tenderness toward others.

BUT HE'LL STARVE!

After I finished speaking to a moms' group recently, I noticed one of the moms hanging around as I was repacking my briefcase. "May I help you?" I inquired. "Well, ah-h-h yes," she said as she looked over her shoulder. "I really don't mean to bother you, and I know I should have asked during the session, but I just didn't want to speak up in front of the others."

Immediately, her polite manners and shyness revealed her high "S" personality style. Continuing, she said, "I realize now, after hearing your personality speech, that my five-year-old son runs over me – and I may be the cause. I never thought I could do anything about it, but now I know I must."

Tears began trickling down her face as she explained the demands her son has placed on her. "*He* tells *me* when he's ready for bed (r-i-i-i-i-ight) and what he's going to eat, which is usually just chips or fish crackers and juice. Sometimes he'll eat those little noodle packages."

She was truly devastated and overcome by this child's controlling personality. She proceeded, "What should I do? We battle everything. Most of all, he refuses to eat what I cook every night. I'm worried about his health. How can I get him to eat better?"

"I'm glad you asked. It's actually very simple. Let him know very matter of factly that if he doesn't like what you fix for dinner, he certainly doesn't *have* to eat it. No problem. However, that's all there is to eat for the night. The whole night. No other options. No snacks."

"But, he'll be so *hungry*. He'll *starve*," she protested.

I continued, "Believe me, no child has died of starvation yet because they went a few *hours* overnight without anything to eat. And you can bet – when he's *hungry* – he'll eventually eat what you fix! It's amazing how quickly a child can learn to appreciate vegetables, fruit, and other healthy foods when they don't have junk food options." (They can "Cope and Adjust" to develop healthy eating habits very fast!)

I proceeded to elaborate more on her "S" personality style, and reminded her that the secret to her success was to "pull up" her low "D" personality style to be successful in their relationship. In other words – get tough! (Hit the deck and give me twenty – tough!)

In fact, this sweet mom's high "D" son may have lost respect for her because she wouldn't stand her ground. It was time to gain back the power and control that *he* had captured so naturally. No wonder "S" personality styles require more "mental health" days!

DON'T POKE YOUR BROTHER'S EYE OUT, OKA-A-A-A-AY?

"S" moms unnecessarily seek affirmation of their discipline, "Sit down now, oka-a-a-ay?" They forewarn their children that discipline's on the way, "Don't do that. Don't *do* that! I'm going to count! Here I go! On-n-n-ne, two-o-o-o-o-o, th-h-h-h...!" It's so hard for an "S" mom to tell someone what to do!

Jake, a high "D" child, is very determined to do things his way. He plays to win and take control of everyone in the family. Sadie, a high "S" mom wanting to avoid conflict with Jake and soft on the discipline, was overheard saying, "Now Jakey, don't poke that stick in David's eye again, oka-a-a-ay?"

"S" moms need to be more forceful with swift, decisive action. A child whose mom has never taken firm control of discipline is being deprived of the ability to comprehend the authority that affects his or her life later on. They will eventually come up against a person of authority such as a teacher, police officer, or boss who will expect (without asking, "Oka-a-a-ay?") orders to be followed. This child may face the real world in denial – completely unprepared and unequipped.

I WANT THESE JEANS NOW!

Samantha works at a trendy store in the mall. During a back-to-school sale, she overheard a mom telling her teenage daughter, "Your father has set a spending budget, honey. You know we're going to have to stay within the limit, okay?"

Ignoring her mother's directions, the daughter spied a pair of expensive, 120-dollar jeans. She immediately turned to her mother and adamantly insisted, "Mother, I *have* to have these jeans!"

Samantha said the mom timidly reminded her daughter that the cost of the jeans was not within their budget. Soon the daughter went berserk, *swearing* at her mom and demanding the jeans. "Honey," whispered the mom, "It's just not within our budget, sweetie."

Samantha said, "The daughter became belligerent, louder and louder, making quite a scene. It was embarrassing to me and all the other customers who couldn't help but overhear." It wasn't long before the frustrated mom caved in, saying, "Okay, sweetie, please quit being upset. I'll call dad and let him know we're spending a little more."

What's wrong with this *picture*? This girl *bulldozed* her mom! Obviously, all respect diminished in this duo. The well-meaning mom folded up like a cheap card table! It's *hard* for a sweet "S" mom to stand firm. They fear conflict and focus on unity, but must dig deep to discover it's truly beneficial to the child (and to her) to stay strong.

The powerful "D" child could essentially take advantage of every person or situation he or she encounters. This child needs to control, but it shouldn't be the mom who's controlled. The "D" child will test you, but it's important that you establish and remain in authority. This will not be natural or easy, but essential.

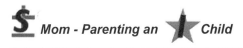

Mom - Parenting an ★ *Child*

> **"S" – PEOPLE-ORIENTED AND RESERVED *MOM*!**
> **"I" – PEOPLE-ORIENTED AND OUTGOING *CHILD*!**
>
> **Strengths**: This is a fun and supportive relationship. The "S" mom can recognize her "I" child's need for attention and help generate positive outlets for expression.
>
> **Struggles**: These two people-oriented family members like to be together, but can neglect to complete tasks or develop necessary organizational skills to get things done.

Because of their love for people, this is a close personal relationship. The "S" mom can offer steadiness and support to the "I" child. She has an appreciative nature that helps the "I" child feel the approval he or she needs to try a new task. The "S" mom is patient with the impulsive high "I" child.

The "I" child brings out the best in the "S" mom by involving her in teamwork and having fun together. This child is a source of amusing entertainment for the normally more subdued "S" mom, providing things aren't too rambunctious. Keeping up with the "I" child can be a challenge! The "I" child has such a difficult time staying still or quiet, exhausting the "S" mom. The "S" mom likes quiet, but the "I" child likes noise.

The "S" mom takes a laid-back approach to parenting, putting effort into helping the attention-seeking "I" child look great! Let them surprise you and experience the fun with them!

GROCERY STORE FIASCOS

Jeanie is a high "S" mom to Corbin, a high "I" child. Not that the infamous grocery store visit is a piece of *cake* for anybody, but every time Jeanie and Corbin go together, it's a piece of *work*! Corbin, as most high "I" children do, loves and wants anything bright colored that he can get his hands on. In fact, he wants these things so badly that he throws a royal fit trying to convince his pleasing high "S" mom to cave in! Jeanie begins her shopping expedition strong and in control, and in the first isle says, "No, not today."

Then (as we know so well) Corbin's demands grow louder and louder.

Jeanie responds, "I said, 'no.'" Then up goes the volume.

Eventually, the public display of conflict becomes overwhelming to Jeanie – until BINGO! Corbin hears the magic words, "Okay, fine! If you'll just *quit* screaming, you can have it!"

Once again, it worked. Actually, it works every time. Jeanie hates the conflict, hates the attention they're generating, and hates letting Corbin down. She hates it so much, in fact, that she'd rather be submissive and give in to avoid the conflict.

In addition, Corbin has no sense of accepting "no" as an answer, or of mastering patience. He's accustomed to having his way, and he'll do whatever it takes to get his way. Corbin's running the house instead of accepting the rules.

This is the scenario a mom who works outside the home can easily fall into as well. It's very difficult to continue with battles like this at the end of a long day when you're tired and worn out. It's so much easier to give in, but so much more detrimental when you do. If you're an "S" mom who feels worn out by the pressure of any personality style, stand your ground. Stay strong and firm. It's worth it in the long run.

LIMIT ONE

Establish your goals in advance. As in the grocery store scenario, remind your child before you walk in the door what the limitations are. And then use this as an opportunity to show praise and reward for your child who stayed in control and obeyed.

I inform my daughter Madison ahead of time (before we enter the store) that she gets to select one (approved) item while we're shopping. It always helps if she knows she can choose one thing and one thing only. (Sometimes she throws me for a loop and selects something like orange juice!) Everything else she can look at, admire, or place on her "next time" list. If she chooses to throw a fit, she's chosen to have a consequence. That is *her* choice. *My* choice is for her to be obedient and respectful.

I also let her know how important it is to me that we have a nice time and enjoy being together. That's my goal, not to be *hassled* but to truly have a good time on our little shopping expedition. I call this "Communication Expectation." Letting your child know what you want and expect up-front enlists their contribution to a successful outcome!

 *Mom - Parenting an* *Child*

> **"S" – PEOPLE-ORIENTED & RESERVED *MOM & CHILD!*
>
> **Strengths**: This is a peaceful and relaxed relationship between mom and child. The easygoing "S" personalities love to be together and support each other, caring and sharing.
>
> **Struggles**: Sometimes the "S" mom can go so far to meet the "S" child's needs that she prevents them from growing and maturing on their own. "Ss" want peace and will give in at all costs to keep it.

This is an easy personal relationship because they are both supportive and loyal. They love to be together, and seek harmony with one another above all else. "Ss" expect friendliness and kindness in others, and dislike disagreement or sarcastic words. They repeatedly stuff their feelings when there's a conflict, which could lead to emotional difficulties (such as depression) further down the road.

A common weakness of "Ss" is that they become overly compliant. "S" moms like to help and support, and derive happiness from meeting their children's needs. If the "S" mom does for her children all the time, they won't learn how to do for themselves. This can foster irresponsible behavior and prevent the child from not only learning responsibility, but also the satisfaction of knowing they can accomplish things for themselves.

TOGETHER AGAIN

Unpretentious and honest, "Ss" naturally evaluate by consistency. They pay attention to each other. The "S" mom can provide the "S" child with instructions or involvement in an area of interest to the child, who lacks the motivation to get it done. Both appreciate a relaxed atmosphere and enjoy hanging out doing nothing. They like to watch television in their lounge chairs, go shopping, or eat together – anything that involves no major decisions.

By many people's standards, this is a pretty dull relationship, but "S" Sarah says about her "S" mom, "My mom and I love hanging out together doing nothing! We're so content." Sarah and her mom may lack in motivation, but lounge in love! Sweet and supportive, they may not accomplish a lot, but they have a very close relationship.

Sarah continues, "When I was young, my mom would sit by the bathtub and read to me every day just because I asked her to. We had a great relationship because we just wanted to be together and support each other." Sarah and her mom spent hours scrap-booking together. Happy to cut, trim, paste, or hunt down just the right picture for her photo albums, Sarah's mom loved to help, and Sarah appreciated her support.

After Sarah married, she and her husband continued to go to her mom's for dinner two or three times a week. Sarah's mom loved to cook for them. However, Sarah's mom made it very clear that Sarah wasn't to invite others to dinner.

"Entertaining others is too much," her mom said. A small, intimate group is enough for – in fact, preferred by – "Ss." Life is good for a cared-for and supported "S" mom-child relationship.

SAVERS

Sentimental "Ss" are savers. They save everything – newspapers, old magazines, letters, and even ten-year-old egg cartons! After all, somebody *might* need them!

Sentimental "Ss" are givers. Joyce said, "When my "S" grandmother passed away recently, we found 49 boxes of oatmeal she had saved – to give away."

Joyce continued, "My grandmother always wanted to be prepared to lend a hand and help others. In case somebody needed oatmeal, she would always be able to support them with their need." "Ss" are always thinking of others.

TIME FOR SOFA – I MEAN – BED!

The "S" child's an easy child to raise -- particularly for an "S" mom who doesn't want to put a lot of energy into disciplining. It's so much easier to give in than battle our kids – initially, anyway!

To avoid conflict and bedtime hassles, "S" mom Jolene chooses to let her "S" daughter Kaitlyn fall asleep on the sofa every night. Jolene knows that otherwise, Kaitlyn would cry if they were separated. "S" moms must model self-discipline to help their children feel secure in knowing they can do the hard things, too. This in turn builds self-assurance and confidence.

NEED MORE...?

"Need more milk? Need more ketchup?" Shelby and Jeff hadn't been married long when Jeff recognized he had an "S" mom-in-law. Jeff said, "When Shelby is sick, her mom doesn't hesitate to drive a hundred miles to cook dinner for her – I'm even referring to a head cold! You name it, and she's here to help."

Shelby, also an "S," really likes it that her mom is so attentive and supportive. Her "C/D" husband continues describing his mother-in-law, "I was blown away by all her attention. It was hard at first. I used to get really upset about her showing up to help. It really helps to know that she's an "S" and just being supportive – not thinking that I can't do anything. Now I expect it and accept it, knowing it means a lot to her to help us. In fact, she's a great cook and I'm learning to appreciate the benefits!"

 **Mom - Parenting a C Child**

"S" – PEOPLE-ORIENTED AND RESERVED *MOM*!
"C" – TASK-ORIENTED AND RESERVED *CHILD*!

Strengths: This combination likes routine. The "S" mom doesn't intrude on the calculating "C" child. She extends kindness, loyalty, and support during this child's task completion!

Struggles: The reserved "C" child doesn't want to waste time chatting and can suffer from a lack of meaningful communication. A critical "C" child could break the heart of a supportive and sweet "S" mom.

Both mom and child tend to be slower paced. This is a proper yet personal relationship because each respects the rights and privacy of the other person. Preferring quiet time, they don't intrude on one another. The "S" mom extends kindness, loyalty, and acceptance in a way that the reserved and independent "C" child can receive and respect. The "S" mom effortlessly supports her "C" child when he or she is involved in tasks that need to be completed.

Even with the best of suggestions and ideas, don't force "C" children to agree with you. Allow them time to contemplate your request without becoming too critical. If they do give in to your rules and corrections without voicing their opinion, they could eventually quit sharing how they really feel. Let "Cs" have plenty of time to make their own choices (even if it's not as *thoughtful* as the one the "S" mom would have made).

HOW WAS SCHOOL TODAY?

High "S" Faith was always so excited for her son, Frank, to arrive home from school. She eagerly waited to hear about the friends he had played with and if anything exciting had happened that day. She wanted to make sure he was happy and content. But Faith was soon disappointed by her "C" son's lack of enthusiasm to talk.

Faith said, "As soon as Frank walked in the door, I greeted him with a hug and eagerly asked about his day, but he usually kind of grumbled and headed for his toys. It really hurt my feelings that he was holding back from me."

After Faith learned about their personality differences, she realized that Frank wasn't avoiding her but needed quiet time for himself. "C" children need time to think about situations and occurrences before they talk. Allow them time to be by themselves, particularly after a stressful day. You can express to them that you'd like to talk about it later when they're ready, but don't push. If they have a concern or question, be prepared to give them all the details and plenty of time to think about it.

AVOID AVOIDING

The "C" child is accurate and dependable, picky and critical. While the "S" mom is pleasing, the "C" child can be hard to please. The "C" child has a strong respect for rules and authority, something difficult for the "S" mom to administer. When the critical "C" child withdraws, the "S" mom's feelings can get hurt, causing her to avoid the situation – or the child.

Theresa said, "When my son, Ryan, gets upset because things aren't perfect, I would rather not hear his moaning and groaning, so I stay away from him and his criticism." Give your "C" child a chance to be alone, but don't give up on helping him recognize a more positive perspective when he's ready to open up.

The "S" mom is a trustworthy supporter when the "C" child feels he or she didn't meet high expectations of perfection. However, a word of caution – an "S" mom could be so *supportive* that she misses the opportunity to propel the "C" child into trying things that are not *natural* for him or her.

It takes energy and a step of faith for the cautious "C" child to reach out and try something that he or she hasn't proven to be "correct" at yet. Use your gift of patience and give your "C" child ample time to find the courage.

INSIGHT FOR "S" MOMS

The "S" mom nurtures and cares for her children. She is always on the lookout for their protection and sense of security. Holidays and special occasions are at their finest with the predictable "S" mom's strong sense of family traditions and routines.

Now let's take a look at Chapter 22 and find out more about the Cautious "**C**" *Parenting Style* with *each* type of personality!

22

D-I-S-COVER THE C PARENTING STYLE WITH A...

*P*ERSONALITY CAPSULE FOCUS:

TYPE:	THOUGHT PATTERN:	BASIC NEED:	IDENTIFIER:
"D"	What?	Control	Dominance
"I"	Who?	Recognition	Interaction
"S"	How?	Appreciation	Support
"C"	Why?	Quality Answers	Correctness

- **Cautious**
- **Calculating**
- **Competent**
- **Conscientious**
- **Contemplative**
- **Careful**

Basic Need: *QUALITY ANSWERS!*

"C" MOM – THINKS, "WHY?"

The task-oriented and efficient "C" mom establishes plans and sees to it that things get done. She thinks, "Why? Why is it this way?" This organized mom is great at home schooling. Spending all day in the task mode is energizing and stimulating for a "C" mom.

Disciplined and structured "C" moms are focused on (obsessed with) completing tasks and working on projects, placing relationships as a lower priority. If you're a "C" mom, remember to let your children recognize you by your beautiful face, not the back of your head!

Rules are as essential as brushing your teeth to a "C" mom. In fact, brushing your teeth *is* a rule! Rules rule! Everything else comes in second, including communicating what she wants. The "C" mom would be content to judiciously post rules on the refrigerator. Just read them and follow them. There's no use talking about them or communicating what the rules mean or why we live by them.

The "C" mom might have obedient children, but they might not develop a personal responsibility or understanding of the "why," or guiding principle, of her rules and procedures.

"C" MOM IN PARENTING RELATIONSHIPS

 *Mom - Parenting a* **D** *Child*

> **"C" – TASK-ORIENTED AND RESERVED *MOM*!**
> **"D" – TASK-ORIENTED AND OUTGOING *CHILD*!**
>
> **Strengths**: Both are naturally organized and enjoy tasks. This cautious "C" mom can help organize steps and procedures toward the "D" child's goals and strong leadership ability.
>
> **Struggles**: The "C" mom's perfectionistic tendency could stifle the "D" child's high achievement and need for accomplishment. Allow the "D" child plenty of physical activity to avoid getting physically and mentally run over!

This is a highly task-oriented relationship. The "C" mom aspires to do things right – after enough time to contemplate whether the outcome will indeed *be* right! "Cs" need to remember that it's okay to *not* be perfect. Your "D" child likes responsibility, making decisions, and getting things done quickly!

A "C" mom's "D" child, who loves challenges and *challenging*, could wreak havoc on perfectly laid out plans and rules! Be flexible; make a commitment to the relationship, not rules, schedules, or preconceived ideas. Place value on commitments and plans, recognizing you're making memories (positive or negative) each day. Ask yourself, what's most important?

Make it a *priority* to develop relationships and make *positive* memories each day. Make a commitment and let it be known that you *want* your family together (having *fun*!) for birthdays, holidays, church, or special occasions.

BACK OUT BEFORE BURNOUT

The high-energy, active "D" child loves to be involved in sports, activities, and anything competitive. The cautious "C" mom's nature is to be more reserved and slower paced. Negotiate a schedule that accommodates activity with room for flexibility. If the "C" mom over commits, soon she will feel worn out, stressed out, and burned out! If the "C" mom overbooks, she will soon feel overloaded!

"D" Michael insists on being involved in three to four activities or sports each season. "C" mom Opal appreciates her son's athletic ability and dedication to sports; however, with two other children to shuffle and manage schedules around, there's chaos in their family! So Opal established a *rule* that each child could participate in only one sport per season – along with remaining faithful to their church activities each week.

Initially, Opal battled the typical moans and groans, but found that having dinners together once in a while (that didn't consist of fast food wrappers strewn all over the back seat of her van) and the opportunity to cheer for one another as they participated in their sports was a benefit worth maintaining. In addition to a calmer, less chaotic home environment, their schoolwork was completed earlier each night, and they were less sleep deprived. Eventually, Michael agreed it was a good plan after all.

"C" MOM DIDN'T SPEAK TO "D" CHILD FOR YEARS

From a very early age, high "D/I" traits were apparent in Deborah. She recalls, "My excitable and driven personality style drove my mom crazy! What I remember most about my childhood is that my 'C/S' mom was really upset with me a lot. I left home after my graduation, and we basically had nothing to do with each other for sixteen years – until I learned the D-I-S-C personality information. From that day on, I began to understand why my mom and I are so completely different. I also learned that it's *okay* for a mom and daughter to be different!"

Shortly after the personality training, Deborah contacted her mom and explained the D-I-S-C personality styles. Deborah said, "My mom was as astonished as I was to learn the dynamics behind our personality differences and how it all makes sense now. We cried, laughed, and cried again. We finally – after all these years – mended the pain of our past. Now our relationship is very good."

Deborah continued, "What a difference it makes to understand each other! I now know she expected me to do everything perfectly because of *her* "C" personality style, not because she wanted to irritate me. And she now understands that I was so driven and determined because of *my* "D" personality style, not because I wanted to act obnoxious or drive her crazy."

Rather than concentrate on how someone else acts, we can focus on controlling our responses. Deborah shared through tears, "It's like a miracle. For years, my mom and I didn't understand our differences, didn't speak, and had no relationship. But now we *appreciate* each other for who we are, and have restored our mother-daughter relationship to a level I never dreamed possible."

C *Mom - Parenting an* ★ *Child*

"C" – TASK-ORIENTED AND RESERVED *MOM*!
"I" – PEOPLE-ORIENTED AND OUTGOING *CHILD*!

Strengths: The structured "C" mom can keep her "I" child organized as well as broaden her own horizons by enjoying the fun loving "I" child's charming personality and spontaneity.

Struggles: If too perfectionistic, this "C" mom may keep a perfect house, but there's no fun in her house. "Is" need and want attention so desperately, they'll settle for negative attention if necessary.

This is a challenging relationship because mom and child are so different. If mom or child is out of control and self-focused, they could bring out the worst in each other! The "C" mom is naturally organized and disciplined, expecting her child to do things correctly and in a timely manner. That's not the program of thinking for the "I" child. The whirlwind "I" child can spawn a mess in the blink of an eye, pushing the "C" mom to the brink of impatience – getting on her perfectionistic nerves.

The "I" child, nonetheless, can bring fun into the home and exhilarate the "C" mom's life. This child inspires her to laugh more, play more, and be on the go more. Nagging or criticizing can defeat an "I" child as quickly as deflating a balloon. Help him or her learn without criticism, or you will shut this child down. The "I" child needs appreciative listening and a watchful audience.

QUIET!

The "C" mom strives for peace and quiet, keeping things in order. Dirty dishes, strewn toys, shoes and clothes in disarray, promptly drive a "C" mom wild. (That is about the *extent* of her wildness!) The "I" child thrives on excitement and high energy, loud television and music, bright lights, and lots of action! A quiet and dimly lit room is peaceful to a "C" mom, but depressing to the "I" child.

As a young child, Russ was found crying whenever he had no friends to play with. This may not make sense to a "C" mom, but understanding her child's love for people and having fun helps the "C" mom to sympathize – or better yet, empathize.

As a teenager today, Russ says his mom is forever complaining, "Turn down the music, turn off the lights, quiet down, and slow down! It's too unruly!" Russ says, "I would much rather be at my friend's house, where his mom is fun, jokes around, and plays loud music even when she's home by herself!"

"C" moms want clean homes, good books to read, and solitude – neglecting to relate to their "I" children's desires. "I" children want to go out into the world to socialize and have fun! "C" moms don't always show affection or let it be known that they're glad their children are home. An "I" child wants to know this, feel this, and will hunt it down in some home somewhere.

The "I" child loves "I" adults. This could result in the "C" mom feeling unloved if she doesn't work at finding a "happy" medium together.

ATTENTION, ATTENTION!

With high "I," eight-year-old Mariah's short attention span, her "C" mom, Trisha, would try to give her directions or explain how to do something to no avail. "Sure, sure, I understand, Mom," Mariah responded, not paying attention. Normally able to exhibit composure, Trisha was becoming so frustrated with Mariah that she found herself losing control.

Eventually, because Trisha began to grasp the concept of the D-I-S-C personality styles, she learned to make her instructions and details short and to the point. She instructed on a need-to-know basis only. When possible, she made it fun and a game out of it – because "Is" are passionate about having fun!

Trisha also began taking Mariah with her to run errands and go places. By doing so, this highly committed mom was able to entice her daughter to finish her tasks first – then they could *go* run errands! "C" moms need to finish things and "Is" need to go, regardless of where *go* is!

FOOTBALL TALK

Recently, we were at a second grade boys' Upward Football Game. The "C" mom sitting next to us was frustrated during the whole game. She continually criticized her high "I" son, "Zack, why can't you stand still in the huddle? Zack, keep that mouthpiece in. Zack, quit jumping around. Zack, quit talking all the time!"

Zack was a really good player, but struggled throughout each quarter with bouncing around, not listening to the calls, and talking. He removed his mouthpiece about 50 times so he could talk to his teammates! This "C" mom was beside herself. When the game was over, she shook her head and said, "I just don't understand him. His games infuriate me."

This is a mom who needs to "tackle" understanding the personality styles!

SIT STILL AND DO YOUR HOMEWORK

Naturally organized "C" moms expect their children to do things correctly, logically, and on time. My neighbor, Kerri, says she often found herself complaining to her procrastinating high "I" daughter, Sydney, "I don't understand why it takes you so long to do your homework. You're always moving around. Why don't you just sit down and get it done?"

But now "C" Kerri is aware that she needs to praise her child for writing a paper, rather than criticize and damage her self-esteem. "Our whole relationship has changed by understanding our personality styles. I realize now I was always stressing her out!" says Kerri.

"Is" expect loose reigns and flexibility in other people. What is a scheduled appointment or time to leave to a "C" is usually a *tentative* arrangement to an "I"! A few years ago, Sydney kept dragging her feet, procrastinating getting dressed each morning to go to day care, and often causing Kerri to be late for work – which is very stressful for any high "C" mom!

Harried most mornings, Kerri developed a plan (as high "Cs" love to do). She forewarned Sydney that they would be leaving at a designated time the next morning and if Sydney procrastinated, she would have to go to the day care in her pajamas, making it clear that it was Sydney's choice what she would wear upon arriving at school.

Kerri said, "When it was time to leave the next morning, Sydney was still lying in bed – as usual – procrastinating. So, as I had warned, I loaded up Sydney in her pajamas and took her to the day care. There was one glitch, though – the day turned out to be *picture day*!"

To this day, they still struggle somewhat with Sydney's procrastination, but almost every morning now – a few years later – I see Sydney ready to walk to school with the other girls – *fully* dressed! (Unless, of course – it's pajama day at school. Oh, what a fun day that is for high "Is"!)

HOMEWORK HASSLES

As a "C" mom, you can become a great asset in helping your "I" child do their homework. After all, if a term paper was assigned six weeks ago, when does your high "I" child typically sit down to do it? Yes, the night before it's due! And then they're angry with the teacher for imposing such restrictions and limitations on them! They actually march into the classroom acting huffy, claiming the teacher's expectations are *unrealistic*!

If little "I" drama queens would settle down for a minute, they would understand that procrastination is a behavior that's out of control for them. A conscientious "C" mom can direct, lead, and help her "I" child develop meticulous habits. She can work some fun into the assignment, too, with room for recognition and fun after completion.

Teach the high "I" child to use a more productive, less stressful, pre-planned concept and lifestyle. This can affect her entire future with her own children, when reports are due at work, organizing projects, etc. Promote the discipline and joy of learning, not perfectionism.

ENTERTAINMENT DELIGHT

High "I" Jeread's family lived out of town, so one particular Easter Sunday he came to our house for dinner. His entertaining personality magically transformed our dining room into a dinner theater! Onstage during the meal, Jeread sang many songs, recited television commercials, quoted numerous movie lines, and entertained us nonstop. Hilarious and talented, he kept us in stitches through dessert!

"How does your family get through meals at home," we quizzed? To our surprise, he said, "Actually, my parents have never heard me say or do any of this. They're much more conservative and reserved, so I've never acted this way in front of them. They don't even know I know this stuff, and they certainly wouldn't think it was funny. They're the serious type. I'm sure that Easter dinner at my parents' house today will be typically quiet and subdued."

My heart ached for Jeread's mom, and I didn't even know her. Her reserved style has kept her from knowing and fully experiencing her fun-loving "I" son. It's not easy when your personality styles are polarized opposites, but it's important to know and appreciate your child for who they are. Sad to say, Jeread's mom has missed out on his humor.

Is it any surprise that he stayed in town for Easter? He had revealed that he didn't want to go home for Easter. "Going home is stressful, boring, and sad," said high "I" Jeread. If you're a "C" mom with an "I" child, do you sanction an environment that he or she wants to come home to?

Mom - Parenting an Child

> **"C" – TASK-ORIENTED AND RESERVED *MOM*!**
> **"S" – PEOPLE-ORIENTED AND RESERVED *CHILD*!**
>
> **Strengths**: Preferring stability and sameness, the quiet "S" child feels secure with the organized and consistent "C" mom and the dependability she brings.
>
> **Struggles**: The "C" mom typically offers praise and support for "perfectly" completed jobs, but the "S" child needs to feel supported and encouraged regardless of perfect results.

A "C" mom expects everyone – including herself – to play by the rules and live by her excellent standards. They prefer being around others who operate on a mission of excellence, and therefore evaluate you accordingly. "C" moms ask a lot of questions, and "S" children are happy to oblige with answers to support their moms' quests.

This reserved mom and reserved child combination prefers accomplishing tasks and doing things ("C" mom) while they can be together ("S" child) at home. This mom will offer opportunities for her child to perfect cultural interests in art, music, dancing and intellectual achievements. If the "S" child has no interest or the "C" mom's standards are set too high, this child could feel overwhelmed and discouraged if his or her efforts are not validated.

Remember, "Ss" *stuff* their feelings and hesitate to speak up. More than any other type, the "C" mom's reserved nature can be damaging with her nonverbal gestures of disapproval. The "C" mom particularly, by demonstrating her confirmation and love, can encourage and endorse her "S" child to achieve a reachable level that he or she might not otherwise have sought out.

NO MRS. FIELDS

As a high "C/D" mom, Margie was one *tough* analytical and critical *cookie*. She lived a difficult life with an alcoholic husband and raising three children. Her "C" personality style expected her children to follow her rules and directions, and do the right thing – contingent upon her judgment at the time.

Margie's son, Jess, felt he could never please his mom. With her critical nature and negative attitude – and as a decisive "D" child – he left home the week after graduation. Determined to move away and stay away, he hardly has a relationship with his mother today.

Jess's "S" sister, Janis, however, desperately sought to please and support her "C" mom – even though it was virtually impossible. Throughout her childhood, Janis suffered great emotional pain and blame. As an adult, Janis struggles with a lack of decision-making skills, and depression. As "Ss" can do, she stuffs her feelings rather than face the conflict of approaching a controversial issue.

Previously suicidal, "S" Janis sought counseling and chose to go forward by working on the positive aspects in her relationship with her mom. Although the pain hasn't completely subsided, their relationship is healing because now Janis understands Margie's temperament. It still hurts, but it's healthy that Janis no longer feels responsible for the emotionally destructive situation in her home life as a child.

Please don't misunderstand. I'm not blaming Margie for Janis's emotional accountability. As adults, each of us has an opportunity to put the past in the past, slap a lid on it, and forget about it. We can choose to blame, harbor emotional pain, and self-destruct, or go forward with the knowledge we've gained and the opportunity to make positive changes – as Janis did.

Mom - Parenting a Child

"C" – TASK-ORIENTED & RESERVED *MOM & CHILD*!

Strengths: This combination enjoys quiet time with an opportunity to recharge by reading, working on a project, thinking and processing. It's an analytical dream team who enjoys accountability and doing things the right way.

Struggles: Methodical and implementing correctness in life, these two perfectionists may never measure up to one another's high standards. Tasks and projects could become more important than the relationship.

This double "C" combination is great at completing tasks on time, finishing homework on time, doing anything on time! They're slower at making decisions because they conscientiously play by the rules. With a quest for excellence and living by precise standards, these two could be too critical when things aren't perfect (which is most of the time)!

"Cs" are so task-oriented, they can slack when it comes to relationship concerns. Both enjoy order and neatness and have a definite method of doing things the right way. "C" moms naturally evaluate their children by accuracy and excellence.

CRAFTY TOGETHER

"Cs" struggle with leaving their comfort zones, and get worn out from too many outgoing or physical activities. This mom and child would prefer alone time, reading or working for hours on a craft or project. Organizing a closet or sock drawer is a better definition of fun for "Cs."

High "I" Melissa didn't understand why her "C" mom, Deanna, and "C" sister, Melanie, never wanted to go places and visit friends – as she did. Melissa said, "I felt ostracized and stuck at home – bored. Once I was old enough to drive my own car, our personality differences were easier to handle.

I could have freedom!" (I wonder if she drove a Ford "*Escape*"!)

As a family attending church together every Sunday, high "I" Melissa (not wanting to miss a *thing*), preferred being the last one to leave, while her "C" mom and sister anxiously hurried to the car at the first opportunity.

Melissa didn't understand her "C" mom's comment, "I don't want to visit or chat after church all the time. Sometimes I just want to stay in my shell and *think* about things, not *talk* about things." As soon as Melanie and Deanna arrived home, they took deep breaths, slipped into something comfortable (regardless of how cute — or *not*), and enjoyed reading or working on a craft or project together.

Now that Melissa understands the personality differences, she no longer gets offended, and vice versa. They've learned to understand and appreciate one another. In addition, if Melissa wants to spend time with her "C" family, she now opts for watching a movie or joining them on a project or craft as a way to *bond* together. It works like *glue*. (Sorry.)

INSIGHTS FOR "C" MOMS

"C" moms establish rules and methods of achieving plans, preferring to work independently. Children who are not of the "C" personality style enjoy working together, communicating, and having their moms' assistance. A "C" mom can learn to show openness to far-fetched ideas and suggestions, even if it's not the correct decision that this mom would normally make.

"C" moms, listen up! You *can* be fun! Ah-h-h, go fly a kite. Seriously! Lead your child on a scavenger hunt, take a slow walk, or simply take time to watch the snowfall. Do something for no reason at all. Do it because it's fun, not a means to an end!

Now let's take a look at Chapter 23 to find out how to handle *Conflict and D-I-S-Cipline*!

23

D-I-S-COVER HOW TO HANDLE CONFLICT & D-I-S-CIPLINE

*W*e work hard to become a lot of things in life, but isn't it amazing how *easy* it is to become a *mom*? (Of course, I'm not discounting the body-wrecking, excruciatingly painful experience called childbirth, where you want to grab your husband by the throat and threaten in your exorcist voice, *"Don't ever touch me again!!!!"*)

We have to become *certified*, pass meticulous *exams*, succumb to extensive interviews, or earn a monumental *degree* in about any other profession to perfect the knowledge and understanding of how to comprehend and handle any confines or limitations we're about to encounter for everything *else*! But motherhood can happen almost overnight! One morning we anxiously look at that trusty little test stick, anticipating a positive reading – or we receive that suspenseful telephone call – or we take that "step" – and we're off and running a lifetime marathon called motherhood!

So now what?

You grab a few books; talk to a few friends, experienced moms, or family members; and follow your intuition. You instinctively learn how to handle feeding schedules, diaper changes, doctors' appointments, play dates, birthday parties, loose teeth, and more. You find yourself humming silly veggie songs throughout the day. You learn how to distinguish which future babysitter – er, ah, I mean character on television – is Barney, BJ, or Baby Bop, how to translate the rare Teletubbie language (or lack thereof), and whether SpongeBob really does have square pants!

But as your child gets older and some things become easier, unfortunately some things become harder! For example – throw in a brother or sister and you've entered a mine-infested, grenade-carrying war zone. Sibling rivalry sparks a battle in every direction. It's called "Sible War"! It's conflict at its best. Negotiation alert! Power struggles and conflict sited just ahead!

Conflict and clashes are inevitable as long as more than one person lives in the home (or, if you're a "D," you might argue with *yourself* just because "Ds" like conflict)! So, how do we handle conflict without clashing? We need to pass "Conflict Resolution 101" courses to earn status as fully operational occupational moms – renewable every four years – just as we study and test for and renew our drivers' licenses!

LIKE PIECES OF A PUZZLE

Determining how to understand conflict and differences in personality styles is somewhat like sitting down and determining how to piece together a new puzzle. If you have no idea what to expect the final picture to look like, things may seem confusing and not make sense until a pattern has been established. However, if you can see the picture on the box lid, you can start putting the pieces together rather strategically and proficiently.

In fact, once you begin to understand how the pieces of the puzzle fit together and you know what picture to expect, it can become a fairly simple task. As with understanding our personality styles, once we understand why we do what we do and why our children do what they do, the puzzle pieces start to fit together as expected. Get the picture?

Now imagine your home environment with *your* family while working on this puzzle. *If* the dominant "D" child is still sitting, he or she may be directing you to assemble the puzzle quickly and according to his or her directions. The "D" likes the challenge (sometimes preferring to *not* look at the picture on the lid) and accomplishment, but will soon get bored or anxious and prefer to move on to a more challenging puzzle or a new project.

The active and interactive "I" child is also having a hard time sitting still, but happy to be with others, talking constantly, of course, and striving for a fun, friendly, and exciting time! The "I" child may even toss a few pieces in the air to make it more fun or – would that possibly be to get more attention?

The steady "S" child is really enjoying a quiet evening at home with loved ones. He or she may have preferred snuggling or watching a good movie together, but happy to assist the family. So, this low-key puzzle will do, just as long as you're all together.

The contemplative "C" child enjoys a quiet evening at home, too – with or without others. The task-oriented "C" will calculate every move, observing the number of pieces, their shapes and colors, and strategically place each piece of the puzzle in its proper position. The "C" cautiously prepares for the next insert – anxious to complete the project.

Whatever puzzle or project you encounter, it's not *puzzling* as long as you keep in mind, "Ds" do it, "Is" talk about it, "Ss" help you do it , and "Cs" think about it!

IDEAL ENVIRONMENT

 ...Upbeat, Fast, Powerful!

 ...Fun, Friendly, Exciting!

 ...Predictable, Stable, Harmonious!

 ...Structured with Procedures, Accuracy!

GENERAL STRESS AND CONFLICT REACTIONS

Whether your personality styles are similar or different, conflict happens! The differences in personality styles have been discussed at great length, but what about those of us who have children with the *same* personality style as ours? That can be an interesting source of conflict as well!

If you *and* your child are both high "Ds," I'll stop right now and pray for you, because you *will* battle for power and control in your home. A high "I" mom and child may indirectly compete for the spotlight! (Excuse me, would that be "indirect lighting"?) If the mom and child are both high "Ss," things may move a little too slowly to ever get anything accomplished! And a "C" mom with a "C" child may analytically fight to be right!

DETERMINE THE SOURCE

Determine the source of conflict – for you and for your child. Is your child acting and responding like you, or does your child act and respond completely differently? Did you have expectations or preconceptions that he or she will act like you? Does your child remind you of yourself when you were a child? Do you associate that precious, adorable child's personality style with that of their father's personality style? (Um-m-m-huh...)

We have personality style connotations and associations, but are they positive or negative with what we're comparing those behaviors to? In other words, are they pushing our *hot buttons*?!?! Remember, we've learned that by understanding our own personality styles and understanding the personality styles of others, we can become *pro*active rather than *re*active in our thinking and attributions! (This, Martha dear, is a good thing!)

PLACE SETTINGS FOR 300

I often write while eating a late lunch, and find myself in the middle of various restaurant occurrences. Recently at a restaurant, a group of employees were gathered around a huge display of beautiful and elegant china samples. On a mission to select their new, twenty-fifth anniversary china, the selection process took on an array of obvious personality styles.

Analyzing several of the place settings, the "C" said, "This one is good. I like it because it's simple and plain. It doesn't draw a lot of attention." (Sounds correct and concise to me.) At the same time, the "I" was exclaiming, "Oh, I *love* this one, it's so fun and colorful!" (It looked like a Mardi Gras street party on a plate!) Just then, another "I" shrieked, "Oh, my gosh, look! This is awesome! I can see myself!" She discovered that the charger (large plate below the place setting) was a mirror. The "C" said, "No way! I would *never* be able to eat if I had to look at myself in the mirror each time I took a bite."

The "S" patiently and thoughtfully viewed the beautiful place settings, and then when prompted commented, "Oh, I don't know, it's all pretty and I really don't want to make a decision. You all pick." Obviously unaware of who was who, the china representative walked up to the "S" and asked if she was one of the managers. Her blushing "S" response was, "Oh, no, no. I'm not a manager. I'm not manager material.

You know, I never have been. I would never want to tell people what to do. I don't understand why. That's just how I am."

The "D" manager stood there with his hands on his hips, "All right! All right! Just pick one." (Sort of like, "Ju-u-u-u-st bottom line it!") I've got a lot to do today. Pick one, and we'll make it work."

During this time they forgot about me, their lone customer. But never fear; the "S" came running over, apologizing profusely for everyone, fetching fresh iced tea with a warm smile, saying, "I am so-o-o sorry! I feel so bad," while offering me everything but her firstborn son (probably because he's a "D"). She wasn't even my server, but humbly took all the blame upon herself, while my high "I" server was still enjoying the view in the mirror.

All work places have a variety of personality styles to contend with. By the way, I had no idea this sort of thing occurred at restaurants between regular mealtimes! I can't wait to see what they selected! (Believe me, it was hard to resist offering my opinion!)

CONFLICT VARIES IN PERSONALITIES

When a "D" faces conflict, he or she may become even more demanding, determined, angry, or controlling. When "Ds" sense a losing battle, they may go to the other extreme and work alone, avoiding people and situations they cannot control.

"Is," desiring to maintain popularity, will keep on smiling and telling jokes to defuse the tension in conflict. The "I" style may join in or agree, to keep from losing friends.

"Ss" may withdraw, retreat, suppress, give in, or find a shell to hide their head. "Ss" may give in, sweep their feelings under the rug, and eventually stuff their own desires or preferences in order to avoid conflict.

The "C" avoids conflict by ignoring the situation until he or she "thinks" of the right answer or the best course of action. Otherwise, if forced to deal with the conflict head-on, "Cs" may strictly impose their "right" or exceedingly high standards on others.

TESTING, TESTING!

Be prepared that children will test to determine the limits! If one discipline technique doesn't work, try another one. And keep trying until you find success. All kinds of wonderful discipline books are available offering new (and old) options and fresh ideas.

Time-out and loss of privileges, as well as reward options, need to be monitored and administered in love and fairness. If need be, temporarily (or permanently) remove television sets, videos, favorite toys, and games. Better yet, let them help you take and give it to a shelter where it's appreciated! One such experience can have a huge impact on future conflict responses.

D-I-S-CIPLINE TECHNIQUES

Discipline techniques that work for one personality style don't necessarily work well for another. It's important to alert moms that in times of stress, each person will become even more dependent on his or her preferred personality style. For example, a "C" or "S" will want more solitary time, while the "D" or "I" will need more action or interaction.

To avoid developing or attributing to negative patterns, we need to be more flexible in using our underdeveloped side, even though our natural tendency is to rely on our preferred style.

CONFLICT WITH AUTHORITY

In the real world, we stop on red and go on green. That's also the way it is when it comes to rules and authority – and our children need to understand this. We can't predict their futures, but we can influence it by boundaries and restrictions administered in love.

Oftentimes, conflict is a battle to gain power and control. If your child perceives that the power or control has been taken away, he or she will initially rebel or battle harder, making the situation much more difficult.

Children will repeatedly test you to have things their way. For example, a dog on a leash for the first time initially will pull and pull, harder and harder, sure to break free and expand those boundary lines! Eventually, however, after consistent opposition and futile attempts, the dog accepts, succumbs, and submits to the circumstances of not having total power or control after all.

Children will do the same if new discipline is doled out, but you must not budge or give in. Giving in increases the odds of their success, and promotes bantering or begging. On top of that, studies have shown that as long as children know what to expect and stay within discipline boundaries, they actually feel more secure and confident.

A BREATH OF FRESH AIR

By knowing what pushes one's hot buttons when dealing with conflict, we can be instrumental in producing results that encourage working together, not against one another. Decompress. Taking care of a child as well as other duties, such as caring for the household, can be exhausting. Give yourself time to enjoy – relax or play (a mom's version of time-out). First and foremost, take care of yourself. No one can do this for you.

The airlines have clear instructions along those lines. In case of the need for oxygen, who is supposed to be taken care of first? Not that the adult is *more* important, but we ourselves need to be equipped and prepared in order to help our children appropriately navigate and handle the conflict and clashes they most assuredly will encounter.

One more thing: If you sense your child has acted out of character and is frustrated, stressed, or tired from an abundance of conflict issues or stressors, then consider treating him or her to your time, *instead* of time-out. There's no greater value, and it works like a breath of fresh air (or fresh oxygen!) in your relationship.

Remember that most of the time, our children are not trying to stir up conflict or do something *to* us, but *for* themselves. They don't always understand why – just what – they do. We can help them understand *what* they do according to *why* – that they're operating in conjunction with their personality styles.

Let's take a look at *Conflict and D-I-S-Cipline* among the four personality styles in more detail throughout the following Chapters 24-27!

24

HOW TO HANDLE CONFLICT WITH A "D" CHILD

IDEAL ENVIRONMENT

 ...Upbeat, Fast, Powerful!

Conflict with the "D" Child

"Ds" insist on power and control. Adventurous, strong-willed, and competitive, they play the game to win. Self-confident and independent, they don't fear hurting your feelings in conflict. If you can work out the conflict, they're a strong ally; otherwise, you're dealing with a powerful adversary.

Hearing "no" only means they'll ask again a little bit later. When conflict arises, outspoken "Ds" begin demanding that others respond a certain way (that, of course, being *their* way). Angry and controlling when they're boiling mad, they steam like a teakettle. If this determined personality style doesn't foresee a victory in process, or feels you're taking advantage of them, they will swiftly withdraw or walk away from the situation. They don't like their judgment to be questioned and if necessary, will take care of the situation on their own. They will then *find* someone who will help them succeed, turning their efforts toward your loss if necessary.

"Ds" enjoy bucking the system – even creating conflict at times! However, "D" children often find themselves in trouble for being unwilling to submit to authority. If your child does get into trouble with an authority figure, lay low and consider it an "opportunity." Let the "authority" be the heavy while you are supportive, showing empathy and concern. Let the *situation* dictate the negative consequences when possible.

Let "Ds" know you're on their side. For example, you can say to your "D" child, "Oh, it's too bad you didn't win the class president election. I bet you're disappointed." But don't say, "I knew you wouldn't win. Maybe next year you will show kindness and concern to your classmates instead of *bossing them around all the time*!" That may be what you *want* to say; how-w-w-w-ever, show compassion instead. Ask your "D" child questions that promote self-evaluation, such as, "What would you do differently if you could do it over?"

If your "D" teenager is exhausted from staying up too late, let the consequence come from the experience by way of the obvious or likely consequence. Focus on reinforcing that *you're* on their team! You could say, "Oh, too bad you're so tired. That's an awful feeling, isn't it? Maybe next time it really would be best if you got to bed earlier. How many hours of sleep do you think you need to not feel like this?"

I'm not trying to get you to shrug off the responsibility of being the authority in your home, but to find opportunities to enlist the natural or obvious consequences to reinforce your cause and make the "mom" job a bit easier! (Sort of like having an assistant!)

SALTY FRIES

Over the years, we've enjoyed eating at our eight-year-old daughter, Madison's, favorite "cowboy" restaurant. One particular dinner (yes, yes, it happened to be during PMS), I was using the much-needed salt for my much-needed starchy french fries. (I know that you know.) I always try to deter Madison from using salt, but this night she was mega bugging us to use the salt.

Now, I could have stood my ground, fought the battle (until repeated the next time), and even won. Or, I could have chosen to let her have all-l-l-l-l the salt she wanted on that itty-bitty french fry – shake, shake, shake – and see what happens. (Yep, obvious consequence.)

My response? "Oh, gee. It's too bad that the french fry doesn't taste so good after all. Hum-m-m. I guess that it's probably best to listen to mom's suggestions, huh?" That was the last time she ever begged me for salt!

I didn't *have* to be the heavy – the "Do it my way or the highway" approach that we "Ds" like to take. I let the "salt" be the heavy in the situation (so to speak). (However, if I keep eating those fries like that, I'll soon become the *heavy*!)

BASIC CONTROL FOR A "D"

IN CONTROL	OUT OF CONTROL
COURAGEOUS	RECKLESS
QUICK TO RESPOND	RUDE
GOAL-ORIENTED	IMPATIENT
RESULTS-ORIENTED	PUSHY
DELIBERATE	DICTATORIAL
SELF-CONFIDENT	CONCEITED
DIRECT	OFFENSIVE
SELF-RELIANT	ARROGANT
STRAIGHTFORWARD	ABRASIVE
COMPETITIVE	RUTHLESS

D-I-S-CIPLINE TIPS FOR THE "D" CHILD

"Ds" will inherently and seemingly *find* a way to do the impossible, but if they incessantly battle you until they "win," they've learned manipulation and control. Stay calm (hard to do when dealing with a "D"), but they *gain* power and control if you *lose* yours. Vying for power and control can result in a battleground to prove who really is boss.

Time-out generally has worked well at our house, as long as my child was secluded in the laundry room or dining room where there was nothing to do or look at until the timer went off (one minute for each year old). My two "C" daughters seldom visited the time-out chair, mortified when they didn't live up to their self-imposed high standards, and preferring to "correct" the situation as soon as possible.

With my "D" son, Scott, however, time-out was a different story. Worse, he could become quite *productive* while in time-out, developing action plans for his next coup attempt. He was determined to *not* show that he hated time-out. In fact, he often announced how much he enjoyed it! He *must* have enjoyed it. He spent a great deal of time there! Time-out wasn't always the best source of discipline for my high "D" child, but if I banned him from riding his bike, prohibited him from building or working on his fort, or from playing sports with the neighbor kids – now *that* was painful!

Find what means something to your children if they were to lose it – and use it. Leverage works! Make rules very clear and stay firm with the discipline. *You* be the one who determines what they're going to control – because they *will* control! You can give them control by sitting down together (but not in the heat of the moment) and designing a contract that spells out expectations, consequences, and rewards. This gives your child control and "ownership" of the agreed-upon consequences.

If faced with conflict and you confront a "D" child, what he or she will really hear is, "Wanna fight?" Remember, "Ds" walk around with their dukes up! They can – and need – to learn how to show their emotions without blowing up. Their short fuses get them into trouble.

When faced with this opposition, you must choose between responding and reacting – there is a big difference! When we respond, rather than react (especially over-react), we remain in control. Learning to respond properly is perhaps the greatest challenge for a "D" child or "D" mom. But remember, "Ds" love a challenge!

CONFLICT NEGOTIATIONS
Thirteen-year-old high "D" Carrie (now that's a scary combination) refused to go to church. She wanted to stay up

late on Saturday night and didn't want to get up early on Sunday morning. It was a weekly source of conflict. When her "C" mom asked me what to do, I said, "Remember, it's very important to a high "D" to feel they have power and control. If you tell them what to do, they'll shoot to do the opposite."

I suggested that they give Carrie a choice and let her know that she doesn't have to go to church. She can stay home and sleep. After Carrie's mom closed her jaw, I asked, "What are some of Carrie's favorite activities?"

A short list was compiled, generating the top item on her list – chatting on the computer with her friends. Carrie was then given a choice. Each day she could chat for either ten minutes or two hours – once homework was done. This was contingent upon whether or not she had attended church the previous Sunday.

It wasn't long before the choice was made and the conflict was over. Carrie was miraculously able to get up on time for church every Sunday after that. The conflict was over.

HOW TO RESPOND TO A "D" CHILD

"Ds," focused and determined to achieve their goals, are generally unaware of their overpowering nature in conflict. The "D" personality styles need physical activity to recover from conflict or stress. They may need to go for a walk or get some exercise in a favorite sport.

For a "D" mom, that physical activity could bring positive results. It could mean physical exertion around the house in a different capacity – cleaning, organizing the closets, straightening the garage, or landscaping. (Digging a hole in the yard is better than digging a hole in a relationship!)

MRS. CLEAN

I first recognized this "under stress cleaning frenzy" in my own "D" personality style several years ago when my kids were much younger. If I were on a cleaning frenzy (not something that happened very often, obviously), my kids would invariably ask me if something was wrong! I didn't realize it, but I would de-stress by mega power cleaning around the house, and they recognized it.

As a "D" mom, there's no way I can sit still and "think about it." After praying about it, I have to take action, take the bull by the horns, and hope I don't get bucked off! Look at it this way: If you or your child is a "D" experiencing stress or conflict, what a great opportunity to get things done! When there's conflict at my house, there's a clean closet or cupboard just around the corner!

Now let's take a look at Chapter 25 to see how to handle *Conflict and **D-I-S-C**ipline* with the outgoing, people-oriented, and inspiring "I" child!

25

HOW TO HANDLE CONFLICT WITH AN "I" CHILD

 DEAL ENVIRONMENT

 ...Fun, Friendly, Exciting!

Conflict with the "I" Child

Desiring to be with friends and to be noticed and adored, the "I" child's needs are mostly social. "Is" are filled with naïve optimism and a fun sense of humor. Boredom is a plague and rejection is a killer. In conflict, what "Is" fear most is losing social recognition and popularity.

If you make them look bad in front of a group, they may overreact with a flood of emotion. And watch out. In the heat of the moment and with their wit and keen sense of humor, they can zap one back, making *you* look bad and damaging your relationship as a result.

Conflict arises for "I" children in simple repetition and daily mundane tasks. Chores, such as emptying the trash or picking up after themselves, are too monotonous. Unorganized and late, "Is" will get there when they get there, spending half their lives apologizing for being late! In addition, they may not hesitate to elaborate in telling the story behind *why* they're late. They don't me-e-e-an to tell those little white lies, they just want their stories to be really exciting. With a tendency to exaggerate, they *shoot* for the stars – desiring to *sound* like a star!

"Is" have conflict and struggle with budgeting issues. They will buy something if they want it (especially if they feel stressed out). After all, a new item will make them look good! That's all the break-the-bank budgeting rationale they need. Teach them how to handle money wisely; otherwise, the "I" will spend without thinking, planning, or needing. These influencing salespeople sell *themselves* on the idea that "It's new, it's fun, and it's mine!"

LET'S TALK – NOT!

High "C" Connie worked as a technical supervisor interacting with people all day, which is ideal for an "I" but stressful and draining for a "C." Her "D" son, Charlie, retained pent-up energy to burn after sitting in a chair most of day at school (especially if he lost recess time). As soon as he arrived home, Charlie needed to physically run and play outside as soon as possible to exert energy. He industriously built new bridges and roads in his sandbox; climbed swing set mountains, or played sports.

But with Connie's high "I" daughter, LeAnn, it was a different story. Connie said, "After I arrived home each day, my daughter excitedly met me at the door with an abundance of energy to tell me every detail of her day. Talking fast and *nonstop*, LeAnn described the first moment she arrived at school, whom she talked to, what happened in each class, whom she talked to in each class, and she told me about any new friends she met – and, of course, what they talked about. She performed a play-by-play of every conversation with her friends on the way home after school and details about *their* day!"

Reserved and task-oriented "C" mom Connie, on the other hand, arrived home desperately in need of a *break*, to read the newspaper and engage in alone time to recharge. Feeling *attacked* by her daughter's conflicting personality style upon walking in the door, Connie found herself short and impatient – almost resenting LeAnn. She realized that because of this situation, the air was getting thick between them – and the wall was getting even thicker. That is, until she began to understand their personality differences and recognized them as the source of the clash in their relationship.

Sensitive to their polarized personality styles and recognizing the resulting conflict, Connie made a plan (as "C" moms do so well). She chose to give LeAnn fifteen minutes of her time to talk about her day when she first arrived home. In exchange, LeAnn then had to grant her mom quiet time for thirty minutes. Then they reconvened again to prepare dinner together, giving LeAnn the opportunity to finish telling all the other details of her day.

This plan was reassuring to Connie that she would have her down time to recharge each day after arriving home, and it was exciting to LeAnn that her mom would offer an attentive ear to hear more, more, more! It worked well for both of them, while Charlie continued to build, conquer, and forge ahead building his sand box empire!

BASIC CONTROL FOR AN "I"

IN CONTROL	OUT OF CONTROL
OPTIMISTIC	UNREALISTIC
PERSUASIVE	MANIPULATIVE
EXCITED	EMOTIONAL
COMMUNICATIVE	GOSSIPY
SPONTANEOUS	IMPULSIVE
OUTGOING	UNFOCUSED
EXPRESSIVE	EXCITABLE
INVOLVED	DIRECTIONLESS
IMAGINATIVE	DAYDREAMER
WARM/FRIENDLY	PURPOSELESS

D-I-S-CIPLINE TIPS FOR THE "I" CHILD

"I" children are always going to seek attention. They *want* attention, *need* attention, and will *get* attention one way or another. In fact, the "I" child will find a way to get it – positively or negatively. They will crave and command your attention to the extreme – regardless if the results are receiving a verbal complaint, a spanking, or explosive anger from you. (Witnessing an adult temper tantrum will do – it's still attention!) If you remain cool, calm, and collected, but *watch* your child throw a temper tantrum – it is *still* attention!

Time-out for an "I" child can be murder for them. Sitting still while listening to the countdown ticking of the kitchen timer, with no one to talk to and no one to look at – and worse, no one to look at them – is torture! (Warning: Sometimes they sing or perform while in time-out.)

If you give your child a time-out while in public, an "I" child may engage a watchful audience by yelling real-l-l-l-ly loudly. Again, it's attention! In this situation, stand your ground, remain calm, and don't give in. If you place your children in time-out and look the other way until they calm down, they will soon learn that it's not worth throwing a fit if there's no audience! Remind your child, "When you're *through* throwing a fit, let me know and we can have fun again."

When the time-out is over, teach your child to apologize for the inappropriate behavior, asking for forgiveness. Then they can enthusiastically join you again. Affirm how much you love them, even when they mess up.

Taking away telephone privileges or forbidding them to spend time with friends is an effective source of discipline for your older high "I" child. They'll think twice about what they have to lose when it's of such high value! Telephone restrictions don't always work for a "D" child, though. They'll think, "You can keep your phone. I'll buy my own someday. In fact, I'll probably own my own telephone company!"

GET ME OUT OF TROUBLE!

"I" personality styles have an extravagant or quick answer for everything and don't want to be held accountable for their own actions. Instead of getting ready for school, Angie talked on the telephone (what a surprise) every morning for about fifteen minutes. Slamming the telephone down upon realizing how late she would be, she hollered, "Mo-o-o-om, help! I need a note! I'm late! I need to make up some excuse!"

Angie's mom said it was painfully hard when faced with this conflict, but she responded with, "Why? Does your car not start? Is your alarm not working this morning – no electricity? Angie, are you asking me to lie?" She refused to write the note and chose to let Angie suffer the consequences.

We have to teach our children that they must take responsibility for making poor choices. Angie had *chosen* to talk on the telephone, so she *chose* to be late. Will she do that again? Probably not – as long as mom won't bail her out! More than likely, Angie will learn to be more responsible.

HOW TO RESPOND TO AN "I" CHILD

The "I" personality style responds differently when under stress than the task-oriented "D" or "C," and with much more energy than the "S." The "I" needs social activity to recover under stress. This may mean going out to play with friends or to the mall – with friends. In other words, *out* somewhere – with friends. For an "I," being able to *talk* through the conflict helps!

When you see that your "I" child is having conflict or is under stress, respond by being friendly and positive. Allow for informal dialogue and show an interest. Compliment "Is," plan fun, and laugh at their jokes! With their easygoing and "lighten up" attitude, as soon as they jump off their emotional roller coaster ride, they will immediately implement their "don't worry, be happy" philosophy.

Now let's take a look at Chapter 26 to see how to handle *Conflict and D-I-S-Cipline* with the reserved, people-oriented, and supportive "**S**" child!

26

HOW TO HANDLE CONFLICT WITH AN "S" CHILD

 IDEAL ENVIRONMENT

 ...Predictable, Stable, Harmonious!

Conflict with the "S" Child

"S" personality styles dislike and will avoid conflict at all costs! Preferring stability and status quo, they perceive as conflict (in fact feel threatened) when you implement changes, particularly if you surprise them. However, those feelings often fly under the radar and are "stuffed." Instead of reacting toward you, they shut down and find escape in withdrawal, excessive sleep, comfort food, or depression. "Ss" devote their lives to pleasing and keeping the peace.

As patient and attentive listeners, they'll discuss issues – as long as you're doing the discussing and they're doing the listening. They lack enthusiasm or energy in making decisions because they don't want to disappoint anybody. However, they may end up being the one disappointed by not speaking up and verbalizing their requests.

"Ss" need help with establishing goals; they won't be impulsive or offensive. If you choose to "fire up" your "S" child with suggestions against their will, you may eventually receive a surprise response. Goals or suggestions may be appreciated for a while, but don't push. "Ss" hold feelings in a lot, until they can't hold them in anymore.

For example, let's say your child begs you to blow up a balloon, "Make it bigger, Mommy!" So you blow in some more air and they want it even bigger. You huff and you puff (doing your best imitation of the big bad wolf) until *pow*! It *pops*! If you push an "S" too far and the conflict is too much, he or she may build up resentment and eventually over-react, even explode!

WHAT BIKE?

When my older daughter, Stacia, was a pre-teen, she didn't like riding bikes (one of my very *favorite* things to do). With a secondary "S" personality style, Stacia avoided the conflict of continually trying to convince me that she simply didn't *want* to ride bikes on the trails. (Believe me, she *told* me several times, but I just didn't *get* it.) One day her bike mysteriously *disappeared* (quite conveniently, I might say). We couldn't find it anywhere! Hum-m-m.

Another "S" word definition we could use is "***Sneaky***"! Rather than face the fire up front, "Ss" will sneak around (in a nice way) to avoid conflict. Not because they're devious and outright sneaky, but because they're avoiding the discomfort of the conflict.

Well, there was no conflict to ride when she couldn't find her bike! Coincidentally, about two years later, I was at the neighborhood garage sale and saw her bike with a "For Sale" sign on it at her best friend's house! In order to avoid my determined-to-get-her-to-love-riding-bikes "D" insistence, she figured out a solution (I'm not a proponent of this, of course) and avoided the conflict for two years!

BASIC CONTROL FOR AN "S"

IN CONTROL	OUT OF CONTROL
RELAXED	LACKING INITIATIVE
RELIABLE	DEPENDENT
COOPERATIVE	A SUCKER
STABLE	INDECISIVE
GOOD LISTENER	UNCOMMUNICATIVE
SINGLE-MINDED	INFLEXIBLE
STEADFAST	RESISTANT TO CHANGE
SOFTHEARTED	EASILY MANIPULATED
SYSTEMATIC	SLOW
AMIABLE	RESENTFUL

D-I-S-CIPLINE TIPS FOR THE "S" CHILD

Since the "S" child loves watching television, reading, or spending one-on-one time with a special friend, what would the obvious discipline of choice be? Time-out would work, except for looking at their sad little faces given that they disappointed you. Preferring a peaceful environment, an "S" child actually might *enjoy* the time-out down time, though!

Eliminating one-on-one time with a special friend, favorite toys or games, or losing television privileges would be effective discipline for the more reserved "S" child. It doesn't take much. "S" children need stability and security, and they don't want anyone to rock their boat. (It's not a sailboat or yacht, but more like a cute, little paddleboat.) Keep them sailing, even in high waters.

FAMILY FRAGMENTATION

If "Ss" are forced out of their comfort zones, the need for stability and security can become a weakness. Stacy and her husband experienced an unpleasant divorce two years ago. Their three children have suffered emotionally through the fragmentation of their familiar family unit. Divorce is hard on everyone involved, but it can take a particularly hard toll on teenage children.

Stacy's "S" son, Kevin, was 15 at the time of her divorce. He dealt with the conflict by plunging into despair, resorting to depression, alcohol consumption, and drug use. Stacy said, "Kevin used every kind of drug you can imagine – even the very serious and dangerous kind. It was so hard to imagine because Kevin had always been so sweet, quiet, and compliant. Growing up, he loved being together as a family and was obedient and helpful. Kevin became passive-aggressive (as "Ss" can do to avoid conflict) after the divorce. He literally paced the floor every time we were in the room together, and wouldn't sit down or look me in the eye. Sometimes Kevin shouted bursts of angry words about things that I had no idea he felt."

Stacy continued to explain that one day, a girl whom Kevin had had a crush on since second grade, invited him to a youth group that met at her house. Stacy said, "This girl's family is very strict and religious, and spends a lot of time with their kids. Kevin wanted to go to youth group at first just to see this girl. When they started dating, I saw him transform dramatically. He turned his life around because he felt secure and wanted to please this girl and her family. He said he liked what her 'stable family' had to offer. His drug use literally stopped overnight. It was amazing! Kevin is still unhappy with our family's situation, but we've learned to talk about it and we've learned to support each other."

Loyalty with family and friends is an important element of security and stability for an "S" child at any age. Be patient and understanding by allowing them time to adjust to ideas or changes. Allow them time to *process* emotional situations. Show encouragement, affirming that they can get through difficult circumstances and conflict. Assure them you'll be with them through the good times and the tough times.

HOW TO RESPOND TO AN "S" CHILD

"Ss" need undirected activity to recover under stress. This may mean piddling around the house or watching a movie they have seen over and over. (They love predicting every word!) A rainy day is a welcome relief on a lazy afternoon for an "S" because there's no pressure to go out and achieve something.

Since "Ss" are slow starters and need more time to process change, patiently accommodate their desire for security and stability. Remember, they prefer status quo and fear sudden changes! With trepidation toward confrontation, you need to show kindness and a friendly response (both verbally and nonverbally) when facing conflict with your "S" child. Encourage and reinforce a sense of appreciation and support for what your child is experiencing. As the S" child feels appreciated and valued as a person, there is no limit to what this little supporter would do to please you.

Now let's take a look at Chapter 27 to see how to handle *Conflict and D-I-S-Cipline* with the reserved, task-oriented, and cautious "**C**" child!

27

HOW TO HANDLE CONFLICT WITH A "C" CHILD!

*I*DEAL ENVIRONMENT

...Structured with Procedures

and Accuracy!

Conflict with the "C" Child

"Cs" put a lot of thought into carefully doing things correctly and perfectly. Conflict arises because they (and others) *must* do things right! They want to know "why" or "what if...?" Cautious "Cs" categorize, theorize, organize, and analyze! But as the expression goes, "over-analysis causes paralysis!"

To excel in their analytical thinking and high standards, "Cs" need space, silence, and organization. They actually feel physically and emotionally uncomfortable in an unorganized environment!

These reserved, more serious organized planners want predictability and dislike spontaneity. They need time to think about a new idea or suggestion. If you push, it can be counterproductive.

"Cs" are great with details and are generally very mannerly, but they have nightmares about making mistakes! They worry that things aren't perfect (or are mediocre). Too much time spent worrying about things going wrong can develop into "stinkin' thinkin'." "Cs" can be hard to please, and moody if their perfectionistic expectations aren't met.

CRINKLED PAPER

Mrs. Young, Justin's teacher, was quite concerned about her student's obsession with perfectionism. She said, "Each morning, Justin sharpens his pencils until all five are the exact same length, and then lines them up in a perfect row at the top of his desk. I noticed that he thinks his papers have to be perfect, his clothes have to be perfect, the toys have to be played with perfectly, and his lunch has to be perfect – or he gets really upset."

Not surprisingly, at the parent-teacher conference, Justin's mom, Sheila (also a "C"), walked in wearing a perfectly groomed outfit, perfectly combed hair, and a file folder in her perfectly manicured hands. With stiff posture and a serious expression, Justin's mom revealed an organized list of details to check off as they conversed. "She had many questions and needed many answers," said Mrs. Young.

Mrs. Young began the conference by saying, "Justin is very mannerly, always gets his work done on time, and never misses a detail." (In other words, Justin *definitely* colors within the lines!) Sheila confided to Mrs. Young that Justin is always such a perfectionist at home and he worries and frets all the time.   She said that she didn't know why he was so perfectionistic and she was worried about him. (Isn't there an expression about an apple not falling far from the tree? Uh-hum.)

A few days after the conference and to help Justin relax a little on the perfectionism, Mrs. Young devised a well-thought-out, strategic, ingenious, brilliant, almost scientific plan. She purposely handed back Justin's paper – *crinkled!* Yes! That's right – *crinkled!* It was shocking. Justin was mortified – and then his mom, Sheila, was mortified (even angry at first)!

It was a great learning experience. Feeling foolish for their anger, Sheila and Justin had an "opportunity" to figure out that he (and she) dealt with an *imperfect* paper, and everything still turned out okay.   They realized their perfectionism and critical thinking were out of control.

Justin is in high school now, but they all still laugh about the "day of the crinkled paper"! He and his mom realize how one small incident of conflict really changed their perspective on what's important each day, and moved them to learn to lighten up.   It's funny how little things can make a big difference!

BASIC CONTROL FOR A "C"

IN CONTROL	OUT OF CONTROL
ORDERLY	COMPULSIVE
LOGICAL	CRITICAL
INTENSE	UNSOCIABLE
CURIOUS	PRYING
TEACHABLE	EASILY OFFENDED
CAUTIOUS	FEARFUL
CORRECT	INFLEXIBLE
QUESTIONING	DOUBTFUL
CONSCIENTIOUS	WORRISOME
PRECISE	PICKY

D-I-S-CIPLINE TIPS FOR THE "C" CHILD

If you have two kids, you probably have two kids with two ways of thinking. One child may sit alone in the room and color, read, or play games, thinking it's a *perfect* afternoon. The other child, however, considers it a *punishment!*

High "Cs" function best with rules and boundaries that are clearly defined. When implementing discipline for your "C" child, establish detailed plans and a structured environment. Administering discipline to "C" children provokes their fear of criticism. With self-imposed high standards and expectations, the "C" child struggles with unrealistic expectations of themselves (and others).

Time-out for a "C" child is not real painful – after all, it's extra "time to think." With the exception that it's physical evidence that this "C" child's behavior wasn't "perfect," he or she could masterfully think up a storm (as long as it doesn't rain on his or her parade). As moms, we have to admit, we can't prohibit them from that pleasurable accomplishment called thinking!

In addition, losing the privilege of going to a party or hanging out with friends may not be as effective as you'd expect with a "C" child (especially if you place high value on this activity as a high "I" or "S" mom). But, restrict your "C" child from computers, books, games, or projects, and ouch – *that* hurts!

COMPUTER SAVVY – NOT

If you are a conscientious "C" mom, don't be afraid to let your child fail. Learning has a much greater impact when we've allowed them to experience the pain and consequences of their decisions firsthand. Children want to do well and contribute; they actually want guidelines and parameters. Permissiveness causes insecurity and low self-esteem.

I learned this best when my "D/C" son, Scott, was about twelve years old. One evening he was "working" on my computer. The next day I discovered my Word program on my computer wasn't installed anymore – vanished, gone, history.

The "Computer Doctor" whom we bought the computer from was kind enough to make a house call, and upon intense observation said, "Hum-m-m-m. Uh-h hum-m-m, I see. Oh-h-h, ah-h-h, well, well, that explains it." (I was getting worried. I thought I was going to have to call a computer ambulance!)

Apparently, Scott had accidentally erased the Word program when he was "exploring" the night before. Then the "Computer Doctor" said something that I'll never forget. He said, "I'm not going to charge you for reinstalling this program or for the house call. Kids need to feel comfortable trying new things and that it's okay if they make a mistake. If I charged you, your son would never feel comfortable trying new things on the computer again. Instead, he would be reluctant and afraid that he would mess things up."

That was such great advice! Scott knows more about a computer today than I probably ever will. He has never hesitated to dig in and explore, and has continued with the determination to solve computer problems. We need to let our curious children feel comfortable to mess things up while trying to figure things out (obviously within certain boundaries). Life will not come crashing down because of it (but your computer may)!

PLANS AND SCHEDULES

"Cs" love schedules and calendars. I learned the *hard* way (watching Madison throw a royal fit one day on the way to school when she discovered what was being served for lunch) to discuss the lunch menu ahead of time with my "C/D" child.

To avoid undue conflict, I now attach the daily lunch menu, school calendar, and schedules of class activities, sports events, and church activities on the inside of a kitchen cabinet door. This allows Madison the "opportunity" to be *responsible* for checking ahead, and helps her feel confident that things are in order.

We also empty her backpack immediately after she arrives home from school – and *before* a favorite snack (it's *all* about leverage!). We methodically discuss the next day's weather forecast and activities, and hang her backpack on the coat closet door with any new permission slips signed and ready to go. By bedtime, we select her next day's outfit before the lights go out.

Equipped and ready to go, it leaves little room for worry, conflict, or concern (or royal fits). I've had to learn to focus on the importance of this routine and how it contributes to her peace and comfort – for her benefit.

As a side note: On that particular day, Madison insisted on taking her lunch as we were walking to school, but I responded with, "It's too late to make your lunch today. Next time we'll plan ahead."

She "had a cow," but had I given in to Madison's quest (fit) to take her lunch that morning (which would have been a *lot* easier), she would not have learned that fits don't work! It was hard to stand my ground, watching those salty little tears flow down her cheeks (along with deafening wails) all the way to school. But I had to stand my ground.

I could have said, "I'll let you take your lunch *this* time, but *next* time..." But which speaks more loudly, words or actions? We as moms need to teach our children that what we say goes. It's particularly hard to stand firm with strong personalities, but essential and for their good, by preventing them from manipulating and controlling.

HOW TO RESPOND TO A "C" CHILD

"Cs" are very conscious of time. They want to start and finish on time; otherwise, they feel antsy. Being late causes them stress. The "C" personality style needs cognitive activity to recover under stress or during conflict. This may mean reading a magazine or story.

Conflict happens in every home. It's unavoidable. Working on the computer, putting a puzzle together, or working a crossword puzzle enables a "C's" calculating and problem-solving personality to unwind! Give them something positive to "think about." They want encouraging words that are unemotional and accurate. Spend quality time with them.

Clearly explain the details of what the expected behavior is when there is a conflict. Most important, let them know "why" you're asking them to do something. With a "C's" suspicious nature, this child will need plenty of time to think through and analyze the process before they can begin. "Cs" *need* to know the "why."

Patiently be specific with your requests and in responding to theirs, give accurate answers. Your "C" child won't say much until he or she feels sure it is safe or correct.

Needing time to process, this child may initially come across as negative, but allow them the freedom to keep asking questions. Don't push them to agree at first. Suggest a step-by-step plan and reassure your child that there will be no surprises. Even in conflict, maintain high standards and keep a commitment to excellence as a mom.

Now let's take a look at Chapter 28 to discover *Motivation Strategies* for your child according to his or her personality style!

28

D-I-S-COVER MOTIVATION STRATEGIES

*E*very morning, Beverly battles her teenage son, Michael, to get out of bed and get ready for school on time. "What can I do to motivate him? Why isn't he motivated to get going?" she asked in sheer frustration. Sound familiar? Do *your* children need to be motivated? If they're breathing, they do!

So the next question is, "*How* do we motivate them?" In one sense, people are *already* motivated – to do exactly what *they* want to do! It is human nature to do things for our own reasons. As moms, we can create environments that help motivate our children.

For example, Beverly could shout, "Michael, there's a fire spreading in the hallway! It's about to reach your room!" Or a really clever and creative mom could say, "Miiiiichael, the cutest girl in your class is at the front door wanting to walk to school with you!" Then what would happen? Michael would *instantly* be motivated to *jet* out of bed that morning instead of ignoring his alarm clock. The difference? We've created an atmosphere that encourages our child to get *motivated!*

WHAT IS MOTIVATION?

Motivation is not enforcing the discipline or consequences we discussed in the previous "Conflict" chapters. And we don't motivate our children by nagging or making threats – such as grounding them for a month or prohibiting them from television, electronics, toys, etc. Motivation is our inner drive. It's what propels us into action! A mom can, however, *affect* her child's motivation.

Studies have concluded that motivation and desire are more important determinants in our success than talent or ability. Everyone's motivated. We're born motivated. For example, even babies are motivated to crawl. (This, by the way, can be an opportunity for a quick and easy evaluation of our child's personality style. If, for instance, you instruct an exploring baby to not touch an item on the coffee table, you can quickly recognize, by their reaction and the degree of their determination to keep touching, the tendencies toward the baby's personality style.)

If your child is dogmatic and determined to keep touching, watch out. You may have yourself a little "D"! An impressionable "I" baby may touch again and again to see what you'll do, and bask in the attention. The sweet "S" baby will hang his or her little head and drop that bottom lip, feeling bad for having upset you. Cautious "C" babies consider it the correct thing to do to follow the rules, avoid this object, and move on – assuming their curiosity doesn't get the best of their little judgment.

We are instinctively motivated. Watch any baby crawl around the entire house on those hard surface floors, scuffing their little knees, because they're motivated to explore, learn, and discover – regardless of their personality style! We were *born* motivated!

WHAT GENERATES MOTIVATION?

Our motivation is derived from our personality styles, talents, gifts, and exposure. What motivates one personality style may not motivate another. I was able to motivate my "C" daughter Stacia by giving her extra time to watch her favorite television shows or talk on the telephone to a special friend. I saw drastic results! For my "D" son, Scott, planning a bike ride on the trails was a great motivator. Stacia hated riding bikes, and you never caught Scott on the telephone! If you know your child's desires, you know your child's motivator.

I'm not motivated to stand on the hardwood floors in the kitchen for an hour cooking dinner amidst the steam, heat, and hassle because I enjoy preparing a meal. But I have enjoyed hearing my daughter Madison ask for another helping of "the best 'pa'sghetti' in the whole wide world." I am *motivated* to take care of my family and show them love and attention. I can do this by cooking a nice dinner for them. (They've probably felt *un*loved and hungry through the duration of my writing this book!)

I don't like working out (although sometimes it's the only forty minutes I have to myself all day). Who likes all the sweating (glowing), getting hot, and worn out? But I do like the benefits of staying healthy and maintaining slightly smaller thighs than a Sumo wrestler.

Motivation, varying in personality styles, can stem from the desire to win power, be popular, feel cared for, or be correct. It is the spark that ignites the fire inside us. When our dreams are truly realized and the spark intensifies, those fires can ignite and burst into resplendent motivation spontaneous combustion!

HOW DO WE KNOW WHAT MOTIVATES OUR CHILD?

We discover our child's motivation and interests by exposing them to a variety of opportunities, activities, and experiences. We add fuel to their fire by showing our love, support, and interest, too. Establish solid relationships with your children and stay engaged. They'll feel free and have the self-confidence to take advantage of opportunities for learning and exploring.

What is your child's passion? Is your child motivated to win, gain recognition, have a close relationship, or follow rules? Knowing what makes them tick is an important component in developing a great relationship, positioning them in a positive environment where they will thrive.

Be intentional in getting to know your children! Spend time together to find out what motivates them if you're not certain. Do they love to eat pizza (buffet – if he's a teenage boy, of course), ride bikes, or play golf, soccer, baseball, football, tennis, or hike (possibly unlike you)? Do they (again, unlike you) enjoy ballet, concerts, opera, piano, art, antiques, books, or music? Maybe you have a movie buff on your hands. If so, go to the movie with them, sit and listen to their music, take lessons together. Be their cheerleader.

If you and your child have different interests, it can be hard to find something you both enjoy. Sometimes, as moms, we have to mold things with Play-Doh® or build a fort even when we don't have an interest. However, if we're motivated to develop the kinds of relationships with our children that we seek and desire, then we have to rummage around for kindling to ignite that fire.

YOU WANT ME TO DO WHAT?

I didn't know a thing about soccer when my son, Scott, asked me to coach his soccer team. (He was four years old at the time.) However, I volunteered, read the soccer instruction book (even took it to the practices with me), and coached eighteen energy-packed, dirt-diggin', testosterone-driven little boys – for *six* soccer seasons!

I can't say that I ever became a great soccer coach, and we didn't break any outstanding records, but oddly enough, I had a lengthy waiting list each season of boys wanting to be on the team. We had a lot of fun, learned how to play and work together as a team, and even learned a few soccer skills along the way.

As unqualified as I was to coach soccer, the benefit from that coaching experience was developing better relationships with Scott, his friends, and the other parents. I spent time with my son and shared in his "goals." (I know, I know... moan. That was a bad one.) Does your child like to play tennis, make jewelry, shoot hoops; enjoy scrap-booking or painting; or need to practice pitching?

Express an interest in your child's interest. Is he or she an aspiring actor? Go to a play together. Ask for your children's opinions. Soon they'll get the idea that you care about what they're doing, their dreams and goals. Are they sports enthusiasts? Go to a game! Understand and support who *they* are and what motivates *them*. Find a way to participate with an attentive and captivated eye as a proud mom. You don't have to be good (I can vouch for that one), you just have to be connected.

OF COURSE YOU MAY BUY ANYTHING YOU WANT

"Please mom, pleeeeeze," she would plead. Every time we would go shopping, Madison never hesitated to beg for toys in every aisle. (It's such a *breeze* when you shop solo!) This was driving me *crazy*! All the typical efforts to make her reflect and re-evaluate any greediness or lack of appreciation for her life of plenty – didn't *faze* her!

I decided it was time to implement an allowance program. We purchased a Larry Burkett kid's bank and negotiated an earning potential of $5.00 each Saturday. She can earn this if she keeps her room clean, toys picked up, and bed made; sets and clears the table; and escorts Rocky, our new Shih Tzu puppy, outside for "visits."

We spelled out (literally) all-l-l-l the required *details* for our "C" child. Ten percent of the $5.00 goes to her tithe at church (50¢). Half of what's left of the $4.50 goes to her bank savings, and the other $2.25 can go to anything she wants.

Consequently, now when we're shopping and she longs for a treasured item (in other words, gets the "gimmes"), she can buy it if she uses her money. When I hear, "Please mom, pleeeeeze, may I buy my (*147th!!!*) stuffed animal?" I can always reply, "*Yes*, of course! That is, *if* you want to spend *your* own money!"

Oh, what a wonderful solution for those shopping sprees and pleas! It's up to her what she spends all-l-l-l-l that money on. I'm just along for the ride and the teachable moment. This is also a great opportunity to *motivate* Madison to learn math and how to save each week to accumulate for something better! It motivates her to think about and plan (which "Cs" *love* to do) before spending.

DOES EARNING AN ALLOWANCE MOTIVATE?

Allocating an allowance also worked as a motivation for Stacia and Scott, my two now-adult children, when they were in elementary school. (No, I do not continue to give my adult children an allowance. I've made *plenty* of benevolent allowances for them already!)

Every weekend they were required to do chores. I designed an "A List" and a "B List." They alternated the lists each Saturday. The recipient of the "A List" had to vacuum, dust all wood, clean the shower, and vacuum the stairs. The "B List" required cleaning all glass and mirrors, sweeping the kitchen floor, scrubbing toilets, and cleaning sinks. This may sound like a lot, but they managed just fine. (I watched them carefully while I nibbled on my bonbons and sipped my tropical tea. Sure.)

Upon completion of their chores, they earned a whopping $3.00 (that actually got you into a movie fifteen years ago). Also, they could choose to complete the chores on Friday if they had plans for Saturday. However, they couldn't go anywhere on Saturday until their chores were done.

High "D" Scott would always dart around the house, striving to complete his chores fast and first – to win (win what, I'm not sure). High "C" Stacia was a little more apt to follow the rules and get the chores done right, but complained endlessly.

Now, you might be thinking that making a chore list is no big deal, right? If you've seen one chore list, you've seen a hundred, so what? Because they were both highly motivated to participate in things such as skating parties, sleepovers, etc., I found it wasn't a problem in *completing* the chores. That was the easy part. In fact, sometimes they did an amazingly *fast* job – but not an amazingly *good* job!

One more issue I had to deal with each week was their *complaining* about having to do chores. Their lackadaisical attitude about how well they cleaned, and their moaning and groaning was getting to me. So, I added an addendum to the chore list.

Keep in mind, they had to do their chores regardless – cut-and-dried – there was no getting out of it. But it soon became beneficial to complete the chores with a sparkle and a shine in the *house* – and in their *attitude!* Base pay consisted of receiving $3.00 upon completion of their chores. However (here's the kicker), *if* they did their chores and did a *really good job*, they could earn $4.00! And (ready?) *if* they did their chores, and *if* they did a really good job, and *if* they had a *really positive non-complaining-moaning-groaning attitude*, they could earn $5.00!

Guess what they were motivated to do? In addition, they learned the *value* of doing a really good job as well as having a really positive attitude. Just as in the real world, the work force, or life in general – it pays off! Motivation makes a difference!

ROLE MODEL BY DEFAULT

Being a good role model with a can-do attitude can influence and propel your child to reach beyond his or her perceived limits. Teach by example. Moms who are excited about their lives, their jobs, their families, and perceive the *opportunity* to help a neighbor – rather than complaining – can influence their children in a big way.

Does your child want to give up on that math problem before he or she is finished? Help to understand the value in sticking with it, finishing what's started. Surround your children with good role models who can motivate them to continue and persevere – regardless of how difficult or dismal the effort appears at the time.

AFTER SCHOOL

Different personality styles have different approaches and preferences for homework time and playtime after school. The "D" personality style needs to burn pent-up energy, the "I" needs a chance to talk and be around friends, the "S" prefers time to relax, and the "C" needs time away from interaction with people all day – to think.

Homework is a fundamental component toward our children's educational success. Allocate a quiet and uninterrupted environment in a designated study area equipped with supplies and resources. Remind your child that during this special study time, there will be no telephone calls and no "favorite" shows or friends over. Learn more about after-school preferences and alternatives for each personality style in the following four chapters!

THE ART OF MOTIVATION

It's an art to adjust our style (not change who we are) and work with our children to meet their needs, as well as better motivate them according to their natural drives. Some personality styles open up easily and often. Some are more reserved and need time to think about what they have to say before they start chatting about their day.

An opportunity to learn about your children's day and what impacted them often presents itself at bedtime. The routine of snuggling or sitting by their side at the end of the day creates a time for your child to feel safe, secure, and loved at home. One thing I found that helped prompt my kids to discuss their day was simply saying, "Tell me your happy and sad today." Sometimes just one or two things were mentioned, and sometimes the floodgates of communication burst open and astonishing bits of news gushed out.

There is no sure method for motivating your child. However, understanding what motivates your children according to their unique personality styles significantly raises their chances for success. Guiding your children according to their abilities (not manipulating them into something for your own personal gain), promotes fulfillment for your children – and for you as their mom.

Let's take a look at Chapter 29 and learn about exciting *Motivation Strategies* for the determined "**D**" child!

29

MOTIVATION STRATEGIES FOR THE D CHILD!

*M*OTIVATION TECHNIQUES FOR YOUR "D" CHILD

Basic Motivation:

- Challenges
- Choices
- Control

The "D" child is motivated by having a specific plan of action – with control over determining when and what goals to accomplish. With high "Ds'" competitive nature, they are motivated by challenges and results. If we could crawl inside the high "D" child's mind, it would sound like someone revving up a car engine, "rum rum-m-m." "Ds" have an internal drive that *propels* their external objectives into action!

The "D" child likes to do things the *fast* way. "Ds" *need* a contest or challenge where they feel that they have control and can win. Needing opportunities to lead, they will rise to the occasion when given the opportunity (if you don't *tell* them what to do)! They are self-starters and *wake* up *fired* up! They're naturally motivated to be assertive, but out-of-control *assertion* can lead to *aggression*.

COMMUNICATION WITH YOUR "D" CHILD

> To feel connected, we need to communicate and express love in ways that are meaningful. The "**D**" child says:
>
> - "Be direct and clear."
> - "Tell me what you want me to do."
> - "Show me what I can accomplish."
> - "Offer me choices when possible."

The high "D" personality style needs encouraging words that are direct and to the point. Use a confident, firm tone and be brief. You can reinforce the "D" child's ability by giving age-appropriate authority and responsibility with challenges. "Ds" may cut to the chase, but they mean what they say and say what they mean. You can count on them to tell you *exactly* what they're thinking! Direct communication is a strength, but the "D" child needs to learn to be sensitive to others' feelings.

"D" types are full of energy. Something is going on all the time, either inwardly or outwardly. "D" personality styles need us to be consistent and fair with them as much as possible. If there is an issue of opposition between you, it's important that "D" children understand how to verbalize their feelings in a mannerly way. Tell them that as long as they respond with respect, rather than react in anger, you will listen to them.

Remember to create an atmosphere where "Ds" feel you are on their *team*, rather than on their *back*! If your "D" child is motivated to achieve great things together, he or she could be a zealous supporter of your accomplishments and eagerly help you solve any problems along the way!

KITCHEN CABINETS TO CLIMB AND CONQUER

As a toddler, high "D" Hannah was motivated to continually climb onto the kitchen counters, backs of chairs, tables, etc. Her mom, Robin, had a choice. She could yell, "No! No! Don't climb there," over and over again, or she could recognize Hannah's desire for climbing and suggest, "I think you must really like to climb things! Climbing's fun! Would you like me to enroll you in a gymnastics class?" Or, for a more immediate climbing alternative, she could say, "Let's go climb at the park, but not here in the kitchen where you could get hurt."

We can spend the entire day shouting, "No!" – or we can recognize our child's motivation for physical action and offer options that spark a positive response. Making a habit to point out alternatives that are available can promote positive thinking and redirect the behavior rather than launch a battle!

THE "D" CHILD RESPONDS BEST...

...to a Mom Who:

- Provides direct answers.
- Sticks to the bottom line.
- Stresses goals.
- Provides firm, but fair pressure.
- Allows freedom for personal accomplishment.

LABEL BEHAVIOR, NOT THE CHILD

The "D" child is motivated to control and manipulate, but your child's behavior is separate from the child and we should verbalize accordingly. For example, if your "D" child acted bad, let's say bossy and mean to a friend, distinguish the behavior. Place the emphasis on the behavior as bad, and avoid labeling the child as bad.

In other words, you can say, "Your behavior was bad and inappropriate" rather than, "*You* were bad or inappropriate." The child *acted* bad and inappropriate. Actions can be changed. This gives children the opportunity to improve their behavior and separate themselves from the "bad boy" or "bad girl" label.

We can also reinforce that we love our children, regardless of how they act. Our love is unconditional, and every child of every personality style needs to feel they're loved unconditionally regardless of good or bad behavior. We love them simply for who they are (even during those notorious teenage years), not for what they do or don't do!

ENCOURAGE YOUR "D" CHILD

> *Quick & Easy Encouragement for Your "D" Child:*
>
> - "You are confident and quick to respond!"
> - "I like that you tell me exactly what you want!"
> - "You can see a problem and figure out a way to solve it."
> - "When you want to accomplish something, I would be happy to help!"

When parenting determined "Ds," remember that they not only need room to grow, but they also need room to fail. They are more adept at *taking on* a project and creating a vision than following through and *completing* it. Give them clear boundaries – written down – so they understand exactly what is expected.

As their one-track minds detect ownership of the project (control), they will become self-motivated, working *with* you, rather than creating disharmony and working *against* you. Encourage confident and resourceful "D" children to make a difference in this world with their valuable contributions and goal-oriented strengths.

AFTER SCHOOL WITH A "D" CHILD

The outgoing, high-energy "D" child needs to come home after school and burn energy, accomplish something physical and constructive. A long day of sitting still in a chair, being told what to do, and without any control can be very stressful for a high "D" child.

When my "D" son, Scott, arrived home after school, I knew he needed to grab a snack (a sizeable snack) and head outside to burn up some energy right away! Sitting immobile in school during the day was a struggle for him (excelling during recess and P.E. class). By allowing time for a physical energy release, he was better able to sit still again and conquer his homework assignments later.

"Ds" want their own way, will test you, and quickly move into action to push you to see what they can get away with. "D" children demand to control the situation, even enticing power struggles to manipulate. We can help our "D" children achieve and conquer their perceived difficult restrictions placed on them (homework) by recognizing their high-energy personality style and helping them achieve their objectives (graduate from school and become CEO of Planet Earth).

"Ds" live to achieve and need to conquer something (and it's up to you to make sure it's not their little brother or sister)!

METHODS AND MANEUVERS FOR THE "D" CHILD

Risk-taking "D" children love adventure and work for results. They become bored with routine, acting impatient or belligerent. As natural leaders, "Ds" speak out openly. When asked to do something undesirable, they may be argumentative and overstep authority. They can be pushy, and will take control for independence.

Struggles for independence and control are common occurrences. This is particularly true at the notorious bedtime when everybody else is out of gas – and "Ds" are charging full speed ahead to have things *their* way! Are there bedtime battles in your home? You can make getting ready for bed a *fun* ending to the day instead.

For example, since "Ds" are motivated to compete, a great method to get things moving for younger "Ds" is to declare a race to see who can get their pajamas on and brush their teeth first! If you proclaim that you will be the winner, you'll find a competitive contender running past you to *prove* who can get there first!

"Ds" will cooperate with about anything or anybody if it means they can win at something. Let them be a part of the action in making things happen – particularly against all odds. What's a sure-fire method to get "Ds" to do something? Tell them it *can't* be done! Then sit back and watch!

The "D's" motivation comes from being in charge of goals and accomplishments! This decisive "D" personality style is quick to take action while others are still *processing* the situation! They will assertively tackle something (or someone) head on, seeing it through until they're victorious.

HOW DO "Ds" CLEAN THEIR BEDROOMS?

"Ds" clean with snowplows! The "D" child likes to clean (or do anything) the fast way! For example, I had designed a bunk bed "house" with the top mattress as the roof for my "D" son, Scott, when he was about seven years old. When forced to clean his messy room, his method of cleaning was to open the door to the house below and shove everything in – as if he were operating a snowplow. In one fell swoop, he could make scattered toys vanish into the house! Presto! His room was clean!

Confident and goal-oriented "Ds" want quick action, with little time for details that don't pertain to results. They don't need things perfectly organized and put away (unless it will help them accomplish something). They need things done so they can move on to the next item on their agenda!

FEEL THE STRENGTH OF THE "D" DRIVE

Sure, there may be plenty of obstacles, but this achiever will quickly (possibly without thinking) find a way to win! If you parent "D" children, you will feel the strength of their drive. This is a wonderful strength that will allow them to accomplish many things when other personality styles may give up.

Strong, courageous "D" children will be successful in whatever they do because of their determination and dedication to accomplish and succeed. When others fold, the determined "Ds" are motivated to succeed by the strength of their convictions.

There is no limit to what "Ds" can accomplish once they've set their minds to the goal. If they're aiming in the wrong direction, it won't stop them. They'll simply re-aim and continue to blast forward – full speed ahead!

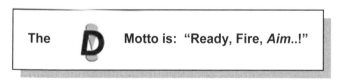

The **D** Motto is: "Ready, Fire, *Aim*..!"

Now let's take a look at Chapter 30 and learn exciting *Motivation Strategies* for the inspiring "**I**" child!

30

MOTIVATION STRATEGIES FOR THE ★ CHILD!

*M*OTIVATION TECHNIQUES FOR YOUR "I" CHILD

Basic Motivation:

- Recognition
- Approval
- Popularity

The "I" child likes flexibility, freedom, and to do things the *fun* way! "Is" are motivated to receive attention and acknowledgment, but can be viewed as the "class clown" for frequently acting as if onstage. If their energy is directed in the right way, "Is" can be outgoing, energetic leaders who love the opportunity to entertain, try new things, and be creative.

"Is" like recognition and rewards. While other personality styles may be *un*comfortable in the spotlight, the "I" personality style is *motivated* by it! If there's conflict brewing in the house, the "I" child will seek to lighten up the situation to make everybody happy!

COMMUNICATION WITH YOUR "I" CHILD

> To feel connected, we need to communicate and express love in ways that are meaningful. The "I" child says:
>
> - "Tell me who else is doing what you want me to do."
> - "Let me talk about what I am feeling."
> - "Be friendly and excited."
> - "Offer me rewards for quick jobs."

Motivate your "I" child by offering praise and fun. Learn to understand this personality style rather than criticize or complain about the muddled state of messiness. To understand doesn't mean to *accept* the disorder, though!

Use friendly voice tones while allowing plenty of time for "I" children to verbalize their feelings. Offer positive reinforcement and incentives for completing tasks (you may have to *supervise*) and communicate positive recognition. They in turn will inspire and motivate others!

THE "I" CHILD RESPONDS BEST...

> **...to a Mom Who:**
>
> - Is fun and fair.
> - Provides social involvement.
> - Provides recognition of abilities.
> - Offers incentives for risk-taking.
> - Creates an atmosphere of excitement.

AND MY MOM...

"Is" talk, and talk, and talk some more. They will tell you every detail about everything and everybody if you'll listen. Don't expect your "I" child to keep personal information personal, or secrets secret. In fact, "Is" at any age tend to *broadcast* all news! For instance, when I was the speaker at a conference recently, I noticed a lady who had arrived early with her four children. She used a nearby table to serve her children a specially-prepared dinner (fast food) before the program started.

One of her little girls spied me, flashed a sparkly smile, took a deep breath, and immediately – with an *amazing* amount of speed and velocity – began talking, "Oh, hi! My name is Jenny. I'm five and I'm in kindergarten and this is my little sister, Brittany, and that's my other little sister, Paige. That's Ms. Cathy over there and Ms. Tracy is over there! Oh, and that's my little baby brother in his infant seat. His name is Michael and he's five months old. It's good he's asleep."

I responded (barely squeezing a word in), "Oh, he sure is cute." Jenny quickly shot back, transmitting *a hundred miles an hour*, "Yeah! He's okay now, but last week Michael had an *ear* infection! My Daddy had a *sinus* infection one time! And right now my mommy has a *yeast* infection!"

Instantly, silence fell on the room as our mouths fell wide open. Horror of all horrors for this poor mom! We heard Jenny's mom *gasp* and then vanish under the table!

"I" children will always repeat what they hear. They are highly motivated to talk – to everyone – about every*thing*! Help them know when, where, and what to say – or to *not* say in public!

ENCOURAGE YOUR "I" CHILD

> ### Quick & Easy Encouragement for Your "I" Child:
>
> - "You are fun to be with and full of surprises!"
> - "I like that you share your thoughts and feelings with me."
> - "You can make others feel so comfortable with your wonderful sense of humor!"
> - "When you are enthusiastic, it's contagious! Let's be enthusiastic together!"

Children need immediate rewards to make a positive connection with a positive behavior. Success is elusive if recognition isn't rewarded soon (as in immediately) for an "I" child. I'm not saying that you shouldn't have long-term goals, they can be fun and challenging too (said the "D" mom), but "Is" easily lose track and lose interest if they experience extensive delays.

APPLAUSE, PLEASE

Five-year-old high "I" Jackson walked into the house after school moaning a bewildered, "Oh hi, mom." While helping him take off his backpack, Jennie asked, "What's wrong, Jackson? Did something happen at school?"

Distressed, Jackson replied, "When I held up my new racecar for show-and-tell today, nobody clapped. They clapped for Charlie's racecar last week. Why didn't anybody clap for *me*?"

Jennie reminded Jackson, "Charlie made his racecar himself and he announced that he won the Pinewood Derby with it. It doesn't mean that your show-and-tell wasn't good, too. They were clapping because he won the race."

Jennie affirmed Jackson's feelings, but reminded him that we don't always get accolades for what we do. Although "I" children are motivated to attain attention for everything, they need to identify that sometimes they need to be the ones doing the applauding to motivate others.

"Is" SEEK RECOGNITION WITHOUT ADO

Determined to help her high "I" son, Michael, succeed, Megan, a high "C," developed a motivation-and-rewards system that would help him complete tasks and accomplish more each month. Michael could earn a star for completing various pre-established requirements. At the end of the month, he could choose an outing or activity for having earned a specific number of stars.

However, Megan soon found a glitch to her concisely developed plan, and realized that it needed to be modified.

"My son liked getting stars and recognition, but after a few days he lost interest and quit trying," said Megan.

After much contemplation, Megan determined that the reward was too drawn out for Michael to fully realize the benefit of the stars he earned. She began instituting more immediate rewards that Michael could achieve and receive right away. Rewards and recognition must be as soon as possible to have an impact for high "Is." Otherwise, the motivation to do well may seem evasive.

AFTER SCHOOL FOR AN "I" CHILD

Remember, "Is" think in terms of "who?" They want a lot of people involved in their projects, and need a fervent hand offering specific guidelines. Give them encouragement, as well as deadlines. For example, if your "I" child has homework assigned on Monday and due on Friday, verify progress every day. Otherwise, he or she will put it off until the last minute, and then be frustrated (or blame the teacher) because the homework is impossible to accomplish in such a *short* amount of time!

Be consistent in homework rules. Make completing homework assignments fun, such as by providing your highly entertaining "I" child an opportunity to act out characters, as though onstage, when practicing for a book report. Your "I" child may have just spent the *entire day* in school with many friends, yet still insist on *more* time with friends after school! Allow ample opportunity for friends as a reward after homework is completed.

MULTIPLICATION HOOPS

My best girlfriend, Dianne, a high "I" mom, can relate perfectly with her high "I" son, Hunter, when he doesn't want to complete his homework – or do anything that's not *fun!* When Hunter began struggling with math in school, Dianne knew she had to do something to help him, so this imaginative high "I" mom came up with a very creative idea to help him learn his multiplication tables.

Given that Hunter *loves* basketball (and all the attention he gets while playing), Dianne created a basketball court on their driveway. She then randomly chalked the answers to multiplication tables in squares drawn all over the driveway. Positioned on the sidelines, she quizzed one math problem at a time, hollering, "What's six times six?" Hunter would then calculate his answer, dart for the chalked number "36," and *shoot*!

Next she asked, "What's seven times eight?" Hunter would then dart to the chalked number "56" and *swish*! The crowd (high "I" Dianne) would cheer wildly in applause and approval. It was a great strategy and a newfound success in math!

METHODS AND MANEUVERS FOR THE "I" CHILD

Supervise your born-procrastinator, easily distracted high "I" child's assignments. "Is" love new and exciting activities and don't want to be left out of the fun, but they over-assess and over-commit what they can actually do! Help your children schedule realistically.

You will want to teach them the advantage of being organized by showing them how to do things. Every move "Is" make is to fuel their desire to have fun. Make things fun by motivating them to make it a game! Inspire them to appreciate the benefit of completing a task and *avoid* their natural ability to talk their way out of doing something! With an inner need for approval, bright-eyed "I" children must remember to get their acts together with their short attention spans and stop the constant chatter.

Possessing many friends, "I" children want to be doing something with somebody all the time. Social acceptance isn't the only form of approval to seek. Emotionally, this may motivate them to get in trouble. With a greater need for affection than any other personality style, this child wants to be hugged, held, and liked so much that they may try to impress others and make bad choices in the heat of the moment.

HOW DO "Is" CLEAN THEIR BEDROOMS?

How do "Is" clean their rooms? They don't! Okay, they do sometimes. Impulsive "Is" lack follow-through. Help these enthusiastic starters focus on short-term assignments. Overly optimistic with a tendency to be unrealistic, they will strive to get the job done, but will be easily distracted from reaching the goal.

Jessica, a first grader, prefers the theatrical approach. Her mom said, "She sings and dances as she cleans, draping blankets and scarves over piles of unorganized toys. Her music is blasting out of her Hello Kitty CD player, and all the dolls and animals applaud after every performance. Seldom does her room get legitimately clean, unless, of course, a friend is coming over who would gossip about her messy room!"

With the difficult task of having to clean their rooms, "Is" can easily feel overwhelmed and unmotivated at the mere thought! Find ways to defeat the "elephant" task (How do you eat an elephant?) by tackling the chore one bite at a time.

First, assign your "I" child to pick up and put away one specific type of item. For example, they could search for all their dollhouse pieces – or all their HOT WHEELS™ – and put only those items away first. Or maybe you could suggest they put away everything that's pink (better make that red for a boy)! Set a timer so they understand that this won't last "forev-v-v-ver." Play music and suggest they dance and sing along! Inspire the "I" child, who so dearly loves to inspire!

FEEL THE STRENGTH OF THE "Is" INSPIRATION

"I" children will soar to new heights when motivated by compliments and approval. Praise them for their warm, friendly openness and amusing behavior. Make chores and assignments fun and exciting, with recognition upon completion by awarding a star – a sticker, certificate, or surprise. "I" types need recognition for *all* they do!

Considering "I" styles think in terms of "who," the more people involved, the more motivated they become. Ask "I" children to help you make things fun when you need to get things done. Make chores and assignments a game. Keep it lively and entertaining – even if it's sweeping the floor!

Spending time together enjoying fun activities will motivate your children to make wise choices by seeking your loving recognition and approval. "Is" love to entertain, laugh, and make *you* laugh! As you continue to parent your "I" child, you will feel like life is an ongoing party. This child will light up your life and bring sunshine into your world!

The   Motto is: "Ready, *Let's Talk*...!"

Now let's take a look at Chapter 31 and learn exciting *Motivation Strategies* for the supportive "**S**" child!

31

MOTIVATION STRATEGIES
FOR THE $ CHILD

ℳ OTIVATION TECHNIQUES FOR YOUR "S" CHILD

> **Basic Motivation:**
>
> - Security
> - Appreciation
> - Assurance

The dependable and loyal "S" child is motivated when appreciated as a team player. They work well under decisive authority, patient and uncomplaining. "Ss" get along well with others, but can please to the extreme. Motivated to comply with everyone else's wishes, they avoid making decisions. Sometimes overly sensitive, they hold their feelings inside.

The "S" child prefers to do things the *traditional* way. Unlike the "D" child, if motivation is engineered by competition against one another, the "S" child may not participate, feeling bad for defeating the other child. The "S" child can be motivated by your offering to spend extra time with him or her as a special reward!

COMMUNICATION WITH YOUR "S" CHILD

> To feel connected, we need to communicate and express love in ways that are meaningful. The "**S**" child says:
>
> - "Tell me how I can help you."
> - "Show me that you care about me."
> - "Be patient and do things with me."
> - "Offer me time to adjust to changes before they happen."

"S" children listen well, but shy away from talking too much. Find ways to break down any communication barriers and build bridges they'll feel comfortable to cross. "Ss" are naturally motivated to go above and beyond the call of duty to help, but could be taken advantage of. Show appreciation and foster an environment of security that will assure the "S" child he or she can communicate with confidence.

The softhearted "S" personality style needs encouraging words that are patient, caring, and not too strong. Because they are easily intimidated, use gentleness to communicate to "S" children that you are there to help and support them.

Never so true how painful words can hurt, as for the sensitive "S" personality style. Communicate without pushing or making off-the-cuff negative remarks. Motivate your "S" child to excel without fear of reprisal or losing your support.

THE "S" CHILD RESPONDS BEST...

...to a Mom Who:

- Is relaxed and amiable.
- Allows time to adjust to change in plans.
- Serves as a helper.
- Allows her child to work at his or her own pace.
- Clearly defines goals as means of reaching them.

Be warm and personable when motivating high "Ss" to be involved in a task. Show sincere appreciation for what they do. Help them speed things up a bit, but don't push too fast or too hard. Stable "Ss" don't like change in schedules or routines.

Make your home environment as stable as possible. Because they prefer things stay status quo, help them to not fear new and exciting changes or opportunities. Allow "Ss" plenty of time to become motivated to take the first step.

BE INVOLVED

Are you concerned your "S" child lives too sedentary a lifestyle? If an "S" child is immobile or lacking initiative, seek to involve this child in activities. Motivate them by involving another little friend, or participate in a group sport to encourage physical activity.

Go for walks. Offer to take a neighbor's baby with you in their stroller! This will give your "S" child the opportunity to fulfill the need to nurture and support, and allow another mom to take a little break at the same time! Weather permitting, you could go to the zoo, ride bikes, fly kites, play an outside game, explore a new hiking trail, go on a scavenger hunt, rake the leaves, build a snowman, play miniature golf, walk around in a children's museum or exhibit, and, of course, hit the parks. (Did I mention – ride bikes?)

Support "S" personality styles by being there *for* them and *with* them. They love being together, part of a special team, and supporting *you*! When doing things together, regularly let them know how much this helps *you* to get out and exercise – and how much you appreciate and enjoy being with them.

To spend time with your "S" child that would entail a *lower*-energy, slower-paced activity, you could explore other new options together. Start your own book club, work on a craft, or take up a new hobby. You could sew a *bag*! (See Motivation Strategies for the "C" Child.)

SAFE, NEW INTERESTS

Our children imitate *our* actions. Downright scary, isn't it? I'm sure you've experienced seeing *yourself* at playtime during role-play (especially with their *own* little babies), emulating your every word and action. To see yourself in action is a wake-up call!

Children imitate how we talk, act, eat, handle anger, show manners and kindness, and our attitudes about situations, chores, work, and life! If we constantly complain that we don't like this or don't like that, they'll pick up on it.

Do you like your job? Do you have a good attitude about it regardless? Do you say, "It's time for Mom to go to work! You have a great day, too!" Children recognize attitudes and emulate the same attitudes toward school (their current "job")! "Oh, hey! It's time to fix dinner!" "It's time for homework!"

Our attitudes reflect and manifest our children's attitudes. Do you enjoy your life? Help your "S" child thrive with a positive "can do" attitude.

ENCOURAGE YOUR "S" CHILD

> ### Quick & Easy Encouragement for Your "S" Child
>
> - "You are a caring listener who can sense someone's needs."
> - "I like that you follow through and finish things so well."
> - "Go ahead and make your decision; you have thought it out well!"
> - "When you patiently give someone the benefit of the doubt, I appreciate your kindness."

The "S" child likes harmony and routine. As you parent sensitive "S" children, you will feel their genuine care for you, so let them know how much *you* care. They love to help, preferring supporting roles instead of stardom. They keep their own pace.

Recognize and appreciate how "Ss" need security and to feel treasured. Express these to them often. Leave encouraging notes of appreciation in their lunch bag, on their dresser to find first thing in the morning, in their bike helmet (if they ride their bike to school), or inside their shoes before leaving for school. Shower sweet, caring "Ss" with thoughtful love notes that take little time and no money. Infiltrate their day by creating an ambiance where they feel loved and secure.

AFTER SCHOOL FOR AN "S" CHILD

Spending the day in a *lot* of activities and around a *lot* of people can cause the cooperative "S" child to feel worn out after school. "Ss" need *down* time upon first arriving home. Time alone with mom can be just what they ordered. Reading together, watching a favorite video or television show, working on a craft, or playing a game can be recharging and refreshing.

You may encounter their reluctance to start a new task or homework, but you can depend on them to finish what's required of them. Nudge, don't push hard. If you push, they may respond with stubborn persistence or hold a grudge against you.

Later, after a snack and completion of homework, your "S" child may choose to have one friend over, not the neighborhood as the "I" child would prefer. One really sweet, good friend is a perfect accommodation. Help "Ss" work through the process to make the choice as to whom they should invite over, taking into consideration the need to avoid hurting anyone's feelings.

METHODS AND MANEUVERS FOR THE "S" CHILD

"S" children are peacemakers. Keeping the peace is so important to them that they may neglect their own legitimate needs. Help them learn to discern objectively the actions and intentions of others, and balance their own needs, too. Understanding their need for time to grow more comfortable with any change is a method that will help encourage them to feel more secure.

Compassionate and obedient, the "S" child is committed to following your rules and meeting expectations. Encourage your child to feel comfortable to lead by setting an example to others to carry out responsibilities and obligations – a preference "Ss" comprehend so naturally.

HOW DO "Ss" CLEAN THEIR BEDROOMS?

The "S" child likes to do things the *traditional* way! "Ss" are not in a hurry – easy does it. They are comfortable with routine and familiarity. This slower-paced child cleans methodically, careful not to discard any valued treasures. It's hard for the "S" personality style to throw anything away, contributing to a stockpile of old coloring books, baby dolls, clothes, worn-out blankets, and more. "Ss" will save everything, including their many fast food toys, books, and dozens of stuffed animals. (Help them toss the used binkies!)

High "S" Molly's mom says, "When Molly is sent to her room to clean, she will spend a great deal of time instead tucking her babies in bed, feeding and dressing them. She has babies and stuffed animals scattered all over the room. She'll do anything to help them feel more comfortable while she's *cleaning*. Molly sees her room as a hospital or classroom to teach the babies and take care of them. She's happy to stay in her room for *hours* when all she needed to do was take a few minutes to pick up a handful items on the floor!"

"Ss" live to nurture, help, and take care of others.

FEEL THE STRENGTH OF THE "Ss" SUPPORT

Motivation for the "S" child stems from their desire to feel peace and security. With their secret longing to be useful, you can best motivate "S" children by providing them with opportunities to help you. Ask them to help you in the kitchen, put clothes away, make file piles, or clean the house together.

Because they fear the unknown, you can enhance their lives with assurance and affection and security in a stabilized environment. You can depend on the reliable "S" child to do what they say they're going to do. It just may take a while to get there! Motivation stems from doing what's expected and asked of them. Happy to comply and support, slow to complete, but patient and loyal until the end.

The **Motto is: "Ready, Ready, *Ready*...!"**

Now let's take a look at Chapter 32 and learn *Motivation Strategies* for the "**C**" child!

32

MOTIVATION STRATEGIES
FOR THE C CHILD

*M*OTIVATION TECHNIQUES FOR YOUR "C" CHILD

Basic Motivation:

- Quality Answers
- Excellence
- Value

"Cs" are naturally motivated to set high principles, complete tasks, and execute a quality job. They want established rules and awareness of the correct procedures. We can admire their consistency to be good organizers, follow directions, and do the *right* thing!

"Cs" expect fairness and high personal standards. Others may not measure up to their expectations or high standards. "C" personality styles may give up on others (or you), placing their focus and interest instead on completing a first-rate task.

It may appear as though they care more about the projects than the relationships (and sometimes they do).

MAKE A BAG?

My "C" child, Madison, recently had a few days off from school for parent-teacher conferences. My personal "D/I" idea of a great day together was to get out of the house and aim for an action-packed fun day. We could go to the mall, eat lunch at a wild and crazy restaurant, ride the carousel, and shop 'til we dropped!

Madison's motivation for sharing a great day together, however, was different than mine. She wanted to make her big sister an early birthday present ("Cs" plan *well* in advance) and responded to my suggestion by saying, "No, I want to stay home and sew a *bag* for Stacia's birthday."

Sew a *bag*? What does *that* mean? Outside of a few Brownie Scout patches, I hadn't sewn much of anything lately. At first I thought this seemed so dull – you know, kind of boring for an outgoing "D/I" mom. I couldn't understand why she wasn't motivated to *go* and have *fun*! But then I reminded myself of *her* personality style. As a "C," she preferred to stay home and work on a task (her definition of a great day).

So, we dragged out scraps of old fabric, ribbon, buttons, lace, and went to work sewing Stacia a cute, pink *bag*! Madison was in her little "C" element. She wasn't trying to spoil my plans or fun ideas; she was enthralled with a task we could do together. When I accepted Madison for who she was – *her* personality style – I found myself happy to oblige and delighted with the memories we were making. Completing a *task* was important to her; riding the carousel will come. (Oh, the ups and downs of the personality styles.)

By understanding Madison's "C" personality style and what motivated her, I was better able to not take it personally that she didn't want to do what I wanted to do on her day off from school. We completed that bag (topped with a pretty pink bow) and surprised her older "C" sister to boot!

COMMUNICATION WITH YOUR "C" CHILD

To feel connected, we need to communicate and express love in ways that are meaningful. The "**C**" child says:

- "Tell me why we need to do something and your expectations."
- "Show me how I fit in and explain guidelines and boundaries."
- "Be logical and careful with me."
- "Offer me quiet time to think and talk alone with you."

As you parent your "C" child who is committed to excellence, you will feel a focus on quality. "Cs" ask so many questions! They want to understand how things work and the proper procedure for everything. Persuade them to communicate how they feel by ensuring them that you're not in a hurry and *you* don't expect perfection.

Worried about life operating *correctly*, "C" children could be gravely affected by problematical relationships or disturbing situations out of their control. Because they are pessimistic at times, remind your serious "Cs" to count their blessings and notice the positive things going on in their lives. With your assistance, they can recognize that the imperfect situation could still offer a pseudo-perfect outcome. Reinforce positive thinking by helping your cautious and critical "C" child make a list (and check it off) noting the promising occurrences each day!

With their consistent desire for perfection (and often our lack of obtaining perfection), "Cs" could come across as abrupt and hurtful. It's not easy for task-oriented "Cs" to verbalize their feelings when they fear failure. They may be primarily focused on superior task completion, but we can teach our "C" children to communicate compassion and understanding. Teach them how to communicate in a way that eases the pain of their frustration. Spending an excess amount of time trying to achieve far-reaching standards does not *guarantee* success as predicted, particularly when it entails ignoring the value of communication.

THE "C" CHILD RESPONDS BEST...

...to a Mom Who:

- Provides reassurance.
- Maintains a supportive atmosphere.
- Provides an open-door policy.
- Defines concise operating standards.
- Is detail-oriented.

If you parent "C" children, you will feel their focus on quality. They ask so many questions because they need so many answers! Hang in there! They want to understand how things work and the proper procedure for everything. Because they are driven for perfection, they take criticism very personally.

How do you know what "C" children like to do, what their interests are, and what motivates them? Spend time. Spend time. Spend time with them. My task-driven "D/C" husband takes our eight-year-old, task-driven "C/D" daughter, Madison, on a daddy-daughter date every two or three weeks. They usually go to Burger King (off limits for *our* dates), and hang out afterwards at home playing board games, cards, puzzles, or constructing some monstrosity with Lego® or Ello™ blocks.

Without this talkative mom around, these two *task*-oriented individuals are forced to carry on their *own* conversations and cultivate a little *people*-oriented bonding time!

ENCOURAGE YOUR "C" CHILD

Quick & Easy Encouragement for Your "C" Child

- "You are so precise and perceptive; I like to know how you feel."
- "I like that you are organized and always try to do your best!"
- "You can catch important details that others may miss."
- "When you work you are so conscientious, and you always look for the best answers."

With your patient yet persistent tone, high "C" personality styles value encouraging words that are accurate and unemotional. Give them special attention by making distinct plans to spend quality time with them. Because they prefer private time, they may have to be persuaded to understand value in spending time together.

"Cs" are responsible and reliable. Reinforce their dependability by expanding their responsibilities around the house. Use carefully chosen words to express encouragement and to reinforce your positive relationship with them. You can help "C" children understand that everyone makes mistakes as they learn and grow; then they can learn to be more tolerant of your mistakes, as well as their own.

Be patient as you encourage them to develop their special gifts. They will usually be much harder on themselves than you would be. Encourage them to express how they feel and in return, share your feelings with them. Remember that they may have difficulty expressing or even recognizing their own feelings.

MOTIVATED FOR TRUTH

Most important, we need to motivate our child to tell the truth. One hot summer afternoon, Madison asked, "Mom, can I have a can of lemonade?" I responded with, "You may drink one-half of a can, because we're going to have dinner shortly." Contrary to what she had been told, Madison fervently devoured the whole can.

A little bit later, she was standing in the kitchen while I was preparing dinner. I said, "So how was your lemonade?" I knew immediately she must have done something wrong – considering her bottom lip was curled down and she couldn't look me in the eye. I asked, "Madison, did you drink half of the lemonade?" and she just stood there (like a deer in headlights) staring at me.

When your child disobeys, it's hard to not feel angry, hurt, or betrayed. I responded with the utmost control (*after* I wiped the steam off of my brow and cleared the smoke from the top of my head). I didn't yell or take it personally that my child had gone against my stipulation. Instead, I said, "Here's the scoop – you tell me the truth and you get one time-out, but if you don't tell me the truth, you get two time-outs. It's your choice." It was difficult, but she finally confessed.

The point is that I wanted to motivate my child to tell the truth *more* than I wanted to give her harsh consequences. She had a consequence for disobedience, regardless, but the benefit to telling the truth was the imposition of a lesser consequence. Granted, we would love it if our children always told the truth because it's the *right* thing to do – but it's just not always in our carnal nature!

Instilling motivation for telling the truth, regardless of their personality style, is essential to helping our children make better choices. Otherwise, we set our kids up to question if a lie might be the better choice (until the *lightning* strikes, of course)! The key is to motivate your child to make better choices in the future, without going overboard or getting too bent out of shape. As moms know, kids are going to test – suffer the consequences, test – suffer the consequences, and eventually get it, *hopefully*! (That "on the knees" thing works miracles, by the way!)

It takes much more patience and commitment to train, guide, motivate, and encourage your child, than to just respond the easy way, such as blowing your top. Remember, your "C" child needs plenty of time to make decisions that are accurate and precise. Patience, my dear mom, patience.

AFTER SCHOOL WITH A "C" CHILD

Task-oriented and reserved "Cs" are good students and enjoy learning, but will be tired, even feel stressed, from interacting with other kids all day. When they first arrive home from school, they may want to postpone talking for a while until after having time to work on a project – or enough time has passed to simply *think* about things. They need time *alone* to think, read, work on a puzzle or computer, or watch a favorite show – all to recharge (particularly if high-energy demands were placed on them during the day).

At the beginning of the year when Madison arrived home from school, I asked, "How was your day? Anything exciting happen today? Did you learn anything new?" But Madison would respond, "I can't remember." Now, I may have a bad memory, but that's really bad! Finally I determined she said this to avoid conversation. I learned that if I waited until dinnertime, she was much more apt to share. You can talk to your "C" children later, but let them have time to themselves first to *calculate* their day before *expressing* their day.

HOMEWORK STANDARDS

The conscientious "C" child will seldom need to be nudged to complete homework assignments. Desiring organized, clear instructions, "Cs" are generally good students with high standards. Many "why" questions float around the curious "C's" homework desk. Help "C" children excel by allowing them to explore logical answers to their questions.

Unwilling to settle for typical answers, the curious "C" mind makes great advances in evaluating new science ideas, technology solutions, and medical advances as he or she approaches new and improved opportunities for new and improved answers. Help a procrastinating "C" child feel comfortable taking on a new idea or project, even if a perfect outcome isn't guaranteed.

METHODS AND MANEUVERS FOR THE "C" CHILD

Overall, analytical and with high personal standards, "Cs" want things done properly. Conscientious "Cs" love to think about or organize things in their heads before ever taking a step of action. You may find they understand some things far better than their peers, especially in an area of interest to them.

Their emotional behavior may come across as capricious – appearing first to be mature, and then suddenly exploding into frustration. Recognize the benefit of the high quality of their work, and motivate them to develop a method to value keeping control under pressure when faced with unmet expectations.

Direct your "C" children toward thinking positively rather than negatively. If they are too critical or complaining, motivate positive comments by thinking of ways to reward them for *not* complaining! Help them to patiently show compassion for those who don't do things right all the time. Remind your "C" child that a friend or sibling didn't *mean* to do something wrong or incorrect.

HOW DO "CS" CLEAN THEIR BEDROOMS?

"Cs" are naturally motivated to be good organizers. They typically follow directions well. Don't get me wrong, there will always be the stray sock showing up a sock size later, or a scary-looking green blob discovered in a dark corner under the bed. (Every mom seems to find at least one!)

Jackie said about her teenage daughter, "Jenell cleans her room like a drill sergeant preparing her troops for war! She likes her socks folded in pairs, her closet is color–coded, her brushes are in a straight line in the drawer, and even her ponytail holders manage to find their way back to the right spot. My 'C' daughter makes me feel like an unorganized mess. She will grab the glass cleaner without being asked or told to! I'm not sure what planet she's from, but I'm not *complaining!*"

"Cs" like their rooms neat and orderly. Oh, sure, they can have their moments of disorganization, but they don't last long. Angie said about her high "C" five-year-old daughter, "Brooklyn can't settle down at night to sleep until everything is in its place. She gets up four or five times a night to rearrange things in her room. She's overly obsessed with keeping everything so tidy!"

A messy, unorganized room (or home) can be stressful to "Cs." They're motivated to discard chaos as soon as possible. They're prone to get rid of a lot of things, in fact. Unlike the "S" savers, "Cs" toss most things without looking back. Order is essential.

> **The *C* Motto is: "Ready, Aim, *Aim*...!"**

MOMS EXTRAORDINAIRE

If you're a mom and you've raised kids, let it be said that you can manage and motivate! In fact, you could probably run any corporation or company by now! Your net worth is off the charts! Your "on the job" training as a mom is what most management seminars teach in exchange for exorbitant fees!

Moms balance many activities in a day and perform numerous job descriptions – teacher, chaperone, chauffeur, nurse, cook, gardener, art director, accountant, interior designer, referee, personality consultant, and motivator of your in-home staff!

Your role as a mom is a great training ground for success and leadership. You've learned to be flexible, understand, listen, and care about the smallest of details. You've now learned to motivate according to the different personality styles and once again how to "Cope and Adjust!"

Now let's take a look at the exciting and concluding chapter of *Personality Insights for Moms*!

33

D-I-S-COVER HOPE
FOR MOMS

"Congratulations! You're going to be a mom!" Remember when you first heard those words revealing the enormous change (which you had no idea of the *magnitude* at the time) you were about to embark upon? Of course, you were so excited that you just had to tell someone right away! (By the way, has your husband ever figured out that your *nail lady* was the first to know?)

I don't know about you, but I dreamed, role-played, and longed for the day that everything in my life would utterly and completely transpire because of the sweetest-smelling, softest, most adorable, and precious little bundle of joy (*alien*) entering my life! Ah-h-h but, children are truly irresistible blessings. And moms! Moms magically develop this innate ability to deeply and unconditionally love and care for their children. (After what they went through to get them here, why *wouldn't* they?)

A mom's deep reservoir of love is astounding. However, as much as we want to *show* our children love, sometimes children don't *feel* loved. If moms don't demonstrate their love in a way that their children can *recognize* it, they may miss it all together. Their children may comprehend a completely *different* message!

HOLD THE ROSES

As we come to a close in this final chapter of ***Personality Insights for Moms***, I want to emphasize that although you've learned your personality style as well as your child's personality style, and have a much broader understanding of why your children (and you) act as they do – well, this may come as a total surprise, but that just doesn't guarantee that life with your children is now going to be a bed of roses. After all, roses do have their thorns, and we can't consider one without the other! Kids are still going to be kids, with their own sets of priorities and peculiar agendas.

However, there's *hope*! Having read this book does mean that the *propensity* to understand yourself and your child better, to communicate better, and to anticipate future interactions better is a definite possibility! There will always be issues of concern in your life, but how you deal with and solve your issues determines the *quality* of your life.

We must use what we have and start where we are. At the end of our lives, we will never regret not having climbed one more step of the corporate ladder, or not having had one more day of a perfectly clean house. However, we might regret not having spent more time with our children, or not having taken more opportunities to demonstrate our love for them and communicate to them that we understand them.

Years from now, our lives will have changed, but we'll still have our children (bigger versions) and we'll still have our memories (for the most part). (However, there is a remote possibility that we may *not* still have our *teeth*.)

INSTILL SELF-ESTEEM

The little-nothing moments in our lives can be so special. Our kids need to feel special – as though there were no one on this earth more loved and understood than they are –

specifically by their moms! Children who feel loved and understood will have higher self-esteem than children who do not feel valued by those closest to them.

A secure mom-child relationship is instrumental in laying a firm foundation for a child's self-esteem. Kids with healthy, positive self-images have a predictably better chance of success in life. Expounding a supportive foundation to build self-esteem must involve new and creative approaches to everyday life situations that can be mastered by all moms, and open the door to a myriad of possibilities.

No, we'll never be *perfect* (sorry, "Cs"), but we can be really *good!* Yes, we may blow it from time to time. We may miss our turn at carpooling, show up twenty minutes late for a parent-teacher conference, or forget an important dentist appointment. (Nothing that a warm batch of brownies can't cover!) Our kids can't expect us to be perfect – just as we can't expect them to be perfect.

YOU'RE HIRED!

Don't give up or feel as though you aren't measuring up. You're doing the most important job in the world. You're a mom. Being a mom is about building a relationship that will last a lifetime – loving the changes our little growing people aspire to, learning and accepting our children as individuals, independent, and eventually enabling them to stand on their own. We also want our children to want to come home long after they leave home – just to visit, of course! (Wait a minute. We spend all of our time raising our kids to *leave* us?)

The most important ingredient to the success of our children is to let them know that their moms are crazy about them! Moms understand value—not monetary value, but the kind that really counts. We don't need to wait a single minute to start improving the world! Don't let anyone ever tell you differently. The job of being a mom is the most important, influential, life-changing job anyone could ever hope to get hired for. Do you realize that a mom's resume would have to be shipped in a hundred-pound carton?

BOTCHES AND BLUNDERS

Somewhere along the path of motherhood, we've fallen prey to the false assumption that just because it's easy to *become* a mom – it's easy to *be* a mom. Let me tell you, I've made so many parenting botches and blunders along the way. I would love to say that I've done it right, made the right discipline choices, and given more than enough time to my kids. I would love to say that I gave them the love and security that they needed just when they needed it, and always acted cool, calm, and collected with my responses. But I can't.

I can say, however, that I truly understand them better now that I understand their personality styles. I truly see them and appreciate them for who they are and why they do what they do! I have a glimpse of insight into why one child and I act and respond to things so differently – and yet another child and I are so much alike!

When I first learned the **D-I-S-C** personality information, it changed my life as a mom. It gave me "ah-has" as to why each child thinks, acts, responds, plans, and plays differently, and our communication is so much more on target! It has shaped my thinking ahead of time and my responses afterwards.

I can say that **D-I-S-C** has truly transformed my relationships. I now understand why my "C" daughter needs every detail for plans well in advance. I understand why my younger "C" daughter questions everything I say and is so much more reserved (and that it's *okay*)! I understand why my "D" son and I went toe-to-toe, head-to-head during his entire upbringing! (I also now understand why some animals eat their young.)

I won't go down in history as the most entertaining mom, the most supportive mom, or the mom with the perfectly mopped kitchen floor. And there's probably even a mom out there who makes better "pa'sghetti"! I don't qualify for the "Supermom" title, but I'm going to do my best with what I know – and you can, too! We're in this mom thing together! We can't change the past, but we can enjoy today – and tomorrow – now that we understand *why* we do what we do and *why* our children do what they do!

FINAL D-I-S-CLOSURE FOR MOMS

Having someone who understands your personality style is a great blessing for you. Being someone who understands personality styles is a great blessing for others.

"D" Moms For all you "D" moms, may you be blessed with accomplishments and success, and remember – don't miss the beauty of the rainbow and all its colors while you're reaching for the pot of gold. Success means looking for the best in our children and giving them the best we have.

Moms maneuver around kids' ups and downs, highs and lows, and everything in between. Your driven personality style can direct your children to climb to greater heights and higher goals in pursuit of success!

"I" Moms Some of you moms are great when you're having a bad day, and some of you are great to share a good laugh. Thankfully, you "I" moms are the all-purpose moms! We never know what to expect with your spontaneity! You avoid dealing with your own messy closets, yet *jump* at the chance to rummage through another mom's second-hand junk!

As an "I" mom, you may be punctuality challenged, but you'll never be boring! And the only problem with being such an *optimistic* mom is that other people don't think you know what's going on! But we know you do! Your personality style can inspire your child to seek out adventure and to discover fun new ways of doing things! You are a breath of fresh air and a commitment to joy!

| **"S" Moms** | For all of you "S" moms, there's an opening for the "Nicest Mom" on Planet Earth, but I'm afraid you're *over*qualified! We can always count on you in times of crisis and in need of assistance. You may not want to lead the pack, run the show, or be CEO of *anything*, but as Mother Teresa said, "We cannot do great things, only small things with great love."

"S" moms are loyal, trustworthy, and keep promises and secrets safely tucked in their hearts. "Ss" are friends who never fade from our lives. Some friends come and go, but "Ss" will remain faithful and loyal, as long as they feel secure. Your sweet personality style with great love and support is immeasurable. (Your support is unrivaled by the best of all pantyhose!) You can support your children to excel in all their dreams. May you, too, be equally supported by the love and security of your families.

| **"C" Moms** | For all you conscientious "C" moms, you keep our lives in order. You may be cautious, but you carefully calculate what's next, what's *best* for your children! You make the rules, make the appointments, and always make the *beds*! But, if your house doesn't look perfect, don't worry about it. Let's face it, when another mom comes to visit you, she's probably *relieved* when she sees that your house is not perfect! It reveals happy playful kids. After all, doing housework while your kids are still growing up is like shoveling the driveway while it's still snowing!

Your attention to details and conscientious style keep your children on their toes – and on time! Your commitment to quality exceeds even beyond my commitment to chocolate! Thank you for always keeping our world in order.

D-I-S-COVER HOPE

The charm of a home is an *outward* manifestation of a mom's *inward* love. When a mom believes in her child, even the impossible seems possible. Parent with purpose for the success of your children. Parent with clarity and evaluate the leverage. Seek balance and loving respect for each other. Is it too late? Never, never is it too late! We have a job to do! I challenge you to come out of the grandstand and run in the race!

I am *passionate* about seeing that moms truly understand that greatness lives within them. Embrace your challenges instead of resenting them. You have a powerful role as a mom! We are champions, persevering until we reach the finish line. We are combatants, fighting for what is right; we are moms (hear us roar)! We can change the world – one personality at a time!

IT'S A GIRL!

Just when I thought I had a fairly good handle on my kids, understood their personality styles and how they uniquely shape our family dynamics, I found out that I was adding more kids to the mix! No, no, no, not that!

During the duration of writing this book, my son, Scott, married his beautiful bride, Erin. So, now I have a new daughter-in-law! Well, of course, I *immediately* had Erin take the **D-I-S-C** Personality Assessment test. (I needed to know right away what I was getting into!)

Guess what?!!! My new daughter-in-law's an "S"! (If *that's* not proof there's a God, I don't know what is!) Yes, a sweet, sentimental, and supportive "S."

An "S" – married to my high "D" son! *Yikes!* That brings on a whole new set of challenges!

So, stay tuned for my next book, **Personality Insights for Couples**, and find out why opposites often *attract* – and then *attack*!

CONGRATULATIONS!

You have now completed your official **Personality Insights for Moms** Training Camp! And we didn't even have to do all the rigorous jumps, stretches, bends, flips, twirls, or endure a stringent diet! (Although, I trust you enjoyed bonbons along the way – or some form of chocolate.) (By the way, did you realize that *five* out of *three* moms love chocolate?)

To all moms who were able to "Cope and Adjust" through the duration of this book without too many alarms going off (or would that be *on?*), my hope and passionate desire is that you have **D-I-S-Co***vered* how to have communication success!

You can now decrease conflict and increase happiness for a lifetime! May God bless you and your children abundantly with peace and joy throughout your prospective personality endeavors!

ABOUT THE AUTHOR

Susan Crook is a wife, mom, and national speaker. As a Certified Human Behavior Consultant, she speaks at women's conferences and events throughout the year. Having graduated Magna Cum Laude, she has a Master's Degree in Speech Communication, a Bachelor of Arts in Business and Human Relations, and an Associate of Arts. She achieved the National Chancellor's List (highest academic honor for graduate students), National Dean's List, Phi Delta Lambda Scholastic Honor Society, Phi Beta Kappa Honor Society, and plans to begin her doctorate degree.

Formerly a successful business owner and the Assistant Director of the NFL Kansas City Chiefs Cheerleaders, Susan is a motivational leader in many respects. Sprinkled with humor, she is an inspirational speaker on various subjects that motivate and encourage others to seek a life full of purpose and joy, to be the best they can be, and to live their best lives *today*! Susan encourages women to live as victorious, world-changing champions seeking passion for God as well as their marriages and families!

Family: Susan has given excruciating, body-wrecking painful birth to three children (who are the joy of her life) and has recently gained a wonderful new daughter-in-law. She is blissfully married to Dale (Jay) Crook – the man who has completely captured her heart forever and true.

To contact Susan for speaking engagements, visit www.SusanCrook.com.

RESOURCE MATERIALS

Adult Personality Profile Assessment
One of the most accurate tools available to D-I-S-Cover your personality style. Complete with charts, graphs, descriptions, goal-setting, team motivation, and management ideas.

Get Real! (Teen Personality Assessment)
One of the most accurate tools available designed to quickly and easily assess the personality styles of teens. It includes occupational suggestions, communication tips, information on learning styles, keys for motivation, and goal-setting ideas for middle school and high school.

All About Bots!™ All About You! (Children ages 4–12)
This is a highly accurate tool for parents, teachers and individuals who work with children to gain an understanding of a child's personality style. Elementary school age children examine stories and "coloring book" pictures of four robot friends. Complete with graph explanations, motivational tips, and pointers on ideal environment and communication.

Parenting Flip Charts *
Easy-to-read and simple to use parenting charts. Each chart represents one of the four basic personality styles for a parent, and how to work effectively with each type of personality style. Charts provide insights on the strengths, struggles, and strategies to overcome potential challenges in working with children.

*Available in Spanish

ORDER ONLINE AT
www.SusanCrook.com

QUICK ORDER FORM
(Photo copy form to place orders)

Postal Orders: Susan Crook Communications, LLC
11936 W. 119th St., #159, Overland Park, KS 66213

Email Orders: order@susancrook.com

Please send _____ copies of the following book.

☐ Personality Insights for Moms! @ $13.95 each.

Please send more information on:

☐ Other Books   ☐ Speaking/Seminars

☐ Email Newsletter   ☐ Consulting

Name: _____
Address: _____
City: _____ State: _____ Zip: _____

Telephone: _____
Email address: _____

Sales tax:: Please add 7.55% for products shipped to Kansas.
Shipping: **U.S.**: $4 for first book, $2 for each additional book.
International: $9 for first book, $5 for each additional book.

Payment Method -   ☐ Check

Credit Card: ☐ Visa   ☐ MasterCard

Credit Card number: _____
Security Code (last 3 digits on back of card by signature) _____

Name on card: _____Exp. Date: _____